VOLTAIRE

AND MADAME DU CHÂTELET

PRINCETON PUBLICATIONS

IN ROMANCE LANGUAGES

VOLTAIRE
AND
MADAME DU CHÂTELET

An ESSAY on
the Intellectual Activity at Cirey

By IRA O. WADE

PRINCETON UNIVERSITY PRESS • PRINCETON
LONDON: HUMPHREY MILFORD: OXFORD UNIVERSITY PRESS
MCM · XLI

This book is published
with the aid of the
Princeton University Research Committee

PRINTED IN THE UNITED STATES OF AMERICA
BY PRINCETON UNIVERSITY PRESS, PRINCETON,
NEW JERSEY

PREFACE

THE present view of the so-called Cirey Period (1733-49) of Voltaire's life is somewhat unsatisfactory in being confined to one aspect. Desnoiresterres in his *Voltaire et la société française au XVIIIᵉ siècle* has treated it either as an amorous escapade or as an incursion into court life. Mr. Lanson in his *Voltaire* has followed the same tendency, while other biographers have continued to play up the Voltaire-Du Châtelet romance, leaving the impression in the student's mind that the years 1733-49 are an amorous interlude, of no particular consequence in the development of Voltaire's thought. Lanson has even branded the latter part of the period as the most sterile of Voltaire's life.

There are difficulties in accepting the Cirey Period as a mere interlude. Being the middle portion of Voltaire's life, it should normally have been a period of maturity. Moreover, since it embraced a span of some sixteen years, when he was between the ages of thirty-nine and fifty-five, it should naturally have been productive. Indeed, when his published output during these years is examined, the period cannot be judged unfruitful. And if it is considered that several works were largely written during the time, though published later, the *Siècle de Louis XIV* and *Essai sur les mœurs*, for instance, the imputation of sterility becomes even less justifiable.

Still, there is a noticeable contrast between the production of the years 1719-33 and that of 1750-78 which our present knowledge of the Cirey Period does not explain. Not that the interval 1733-49 represents a break in the unity of Voltaire's work. It is relatively easy to see in *Alzire* and *Mérope* a continuation of the dramatic tendencies of *Œdipe* and *Zaïre*. The *Mondain* and the

Discours en vers sur l'homme, as well as the *Eléments de la philosophie de Newton,* can be explained for the most part as coming out of the English journey. His histories, particularly the
Siècle de Louis XIV and the *Essai sur les mœurs,* can be in some
measure explained as a logical growth from the *Henriade* and the
Histoire de Charles XII. In short, there is no great difference in
tone or direction between what was published in the Youth or
English Periods and what was published in the Cirey Period.
There is more intensity, more diversity, and more finish to the
products of 1733-49, but not any real increase in breadth of interest, which cannot be explained by Voltaire's previous experiences or interests. It is when his production of 1750-78 is
compared with that of 1719-49 that a real difference is apparent.
There is but little in the earlier periods to indicate a source for
the *Examen important,* or the *Sermon des cinquante,* or any of
the critical deism of the later years. The obvious characteristic
of Voltaire's later work is not only that he has become intensely
philosophical, but that this philosophy is strongly anti-christian,
anti-catholic, and anti-biblical. This fact has already been noted
many times, but an adequate explanation for the phenomenon
has not been found. Lanson was one of the first to make the observation in his *Histoire de la littérature française* that Voltaire
was literary until 1750 and philosophical thereafter. Mr. Torrey
in his *Voltaire and the English Deists* stressed this division when
he pointed out that the effects of English critical deism to which
Voltaire was exposed before 1733 were not apparent until after
1760.

As a result of these observations the Cirey Period seems enigmatic and somewhat illogical. Since it does not mark a clear
transition from the English experience to the violent anti-biblical
criticism of the Berlin-Ferney Periods, which has been thought
to be largely English in origin, critics have assumed that in the
years 1733-49, Voltaire neglected to utilize the greater part of
that experience. They have proposed various explanations for
this neglect on his part. The most naive is that he was in love,

totally preoccupied with the Cirey Idyll, and as a consequence satisfied, like Aeneas at Carthage, to mark time. More plausible is the suggestion that he refrained from this type of criticism for reasons of prudence. But though reasons of prudence may have prevented his publishing his material, it would not prevent him from assembling it. Finally, it has been suggested that he was really ignorant of the critical deistic movement until the Berlin Period. This explanation is the most unlikely of the three. For it has been shown that there was between 1725-50 a widespread interest in critical deism, even in France, and if Voltaire was unaware of its presence until 1760, he was certainly lacking in his usual alertness. None of these theories adequately explains the fact that the Cirey Period fails to mark the logical transition in philosophical thought between English critical deism and the Voltairean critical deism of 1760-78, as it fails likewise to mark the transition between the clandestine French critical deism of 1725-50 and the Voltairean deism of Ferney.

It was precisely considerations of this sort which led me to investigate the Cirey Period anew, with a view to writing its history. But it soon became apparent that I was quite incompetent for the present to grasp the multifarious currents and cross-currents meeting at Cirey. Hence I have limited myself, to a considerable extent, to two figures of the period—the two most important ones, Voltaire and Mme du Châtelet. Even here I was forced to further limitations.

In the present essay, I have made no attempt to elaborate upon the picturesque in their relationship, nor to analyze their love psychology. That task has been capably performed by Maurel in *La Marquise du Châtelet.* Nor have I paid much attention to the social atmosphere at Cirey, since Hamel's work, *An Eighteenth Century Marquise,* has competently treated this aspect. The present essay aims, on the contrary, to present exclusively a discussion of the intellectual activity in which both Voltaire and Mme du Châtelet were engaged during the years 1733-49, and to determine, insofar as it is possible, to what extent the intellectual activity of the latter coincided with and influenced that of the former.

Such an enterprise appeared in its inception relatively simple. In the numerous works dealing with the Lady Newton, there are fairly specific indications of the influence which she exerted upon her lover. I soon realized, however, that these indications, though often repeated, were based more upon surmise, or at best, upon general statements made by her contemporaries, than upon any first-hand acquaintance with her works. Thus, it has often been said that Mme du Châtelet turned Voltaire to the study of physics, or that she inspired him to write history philosophically, and there is good ground for believing that both statements are accurate. But it is more relevant to ask how she turned him to physics or inspired him to write history and more important still, once she had done so, how she contributed to his intellectual progress. This problem has never been clarified.

I thought that some elucidation might be possible through a comparison of the writings of Mme du Châtelet with those of Voltaire. But this immediately brought up another problem: what are the works of Mme du Châtelet? To be sure, every one knows her to be the author of the *Institutions de physique,* which she published in 1740, and a dissertation on the nature of fire which Voltaire had published in the *Mémoires* of the Academy of Sciences. Her *Essai sur le bonheur* which appeared posthumously is not altogether unknown. Therefore a possible comparison seemed to be indicated between the *Institutions de physique* and Voltaire's *Eléments de la philosophie de Newton,* between the *Essai sur le bonheur* and the *Discours en vers sur l'homme.* These comparisons, however, had no positive result, for in each case Mme du Châtelet's work was published after Voltaire's. In fact, it appeared more likely that what was being shown was the way Voltaire influenced Mme du Châtelet.

Now, it is undeniably true that he influenced Mme du Châtelet, as he did all his contemporaries with whom he was associated. But his intellectual influence upon Mme du Châtelet has always been considered a less important aspect of their relationship. It became immediately apparent that if I wished to discover how Mme du Châtelet contributed to the intellectual advancement of Voltaire, I would be forced to shift the emphasis from a simple comparison of what Mme du Châtelet and Voltaire published to a more extended comparison of what they were doing and thinking. This latter change included also what they were writing but not publishing. In other words, although I never refrained from comparing works, attitudes, and even ideas, I ceased making my study a quest for the direct influence of one upon the other and sought to find out in what way they were both contributing to a common intellectual atmosphere.

This entailed a preliminary investigation into what constituted the intellectual atmosphere at Circy. I have attempted to answer this question by analyzing both the activity of Voltaire and Mme du Châtelet. In general I have found that this activity extends over six fields: metaphysics, physics, moral philosophy, critical deism, drama and history. Voltaire's publications of the period fall into five of these six fields, since only critical deism is not adequately represented. Those of Mme du Châtelet, on the contrary, fall into only two of these fields, namely physics and moral philosophy. Further search, however, revealed that she was thought to have written other treatises which have never been published. I have attempted to secure photostats of these treatises and by careful study I have tried to ascertain first, whether she did write them and second, in what way they contributed to the common atmosphere.

I cannot claim to have achieved fully the objective of my study. In my general discussion of the intellectual atmosphere at Cirey, to which I have devoted my first chapter, I am afraid that I have been more sketchy than the subject warranted, particularly regarding the contributions of others than Voltaire and Mme du Châtelet. I felt that, since I was dealing with the two chief figures of the period, I could ill afford to scatter my efforts among the lesser figures who also made important contributions.

And yet some discussion of their influence was necessary to a comprehension of Voltaire and Mme du Châtelet's own efforts. I can only hope that this portion of my study, sketchy though it is, will be deemed adequate. In my study of Mme du Châtelet's work, I regret extremely to have been unable to locate her manuscripts on metaphysics. And I have been unable to ascertain whether she had a hand in the confection of two works whose authorship is uncertain, the *Doutes* and the *Notes* and *Preuves* to the *Religion chrétienne analysée*. However, I think I have thrown some light upon her contributions to the *Traité de métaphysique*, the *Eléments de la philosophie de Newton, Le Mondain,* and the *Discours en vers sur l'homme.*

In examining a second manuscript of Mme du Châtelet, the *Examen de la Genèse,* I have not only attempted completeness, I hope to have achieved it. Indeed, I have devoted more than three-fourths of my essay to a study of this manuscript and its importance to Voltaire. It was originally my intention, after locating it at Troyes, to publish it integrally. Upon further consideration, however, it seemed undesirable to publish the seven hundred thirty-eight pages of biblical criticism at this date, when it has lost all importance as a work of critical exegesis and when its tone is so out of keeping with present-day biblical scholarship. The only importance which the treatise can now have is an historical one. Therefore, it seemed better to make a study of this historical aspect rather than to publish the treatise itself with an historical introduction. This decision did not preclude much necessary investigation concerning the manuscript as well as its content. I have tried to determine upon what grounds the attribution of the authorship to Mme du Châtelet was justified, the date of writing, the nature of the material presented, and the importance of the treatise to Voltaire and his work. Whether I have succeeded in all this remains to be seen.

Only the chapter in which I discuss the content of the *Examen de la Genèse* needs further explanation. The criticism of the *Bible,* which was a lay diversion in the days of the Cirey episode, is happily no longer the fashion. By some it is considered useless; by others, in bad taste; and by all, not a subject for idle conversation. However, in the presentation of Mme du Châtelet's ideas, it was necessary to expound in good faith her objections, her criticism, and insofar as possible, her tone. I have taken scrupulous care neither to add to nor subtract from her views, and indeed to refrain from any personal commentary whatever, in this chapter, save in the concluding paragraphs. To those who still find this analysis insufficient or who might wish to consult the manuscript further, it might be added that a film and transcript of it have been made and deposited in the Princeton University Library.

There only remains for me the pleasant task of expressing my appreciation to all those who have contributed their time, energy, and knowledge to this essay. My thanks are particularly extended to M. Piquard, librarian at the Bibliothèque de Troyes, and his very competent staff who received me with that gracious courtesy which I have learned from experience to regard as the distinguishing characteristic of French librarians. Later, M. Piquard supervised the microfilming of the manuscript. I wish also to thank the librarians of the Public Library of Leningrad who kindly consented to have certain portions of a manuscript now in the Voltaire collection photostated. For undertaking this enterprise, and, indeed, accomplishing it with dispatch and intelligence, I am most grateful to Mr. Cuthbert Lee and his colleagues of the American Documentation Institute. My wife has been tireless in reviewing the text, correcting the expression, and clarifying the ideas. Indeed, I must confess that, although her name does not appear upon the title-page, it is as much her work as my own. To Professor F. J. Crowley, who kindly consented to read my work in an earlier form, I am indebted for some valuable suggestions. And to my former teacher and present colleague, Professor Gilbert Chinard, I owe a debt of gratitude, not only for reading with painstaking care my manuscript, but also for placing at my disposal certain works which I could find nowhere except in his magnificent collection of eighteenth-century treatises. Finally, I wish to express my appreciation to the Research Committee of Princeton University, through whose generosity I have been enabled to publish this essay.

I. O. W.

Department of Modern Languages
Princeton University

CONTENTS

VOLTAIRE AND MADAME DU CHÂTELET

CHAPTER I

THE INTELLECTUAL ATMOSPHERE AT CIREY

So MUCH[1] has been written concerning Mme du Châtelet's romance with Voltaire, her love life with the Marquis de Guébriant, the Duc de Richelieu, and Saint-Lambert, that the one really interesting problem for posterity, namely, the intellectual relationship existing between the "Divine Emilie" and Voltaire has been, if not totally disregarded, at least considerably obscured. Critics never forget that Mme du Châtelet had a skin like a nutmeg-grater, an uncontrollable passion for pompoms, a devastating weakness for gaming, and a violent, though somewhat misplaced, yearning for love. They never overlook the lovers' petty quarrels over a disliked dinner-jacket, a glass of Rhine wine, or a locked door. They rarely fail to mention that the Marquise was a "savante," even on occasion a "pédante," that she knew Latin and English and some Italian, that she explained Leibnitz and Newton with equal facility, that she once bested the scholarly Mairan in a discussion on kinetic energy. However these scholarly achievements are cited primarily as reasons why Voltaire became infatuated with her, they have never been studied as influences upon his intellect. The important thing has al-

[1] See Capefigue, J. B., *La Marquise du Châtelet et les amies des philosophes du XVIIIè siècle,* Paris, 1868; Hamel, F., *An Eighteenth-century Marquise.* N.Y., 1911; Ledeuil d'Enquin, J., *La Marquise du Châtelet et le passage de Voltaire,* Semur, 1892; Maurel, A., *La Marquise du Châtelet,* Paris, 1930; Piot, *Cirey-le-château,* Paris, 1894. The Princeton Library has (3246.766.999) a small book of pamphlets upon Mme du Châtelet. For further small items on the relationship of Voltaire and Mme du Châtelet, see Barr, M. M., *A Bibliography of Writings on Voltaire, 1825-1925,* N.Y., 1929, pp. 21-23.

ways been the character of Mme du Châtelet—"amante" and "savante."

There is some justification for this trend of interest on the part of critics. Practically all of our available information concerning the Cirey Period of Voltaire's career is drawn from sources highly-colored and not entirely reliable.[2] Voltaire himself, in speaking of Emilie, stressed the "savante," while the letter and memoir writers of the time stressed the "amante." Voltaire's testimony can be considered no more valuable than any other lover's, while the assertions of Mme de Créqui, Mme du Deffand, the Abbé Leblanc, Mme de Staal, Mme de Graffigny, the impossible Longchamp, and Collé are scarcely more reliable, but for a different reason. Voltaire sought qualities in his ladylove, while his contemporaries were more interested in defects, the picturesque, or the anecdotal. None of the eighteenth-century writers were interested in the intellectual atmosphere in which the two lovers moved, and lived, and had their being.

Some nineteenth- and twentieth-century writers,[3] however, have touched upon this phase of the Cirey Period, but their treatment of the intellectual influence of Mme du Châtelet upon Voltaire has been indefinite and vague. For instance, it has been pointed out that she was a competent critic of his dramatic production, that she interested him in the more serious pursuits of science, that she urged him to take an inventory of his philosophical beliefs, which procedure led him to write the *Traité de métaphysique,* and that indirectly she turned him, by her criticism of contemporary historical method, to the writing of history in a scientific way. Critics have noted the restraining influence which she exerted over her exuberant friend, and how she continually

[2] Especially Mme de Graffigny, *Vie privée de Voltaire et de Mme du Châtelet,* Paris, 1820; Havard, J. A., *Voltaire et Mme du Châtelet,* Paris, 1863; Longchamp, S. G., [and Wagnière], *Mémoires sur Voltaire et sur ses ouvrages,* Paris, 1826; and the *Mémoires* of D'Argenson, Collé, Hénault, and Voisenon.

[3] See especially Desnoiresterres, G., *Voltaire à Cirey* in *Voltaire et la société française au XVIIIè siècle,* 8 vols., Paris, 1871-76; Lanson, G., *Voltaire,* Paris, 1910; and Bellessort, A., *Essai sur Voltaire,* Paris, 1925.

defended him, as she wrote to D'Argental, against himself, locking the *Traité de métaphysique* and the *Pucelle* under a hundred locks, spiriting the poet away after the publication of the *Mondain,* or defending him against Desfontaines after the appearance of *Le Préservatif.* Thus while the eighteenth century portrayed Mme du Châtelet as "amante" and "savante," the above incidents emphasized by the nineteenth century represent her in the rôle of guardian angel.

It would be manifestly ludicrous to deny that this composite portrait of Mme du Châtelet is false or that our information concerning her romance with Voltaire is distorted. The point is that a superficial portrait of the Marquise and a picturesque account of the life at Cirey give us no idea whatsoever of the really significant aspect of the Cirey episode, Voltaire's intellectual development. Only insofar as Mme du Châtelet's actions, thoughts, and works inspired or influenced Voltaire's works do they assume a greater importance than those of her contemporaries. In short, the fifteen years which were spent by Voltaire at the home, or rather in the company, of Mme du Châtelet were not passed in an aura of romance but in a highly charged intellectual atmosphere. It is not at all important whether, to use the phrase which was once applied more or less maliciously to Fénelon and Mme Guyon, "leur sublime s'amalgama." It is important to know what intellectual pursuits they followed.

In the past, it has been assumed that the task of describing Voltaire's intellectual pursuits from 1733 to 1749 could be performed by giving a chronological list of his major works: the *Lettres philosophiques* of 1734, the *Traité de métaphysique* of the same year, *Alzire* and *Le Mondain* of 1736 and the *Défense du Mondain* of the following year; the *Discours en vers sur l'homme, Les Eléments de la philosophie de Newton,* the *Essai sur la nature du feu,* and *Le Préservatif* of 1738; *Mahomet* of 1742, *Mérope* of 1743, the *Poème de Fontenoy* and the *Temple de la gloire* of 1745, *Le Monde comme il va* of 1746, *Zadig* of 1748, *Sémiramis* of 1748, not to mention numerous épîtres and stanzas, and a voluminous correspondence. Thus metaphysics, moral philosophy, science, drama were the preoccupations of Voltaire during this period. This list of his publications does not tell the whole story, for we know that he was working during these years upon *Le Siècle de Louis XIV,* the *Essai sur les mœurs,* and the *Précis du siècle de Louis XV.* Consequently, to his above-mentioned interests should be added history.

Voltaire's intellectual activity is, however, so complicated during the years 1733-49 that a mere chronological list of his works offers a very insufficient picture of its scope. In metaphysics he puzzles over the four traditional problems of the Paduan School: the proofs of the existence of God, the nature and immortality of the soul, free-will, and the origin of evil. But he is not content to treat these problems in their traditional way; he must needs present the opinions of Leibnitz, Clarke, Locke, and Newton to disprove the opinions of Descartes and Malebranche. Even then, he is not satisfied, for the opinions of the materialists, whoever they are, must be combatted. And from all these conflicting opinions, Voltaire must form one of his own which becomes, as we shall see, singularly complex. In moral philosophy, the one essential problem for him is "bonheur." But it is hard to treat this "bonheur" without breaking it up into several component parts: the nature of pleasure, social good and evil, rewards and punishments, equality, and the relationship between passion and reason. Here again, the traditional way would be for him to merely follow in the path of the seventeenth-century "libertins," Chaulieu, Lafare, St. Evremond, Dehénault and Mme des Houlières, with a strong insistence upon the "petits bonheurs" of Fontenelle. But Locke with his *Essay Concerning Human Understanding* intervenes, Pope becomes all too attractive, the economic school of moral philosophers, Mandeville, Melon, Dutot, exert a certain influence. Once again, opinions pile upon opinions until it becomes necessary to ask what Voltaire himself really thought about moral philosophy. In physics, a similar confusion appears. He steadfastly rejects traditional Cartesianism, but wavers between replacing it by Leibnitz or by Newton. The *Eléments de la philosophie de Newton* is a curious treatise in which at times sufficient reason outweighs cause and effect, deductive philosophy, in spite of the renunciation of Descartes, predominates over experimentalism, and Newton's proofs of the existence of God are extracted from Leibnitz.

It is extremely difficult to understand the dominating force behind this intellectual activity. It is relatively easy to see where Voltaire's interests lay before 1733. He was a poet and playwright, or rather a poet-playwright. After 1733 and until 1749, however, he is no more dramatist than historian, or scientist, or moral philosopher. The striking thing is that he is essaying all these intellectual fields, and gives the two-fold impression first, of not being set and second, of not perceiving clearly the relationship existing between the various fields. This lack of coordination is evident in his work. The *Traité de métaphysique* begins as a treatise on moral philosophy, swiftly turns to metaphysics, and returns finally to moral philosophy. What then, in Voltaire's own mind, is the relative importance of metaphysics and moral philosophy? Does the validity of the latter rest upon the former, or vice versa? The title *Traité de métaphysique* suggests that metaphysics is the key science of philosophy, and this suggestion is confirmed by a reading of the treatise, for in it Voltaire devotes much more attention to problems of metaphysics than to those of moral philosophy. But in the *Discours en vers sur l'homme,* written four years after the *Traité,* the very opposite occurs. He here gives but scant attention to metaphysics, while he strongly stresses moral philosophy. Even in 1747-48, he has not cleared up the confusion, as is evidenced by these different titles given the same work at two stages: *Memnon* (Le Sage) and *Zadig, ou la Destinée.* In the *Eléments,* he devotes the first third of his treatise to metaphysics, leaving the impression that physics is the subordinate science, whereas a reading of his *Essai sur la nature du feu* gives the opposite impression. Evidently, the relationship of metaphysics, moral philosophy, and physics is not clear in his own mind. And when he began to write history, he never clearly distinguished between the historian as moral philosopher and as scientist. One can only conclude that either his intellectual life has lost unity and coherent organization, or that he has deliberately destroyed what unity it formerly possessed in the interest of broadening its scope. The problem immediately arises: whence came the incentive for this rather sudden diversity of interest?

Let us hasten to add that the problem is by no means a new one, nor have suggested solutions to it been lacking. Ever since the overly-categorical statement of Lord Morley, that Voltaire went to England a poet and returned a philosopher, there have been many sound expositions of the influence of English thought upon Voltaire after 1730.[4] It has been shown, not very effectively it is true, but certainly beyond cavil, that his metaphysics, during the Cirey Period at least, owes much to Clarke and Collins. It has been demonstrated more clearly that his moral philosophy resembles Pope's in many respects. No one would be inclined to question, after reading the title of the *Eléments de la philosophie de Newton,* that the English scientist gave the Frenchman a strong incentive for pursuing investigation in the scientific field. And a Shakespearean influence is evident in *Brutus, Zaïre,* and *La Mort de César,* if not in *Alzire, Mérope* and *Mahomet.* English writers and thinkers have left an unmistakable mark[5] upon Voltaire's metaphysics, science, moral philosophy, and dramatic technique during the Cirey Period, but whether this influence is paramount in his work at this time, and whether he brought it back from England on his return, is a much debated question. Certainly, two fields in which we might expect a strong English influence, history and critical deism, have not shown too apparent

---

[4] Especially Torrey, N. L., *Voltaire and the English Deists,* New Haven, 1929. Ballantyne and Sonet are also very helpful.

[5] For a detailed study of these influences see Hoffman, A., *Voltaires Stellung zu Pope,* Königsberg, 1913; Libby, M., *The Attitude of Voltaire to Magic and the Sciences,* New York, 1935; and Lounsbury, T., *Shakespeare and Voltaire,* New York, 1922.

effects of his journey. Hence, the rise of a number of critics who are as categorical in denying the English influence as Morley and a few of his imitators were in affirming it. This group of critics maintain that Voltaire could have found his metaphysics, his interest in science, his moral philosophy, and his interest in history between 1733 and 1749 in the contemporary evolution of French thought. They[6] aver that neither the problem of liberty nor that of good and evil originated with Clarke; that Pope's moral philosophy owed as much to Fontenelle as Voltaire's did to Pope, that Newtonian physics was familiar to many Frenchmen before Voltaire wrote his *Lettres philosophiques;* that Locke's empiricism is in many respects indistinguishable from that of a whole group of French thinkers who flourished around 1722; that Voltaire's interest in history can be traced to the period when he lived with Caumartin at Saint-Ange; and that his critical deism was as solidly grounded in Mirabaud, Fréret, Dumarsais and other French Deists as might be expected.

Categorically stated, the assertions of both schools are incorrect as all categorical statements are prone to be, although in many details they are both correct. The pro-English school errs in assuming that Voltaire concerned himself solely during the Cirey Period with interests acquired during his sojourn in England; the pro-French group assumes, just as falsely, that his interests during the period were exclusively a continuation of those acquired in his youth. The former group is inconsistent in assuming that, if Voltaire sponsored the empiricism of Locke and the mechanics of Newton; if he imitated Pope in his *Discours en vers sur l'homme* and Swift in his "contes"; if he eventually utilized the historical arguments of Middleton, and the ideas of Collins, Woolston, Chubb, and Toland, not to mention

---

[6] For an extreme expression of this point of view see Brunetière, F., *Études critiques.* See also Lanson, G., "Questions diverses" in *R. H. L.,* 1912; Audra, L., *L'Influence française dans l'œuvre de Pope,* Paris, 1931; and Morehouse, A., *Voltaire and Jean Meslier,* New Haven, 1936, where tendencies of a similar sort can be noticed, but where modifications of a very healthy sort have been made in this extreme view.

Bolingbroke—he could not have paid much attention to Bayle and the skeptical Cartesians, nor could he have been impressed by the moral philosophy of Fontenelle, the epicurean tendencies of Chaulieu and Lafare, the historical pursuits of Boulainvilliers, Hénault, and D'Argenson, the ideas of Meslier, Mirabaud, Fréret and Dumarsais. Voltaire, himself, by continually praising the English at the expense of the French, has abetted this view. Those who oppose the view, however, go to the extreme of stressing French influence to the point of forgetting that Voltaire was ever in England, that he knew the English language and had a wide acquaintance with English literature, and that he was greatly impressed by things English in general.

A more reasonable point of view would be that Voltaire, who certainly was not responsible for dividing his life into the five periods which critics ordinarily assign to it, was undoubtedly merging, during this third period of his life which he spent in and around Cirey, influences of the two preceding periods. This merging process, however, consists not so much in his reconciling opposites, such as Newton and Descartes, Locke and Descartes, Shakespeare and Racine, but in his assimilating writers interested in the same subjects, such as Pope and Fontenelle, Bolingbroke and Bayle, Woolston and Meslier. This assimilation is not exclusively characteristic of Voltaire, it is typical of the whole French movement in ideas from 1730 to 1750. In short, the French intellectual atmosphere of 1730-50 was subject to two influences—a strong traditional current and an equally strong English current. Voltaire merely breathed the same air which all intelligent Frenchmen were breathing. Obviously, Cirey was subject to the same influences which were being felt at Paris.

Hence, if we wish to examine carefully the influences motivating Voltaire, we must turn to Cirey, the scene of his idyll with Mme du Châtelet. But the very fact that the idyll was being enacted there makes it difficult to analyse the intellectual atmosphere of Cirey. However, it is possible to classify the interests, ideas and experiences which combine to form this atmosphere in three distinct groups: those surviving from previous periods, those specifically imported from contemporary centers of culture, and finally those created at Cirey. There is no necessity for reviewing the first group. Suffice it to say that it represents the intellectual baggage acquired by Voltaire from the days of the Temple to his return from England. While no effort should be made to minimize its importance, it might be fair to state that this intellectual baggage becomes of primary importance in the Cirey Period only in case it is in a sense recreated or fostered by an increasing continuity of interest on the part of Voltaire. His interest in history, which had its inception during his first imprisonment in the Bastille and continued throughout the English into the Cirey Period, is an excellent example. So is his attentive study of critical deism which began in the days of the Temple and continued throughout the English, Cirey and other Periods of his life. Finally, we may cite his active interest in drama which lasted from his youth until his death, and his interest in Newton and Locke which began not later than the English Period and continued throughout the remainder of his existence. We might even go so far as to assert that this intellectual baggage was Voltaire's great contribution to the Cirey atmosphere.

Voltaire's contribution, however, was no more important than the intellectual stimuli imported from outside cultural centers. It is possible to determine the source of these stimuli, but extremely difficult to measure their extent and intensity. The numerous excursions of Voltaire and Mme du Châtelet to Paris, Lunéville, Brussels, Châlons, Versailles, Sceaux and Anet no doubt afforded them opportunity for an interchange of ideas with others and a consequent incitement to intellectual activity. Correspondence with La Mettrie, Maupertuis, the Abbé Dubos, D'Argental, Algarotti, the Abbé Moussinot, Mairan, and especially Thiériot and Frederick the Great was another important link with the outside world. Still another were the various visits to Cirey by Maupertuis, Kœnig, Clairaut, D'Argental, Algarotti, Kaiserlinck, the Président Hénault, Thiériot, Desmarets,

Lamare, Linant, even Saint-Lambert and the inconsequential Mme de Graffigny. Naturally, the contributions of these individuals differed greatly in extent and importance. No doubt the visits of Hénault, Kœnig, Maupertuis, Clairaut, and Thiériot quickened the Cirey intellectual activity more than those of Linant, Mme de Graffigny, Desmarets, and Saint-Lambert. But each in proportion to his ability undoubtedly contributed something. As far as can be ascertained only M. du Châtelet, Mme de Champbonin, and the Marquis de Trichâteau were totally negligible in their contributions.

The works read by Voltaire during these years would offer an interesting background for his intellectual development. On numerous occasions, he wrote to Moussinot or Thiériot or others asking them to send him various books which he wished to consult. However, he did not incorporate his list of requests in his letters, but enclosed it separately on a slip of paper. It is particularly unfortunate that these lists have been lost, since they would be invaluable in ascertaining his interests at this time. It is definitely known that he consulted certain works, such as Pemberton's treatise on Newton's philosophy, for his own compositions. Our only way of discovering the books with which he was acquainted is to consult his *Correspondance* during the period. However, the fact that Voltaire mentions a book in his letters does not always mean that he has read it. Nor is it fair to assume that he noted in his *Correspondance* every book with which he had become familiar. In any event, a list compiled from his *Correspondance* is a fairly accurate starting-point for an examination of his readings. In a table which we have placed in the appendix, we have arranged the list in three parts: (1) works cited by author and title, (2) works cited anonymously, (3) authors mentioned without the title of their works. In each case we have stated where the reference may be found in Moland, omitting voluntarily only the individual poems of Frederick.

This list, incomplete as it is necessarily, indicates the various trends of Voltaire's interest while at Cirey. As might be suspected, he read extensively in both dramatic and scientific fields, for he was by nature a dramatist, and circumstances were rapidly turning him to scientific studies. The dramatists who seemed to appeal to him most strongly were Crébillon, La Chaussée and Destouches. In the imposing list of his contemporary scientific readings, it is surprising to find that the works of Castel and Mairan figure as prominently as those of Maupertuis. His mention of periodical literature of his day gives us reason to think that he was attempting to bring himself up to date in a thoroughly modern way. Of particular interest in the list are the historical works of Boulainvilliers, Lenglet, and Hénault; the political treatises of Melon and Dutot; and the philosophical dissertations of Leibnitz, Bacon, and Locke. In the field of moral philosophy, Pope is well represented, and not only Cicero, but works upon Cicero are mentioned. A book of rather special interest among these readings is La Bletterie's *Vie de l'Empereur Julien,* which furnished Voltaire with source material for his defense of Julian not only in the *Examen important,* but in the *Défense de l'Empereur Julien* and in the *Histoire de l'établissement du Christianisme.*[7]

Thus, in the years 1733-49, the intellectual atmosphere at Cirey was compounded of a strong English influence (Addison, Pope, Swift, Mandeville, Locke, Newton, Shakespeare, Collins, Clarke, Woolston, and Middleton), a continuous traditional influence (Bayle, Fontenelle, La Fare, Chaulieu, Boulainvilliers, Fréret, Mirabaud, Meslier, Dumarsais, and Calmet), and constant intellectual stimuli from contemporary cultural centers

[7] Voltaire's opinion of La Bletterie's work can be found in a letter to Formont, February 13 [1735]: "Le Père de La Bletterie, en écrivant la *Vie* de Julien, a fait un superstitieux de ce grand homme. Il a adopté les sots contes d'Ammien-Marcellin. Me dire que l'auteur des *Césars* était un païen bigot, c'est vouloir me persuader que Spinosa était bon catholique. La Bletterie devait prendre avec soi le peloton de M. de Saint-Aignan, et s'en servir pour se tirer du labyrinthe où il s'est engagé. Il n'appartient point à un prêtre d'écrire l'histoire; il faut être désintéressé sur tout, et un prêtre ne l'est sur rien." By 1741, Voltaire has adopted his attitude that Julian, if he had lived, would have destroyed Christianity. See XXXVI, 88.

(Paris, Brussels, Lunéville, London, Amsterdam, Anet, and Sceaux) ; contemporary books (Pemberton, Melon, Dutot, La Bletterie), and contemporary acquaintances (Frederick, Hénault, Helvétius, Maupertuis, Clairaut, Mairan). So many individuals, works, interests, currents and cross-currents were meeting, that the natural consequence would be a thickening of the atmosphere. It is precisely this which makes the Cirey Period of Voltaire's life so hard to grasp and so superficial in appearance, for, needless to say, Voltaire, alert as he ever was, endeavored to seize and utilize all these currents and cross-currents. Had he been a more methodical person, Montesquieu for instance, he would have examined them closely, abandoned many as useless or even deleterious, and accepted only those which conformed to a unified intellectual development. It was not, however, in his nature to do so. Since he had no inherent sense of proportion in his intellectual pursuits, the best thing which could happen to him was to meet with some one having the power to control and to organize, rather than to unify, his intellectual energies. That rôle was filled by Mme du Châtelet.

Mme du Châtelet's personal contribution to the atmosphere of Cirey was by no means insignificant since she, too, had a wide range of interests and attainments. Voltaire wrote to Thiériot that she understood English as well as he (Voltaire). Later he wrote (Beuchot XL, 39) : "Tous les ouvrages philosophiques de Cicéron lui étaient familiers. Son goût dominant était pour les mathématiques et pour la métaphysique." To Maupertuis, she confided:[8] ". . . je partage mon temps entre les maçons et M. Locke ; car je cherche le fond des choses tout comme une autre." To Algarotti (*ibid.*, p. 90) she wrote: "Je m'exerce dans l'art de la traduction, pour m'en rendre digne. Je traduis *The Fable of the Bees* de Mandeville." To the same Algarotti, she evinced an interest in Du Resnel's translation of Pope's *Essay on Man*.

[8] Asse, E., *Lettres de la Marquise du Châtelet*, Paris, s. d., p. 28.

When it appeared, a copy was sent her by the author, to whom she addressed the following significant letter:[9]

Rien ne m'a jamais plus flatté—Monsieur, que Votre lettre, je la méritois peutetre par mon estime pour vous, et par le cas que je fais de l'ouvrage que vous voulez bien m'envoyer, le peu que ie sais d'anglais m'a mis a portée de connoitre la difficulté de votre travail, et c'est la seule chose qui puisse donner quelque prix à mon sufrage, j'avoüe que ie croirois les idées metaphisiques aussi peu faites pour notre poësie, que pour notre nation, mais vous m'avez detrompée, vous avez rendu propre aux français un ouvrage dont les beautés étoient perdües pour eux, et vous leur avés apris a faire des poëtes anglais le cas qu'ils meritent, ainsi les deux nations vous ont une obligation Egale, pour moi Monsieur je vous en ay une bien plus grande de m'avoir donné une occasion de vous dire combien je desire votre estime, ie comte parmi les obligations que i'ay a l'amitié de Mr de Voltaire, celle de m'avoir procuré les marques que vous voulés bien m'en donner, ie suis persuadée qu'il lira lessay sur lhomme avec grand plaisir, il m'a toujours parlé de vous avec une estime infinie, ie sais qu'il comte sur votre amitié, et qu'il la merite, soyes bien persuadé, Monsieur, que personne ne fait plus de cas que moi de vos talens, et ne desire plus de vous connoitre combien iay l'honneur d'etre, Monsieur, Votre tres humble et tres obeissante servante

breteuil du chastellet

a Cirey par Vassy en Champagne
le 12 May, *1737.*

Obviously, Mme du Châtelet, as well as Voltaire, was interested in moral philosophy. But not exclusively, for she also had a penchant for metaphysics, which she considered, as she wrote

---

[9] By a curious slip, the letter is marked "Mme du Châtelet to Pope." But a perusal of its contents proves that it could not have been addressed to Pope. The question as to whether Mme du Châtelet did correspond with Pope is treated in Audra, E., *L'Influence française dans l'œuvre de Pope,* Paris, 1931, 77 N. Mr. Audra notes that the *Amateur d'autographes* (1864-65, II, 77) mentions a letter from Mme du Châtelet to Pope on May 12, 1732. Mr. Audra suggests that the letter, which he had not seen, is counterfeit. It seems rather to be a confusion of dates (1732 for 1737) and a confusion of the addressee (Pope for Du Resnel). The letter in question is doubtless the one published here, which was communicated to me by Professor Sherburn.

to Frederick (Asse, p. 384), the foundation of physics. To Maupertuis (Asse, p. 193), she confessed that she was embarrassed by the problem of liberty, "car enfin je me crois libre, et je ne sais si cette quantité de forces toujours la même dans l'univers ne détruit point la liberté." She was also concerned with the problem of the existence of God, for she confided to Richelieu (Asse, p. 40) : "J'ai mené Du Fay à St. Maur, où j'ai passé huit jours : nous avons disputé pendant le chemin sur l'existence de qui vous savez. . . ." She is generally known to have been interested in physics, but there is no truth in the current remark, that she admired Leibnitz without reservation, while Voltaire preferred Newton. For instance, she stated to Maupertuis (Asse, p. 186) : "M. de Leibnitz, à la vérité, n'avait guère raison que sur les forces vives, mais enfin, il les a découvertes, et c'est avoir deviné un des secrets du Créateur." And to Frederick, who complimented her on the publication of her *Institutions de physique*, 1740, she replied (Asse, p. 384) : "J'ai voulu lui donner (*i.e.* to the public), une idée de la métaphysique de M. de Leibnitz, que j'avoue être la seule qui m'ait satisfaite, quoiqu'il me reste encore bien des doutes." Christian Wolff, the intellectual descendant of Leibnitz, she called (Asse, p. 236) "un grand bavard en métaphysique." Thus she occupied herself with moral philosophy, metaphysics, physics. Only in the drama and history did her interests fail to accord with Voltaire's. Yet, even in the field of the drama, she was not disinterested, for he often consulted her about his own plays along with D'Argental, Cideville and Formont; and he had great respect for her judgment, as is proved repeatedly both by his own correspondence and the letters of Mme de Graffigny. It should not be forgotten, either, that it was the playwright Voltaire who first attracted her attention.

The above extracts from Mme du Châtelet's letters indicate that she did not limit herself to the mere discussion and study of moral philosophy, metaphysics and physics. Although she published but one volume during her lifetime,[10] the *Institutions de physique* of 1740, she was constantly busied with writing, and produced extensively for one whose life's span was only forty-three years. After her death in 1749, Voltaire wrote to D'Argental (Moland XXXVII, 67): "Je viens de relire des matériaux immenses de métaphysique que Mme du Châtelet avait assemblés avec une patience et une sagacité qui m'effrayent." Just what these materials were cannot be determined, since they have been apparently lost. Their loss is regrettable, for a comparison between their content and the metaphysical writings of Voltaire during the period would undoubtedly be very revealing. It is already known that Voltaire wrote at her instigation, or at least at her suggestion, his *Traité de métaphysique*. It is less well-known that the whole first section of the *Eléments de la philosophie de Newton* deals with metaphysics rather than with physics. This section which appears in the book as a sort of "hors-d'œuvre," and which in reality was a late addition,[11] has many points in common with the *Traité de métaphysique*. It would be interesting to see what general resemblance existed between the metaphysical ideas of these two treatises and the "matériaux immenses de métaphysique" of the Marquise. Certainly there would be points of agreement between the two. As a matter of fact, there is one striking bit of evidence which indicates absolute coincidence of their views. It will be remembered that in a letter to Frederick, April 17, 1737, Voltaire defined the limits of metaphysics: "Toute la métaphysique, à mon gré, contient deux choses: la première, tout ce que les hommes de bon sens savent; la seconde, ce qu'ils ne sauront jamais." Mme du Châtelet in her *Institutions de physique,* p. 14, gave a similar definition: "La métaphysique contient deux espèces de choses; la première, ce que tous les gens qui font un bon usage de leur

---

[10] Her dissertation on the nature of fire was published in the *Mémoires* of the Academy of Sciences at the request of Voltaire.

[11] See Bengesco, II, 30.

esprit, peuvent savoir; et la seconde, qui est la plus étendue, ce qu'ils ne sauront jamais."

Similarity in definition is by no means the only point of resemblance in the writers' treatment of metaphysical ideas. Mme du Châtelet once expressed in a letter to Frederick her belief that the only sure foundation of physics was metaphysics, and later, in accordance with this assumption, she devoted the opening chapters of her *Institutions de physique* to metaphysical subjects. Professor Lanson has shown that Voltaire adopted this same theory during the Cirey Period and devoted the first third of the *Eléments de la philosophie de Newton* to metaphysics. But even before the publication of these two works, she had encouraged Voltaire to make an inventory of his metaphysical beliefs, which was published in the Kehl edition as the *Traité de métaphysique*. Obviously, while he was making his inventory, she was likewise engaged and hence the accumulation of "matériaux immenses" which amazed him after her death. How closely her ideas resembled Voltaire's can be noted by comparing her chapter of the *Institutions* on the existence of God with a chapter on the same subject in the *Traité de métaphysique*. It would be idle to quote at length passages from the two works, both of which so evidently are derived from Leibnitz. Two quotations, however, will suffice to bring out their similarity:

Traité, XXXVII, 285 (Beuchot): "J'existe, donc quelquechose existe."

Institutions, 39: "Quelquechose existe, puisque j'existe."

Traité, XXXVII, 284 (Beuchot): "Il y a deux manières de parvenir à la notion d'un être qui préside à l'univers. La plus naturelle et la plus parfaite pour les capacités communes est de considérer non seulement l'ordre qui est dans l'univers, mais la fin à laquelle chaque chose paraît se rapporter."

Institutions, 48: "En étudiant la nature, on découvre quelque partie des vûes, et de l'art du Créateur dans la construction de cet univers . . . la connaissance des causes nous élève jusqu'au Créateur, et nous fait entrer dans le mystère de ses desseins, en nous faisant voir l'ordre admirable qui règne dans l'univers et les rapports de ses différentes parties qui ne sont pas seulement des rapports nécessaires de situation, mais des rapports d'un dessein dont tout porte l'empreinte."

The proof of the existence of God is merely one of the metaphysical problems with which Mme du Châtelet was preoccupied. She was also interested in the question of free-will. We have already found her expressing dread to Maupertuis that the solution of the problem of kinetic energy would be a terrible blow to the doctrine of free-will. That she made efforts to preserve the feeling of free-will in the individual is evident from her anxiety. Just what her ideas on the subject were and what arguments she adduced to defend them have never been disclosed.

Nor has anyone ever inquired how free-will, a metaphysical problem, traditional since the Paduan movement,[12] became of paramount importance to Voltaire. Was his interest in it awakened by treatises such as *De la Liberté,* which was circulated clandestinely and eventually printed in the *Nouvelles libertés de penser* of 1743? Or was it Locke's *Essay Concerning Human Understanding* and Clarke's discussion with Leibnitz which made him aware of the problem? Was it he or Mme du Châtelet who brought it up for discussion at Cirey? Presumably he was awakened to a consideration of the doctrine by his combined acquaintance with the clandestine treatises, Locke and Clarke. And Mme du Châtelet must have been familiar with the traditional French treatment as well as with Locke's. Voltaire was prompted to discuss free-will because it was in the atmosphere and, as Marivaux said, he was the "premier homme du monde à dire ce que tout le monde a pensé." It should, however, be noted that he had already treated it in the thirteenth letter of the *Lettres philosophiques* before Mme du Châtelet could have called it to his attention. But it must be admitted that the

[12] Busson, N., *La Pensée religieuse française de Charron à Pascal,* Paris, 1933.

approach in this particular instance is Locke's and not Voltaire's. The first broad consideration which the latter gave free-will is in the *Traité de métaphysique* and not in the *Lettres philosophiques,* and credit for initiating that work has always gone to Mme du Châtelet.[13]

There is now among the Voltaire papers at Leningrad (Tome IX, pp. 61-74) a treatise marked Chapitre 5 and entitled *De la Liberté* (see Caussy, *op. cit.*). At the end of it, a note in handwriting closely resembling Voltaire's reads: "sur la liberté par M^e du chastelet." The position of the treatise in the manuscript, between notes obviously taken by Mme du Châtelet for her scientific work, and three succeeding chapters on grammar, marked Chapters VI, VII, and VIII, would readily lead to the belief that Chapitre 5, *De la Liberté,* is a portion of a work to which the Chapters VI, VII, and VIII also belong. The remaining Chapters I, II, III, and IV, and whatever chapters followed VIII are now lost. All external evidence points to the conclusion that, in the *De la Liberté,* we have Mme du Châtelet's views on free-will.

A perusal of the contents quickly dispels this assumption, for the *De la Liberté* of the manuscript is the article which Voltaire sent to Frederick in October 1737 with a covering letter explaining that it was an "extrait d'un chapitre sur la liberté" (Beuchot LII, 520 ff.). It is inconceivable that Voltaire would send to Frederick as his own, an article by Mme du Châtelet.

---

[13] Once Voltaire had been led to give serious consideration to the problem, it became for him, as apparently for Mme du Châtelet, the central problem of metaphysics. It will be recalled, that having completed the *Traité de métaphysique,* Voltaire offered to send a copy of it to Frederick, an offer which was immediately vetoed by the astute Mme du Châtelet. Seeing the impossibility of transmitting the whole *Traité* to Frederick, Voltaire then extracted from it what he must have considered its most important chapter, that on free-will, and having revised it to give it a unity all its own, he sent a draft to Frederick. And thereupon, a new complication was added to the Cirey atmosphere, for Frederick raised objections to Voltaire's solutions and a lengthy discussion ensued, which did not end until 1749. The main lines of this discussion can be followed in Moland XXXIV, 324, 368, 394, 412, 432, 454.

Besides the unthinkable indiscretion of such an act, there remains the very positive evidence that the ideas in the article are Voltaire's and were repeated not only in the *Traité de métaphysique* and the *Discours en vers sur l'homme* but in the lengthy correspondence between him and Frederick concerning the article. There seems to be absolutely no reason to extract the article from the Voltaire canon and return it to Mme du Châtelet, except the fact that the manuscript occurs in that lady's papers. But another explanation may be proffered for this circumstance.

A close examination of the manuscript reveals that it was redacted previous to the copy sent Frederick, since in the main its corrections and erasures have been observed in the Frederick version. Some errors occurred in making the Frederick copy, due chiefly to hasty copying or an imperfect understanding of the text. In each case where there is divergence, the Leningrad manuscript would seem to be the correct form, except in one case where Voltaire added four words to the printed text. On the other hand, there is considerable rearrangement of the order of presentation in the Frederick version, though all this rearrangement has been indicated in the manuscript. These observations tend to establish the manuscript as the earlier, corrected version of what was sent to Frederick. But the treatise when composed was not intended for Frederick. As a matter of fact, he received it only when Mme du Châtelet refused to allow Voltaire to send a promised copy of the *Traité de métaphysique*.

According to Voltaire, the article was merely an extract from a chapter on free-will. And indeed it was but a portion of a larger work, for besides being marked "Chapitre 5," it is divided in sections beginning with eighty-four and continuing through eighty-seven. We have a part of the end of section eighty-three although it has been scratched out. It reads:

. . . Liberté, et l'on voit aizément que les philosophes qui prétendent que la quantité de mouvement est invariable dans l'univers, nient à l'homme cette faculté soi-mouvante. (Note 1.)

Note 1 which has likewise been scratched out reads:

Note 1. je n'examine point ici si l'opinion (de la conservation d'une égale) qui veut que la quantité de force reste la même dans l'univers est aussi contraire à la liberté que celle d'une égale quantité de mouvement. Voyez sur cela ch. 8.

The initial sentence has also been scratched out and in its place has been substituted the opening sentence as it occurs in Beuchot. However, the sentence as originally written was better adapted to furnish the transition from what had gone before and which was now eliminated. Originally, the opening sentence read:

§ 84. Il est certain que la question de notre liberté (si c'en est une) nous intéresse infiniment plus que toutes celles que l'on peut faire sur la nature du mouvement et sur sa conservation, puisque de cette seule question dépend toute la morale.

From these scratched-out portions of the manuscript, some evidence concerning the nature of the projected work, of which it is only a part, may be deduced. In the first place, one may reasonably assume that it was intended to be a fairly long one. The four sections which we have occupy over fifteen pages in Beuchot. If it progressed at the same rate, it would comprise over three hundred pages before the end of the fifth chapter. But there were at least eight chapters, because note 1 which has been marked out, already referred to a Chapter 8. The Leningrad manuscript also gives a clue concerning the nature of the work. At one point in the argument, the author avers that if man does not have free-will, the Deity cannot possess it either. He refers at this point in the manuscript to a § 15, n. 6. In the copy sent Frederick, the reference does not occur, but two paragraphs are inserted which discuss free-will in the Deity. I assume that these paragraphs are either extracted from § 15, n. 6, or that they give a summary of the discussion of § 15. If this assumption is correct, the first part of the work dealt with the nature and existence of God. What followed this first part cannot be ascertained by any reconstruction. It is none the less certain that there was a subsequent section on the nature and existence of matter. For at the point in the manuscript where Voltaire is refuting the argument of the materialists, who maintain that man's inward feeling of freedom is no proof of its existence because it may be deceptive (Beuchot LII, 530), Mme du Châtelet has appended a note which reads (p. 64):

Note. La reponse a cette seconde objection est presque la même que celle du 3ᵉ argument contre l'existence des corps. Mais cela ne peut être autrement puisque les personnes qui nient la liberté font contre elle une partie des objections que ceux qui nient l'existence des corps font contre cette existence.

The closing lines of Chapter 4 which we have quoted above give an indication of its content. Evidently the subject has again changed from the existence of matter to the more concrete problems in physics of the conservation of matter and kinetic energy. It should be recalled here as particularly significant that Mme du Châtelet had already confessed to Maupertuis that the solution of the problem of kinetic energy was a terrible blow to the doctrine of free-will. Evidently the author of the *De la Liberté* has been led to think likewise, since he follows with a dissertation on free-will, although he admits digressing from his subject (Beuchot LII, 526):

Un aussi grand intérêt mérite bien que je m'éloigne un peu de mon sujet pour entrer dans cette discussion.

This "aussi grand intérêt" proves upon investigation to be none other than the question of "la morale" which was probably discussed in lost Chapters 6 and 7 and certainly discussed in Chapter 8. Hence, with all due allowance for unknown and unverified subject matter, we can assert with a fair degree of assurance that the full work, of which the *De la Liberté* is a portion, dealt with the nature and existence of God, the nature and existence of matter, problems of physics, free-will, and "la morale." But precisely these subjects (along with the question of the soul and the origin of ideas) are treated in the *Traité de métaphysique*. The question immediately arises: was this the real *Traité de métaphysique,* of

which the *Traité de métaphysique* printed by Kehl is but a mutilated version, or was it the first draft of the now-existent, condensed *Traité?* In view of the circumstances surrounding the
discovery and printing of the Kehl *Traité,* and in view also of
the fact that the chapter on free-will in the Leningrad manuscript
is much fuller than the chapter in the printed *Traité,* I am inclined to believe that only a mutilated version of the *Traité de
métaphysique* has been preserved.

At all events, we are now in a position to see more clearly the
relationship of Voltaire and Mme du Châtelet in the confection
of the *Traité de métaphysique.* It has already been known that
Mme du Châtelet suggested the writing of the treatise. But it
now appears that she also presented problems for consideration
and debated them with Voltaire. Moreover, Voltaire gave her
the finished sections for comment and in one case at least she
added a comment. Indeed, this explains why the manuscript was
among her papers. On the other hand, as we shall see, she talked
over with him her translation of Mandeville and handed to him
her finished sections for comment. This explains how so much
of Mandeville and so much more of Mme du Châtelet's additions
to Mandeville entered into the composition of Chapters VIII and
IX of the *Traité.*[14]

Other treatises of Mme du Châtelet have been preserved in
various libraries. The Leningrad Public Library possesses, for
example, among the Voltaire collection of manuscripts,[15] her
preface and translation of Mandeville's *Fable of the Bees,* portions of her *Institutions de physique,* her notes and commentaries
on Descartes, some scattered "pensées," and other material, some
of which she merely copied, such as the *Dissertation sur Elie et
Enoch* and the *Religion* of Dumarsais. Of these works, the most
deserving of attention is her translation of Mandeville's *Fable
of the Bees* which has never been published, except for a few

---

[14] See *infra,* p. 33.
[15] Caussy, F., *Inventaire des manuscrits de la bibliothèque de Voltaire,*
Paris, 1914, pp. 43-44.

pages of Mandeville's own preface which Mme de Graffigny transcribed while at Cirey.[16] Since Mme de Graffigny was at Cirey between December 4, 1738 and February 10, 1739, the translation must have been made by this time. However, Mme de Graffigny commented upon the fact that Mme du Châtelet had composed a preface to the translation in half an hour. Since in all likelihood the preface to the work would be the last portion written, Mme de Graffigny's stay at Cirey gives a terminus for the translation. But it was undoubtedly made some time before, because the preface is now dated 1735. This date comes as a bit of a surprise, for it shows that Mme du Châtelet, and presumably Voltaire, were acquainted with Mandeville before the *Mondain* was written, or rather that they were becoming acquainted with Mandeville while the *Mondain* was being written. Thus, there is now an explanation for the similarity between certain passages in the *Mondain* and Mandeville. Mr. Morize,[17] having noted the parallel passages in the two works, was unwilling to treat Mandeville as a source for the *Mondain,* since there was no evidence of Voltaire's familiarity with the English moralist. It would now appear from the date upon Mme du Châtelet's manuscript that Mandeville was Voltaire's major source for the *Mondain.*

Mme du Châtelet did not translate the poem, called by Mandeville *The Grumbling Hive.* Her reason for not doing so, she explained on pp. 15-16 of her "avertissement":

ie n'ay point traduit la fable des abeilles qui a donné lieu aux remarques parce qu'il faudroit que cette traduction fut en vers et que ie n'en fais point, d'ailleurs elle me paroit peu necessaire, chaque remarque est un petit traité de morale, i'y ay mis des titres au lieu des vers de la fable qui sont dans l'original anglais, et ie crois que ce livre n'en sera pas moins utile et moins agréable au public.

As a matter of fact, all that now remains of her translation is her own *Préface du traducteur* (pp. 1-16), the *Avertissement du*

[16] See *Vie privée de Voltaire et Mme du Châtelet,* Paris, 1820, pp. 146-149.
[17] Morize, A., *Le Mondain et l'Apologie du luxe au XVIIIe siècle,* Paris, 1909, p. 75.

traducteur (pp. 15-16) which we have just quoted, the translation of Mandeville's *Preface* (pp. 17-29), which is in reality the merging of Mandeville's *Preface* to his 1714 edition and his *Introduction;* the translation of Mandeville's *Enquiry into the Origin of Moral Virtue* (pp. 27-47); and of his remarks A to L inclusive (pp. 48-127). Since this translation represents only an infinitesimal amount of the *Remarks,* not to mention the *Essay on Charity and Charity-Schools* and the whole of Part II of the *Fable,* one questions whether Mme du Châtelet abandoned her task after completing so little of it or whether only a small portion of her translation has been preserved in the manuscript now at Leningrad. In view of the fact that she wrote her own preface to the work as if she were preparing it for the printer, and that in 1738-39 she exhibited it to Mme de Graffigny as completed, it would seem that the major portion of the manuscript is now lost. This should occasion no surprise, for of her manuscripts which Voltaire preserved in his own papers (See Caussy, *op. cit.*), not a single one is complete. Apparently, these were not Mme du Châtelet's original manuscripts, but copies of portions of them which she passed to Voltaire for his marginal comments. And not infrequently a comment occurs written in his own hand.

In the translator's preface, which I have published integrally in the appendix (see Appendix III), Mme du Châtelet has disclosed not only her reasons for making the translation, and her method of procedure, but she has offered a veritable plea for woman's rights in literature. Having reached an age at which she is aware of life's brevity, she confesses amazement at her previous concern for her body's care and her neglect of her mental development. Realizing that it is too late to acquire new talents and that she possesses no remarkable talent for creative production, she has resolved to devote herself to translating the works of others, being convinced that a good translation is worth more than a bad French work. Moreover, translators perform a distinct and honorable service as "tradesmen" of literature, and are all the more deserving since they make but little claim to fame.

Their great achievement is rendering ideas available to readers who are unable to do the translating themselves. Locke, for instance, would have been practically unknown on the Continent had it not been for Coste's translation. Their great defect is bad rendering of the original, either because they have not clearly comprehended it or because they have substituted their ideas for the original ones.

Mme du Châtelet attempts to defend her position by stating that, important as translations are, they can only represent a mediocre form of literature. Even so, she thinks people may find it surprising to see a translation undertaken by a woman, for women are only permitted to write comedies. She protests against the injustice of this. For centuries woman has never produced a good tragedy, a good poem, an estimable history, a beautiful painting, a good book on science. Why? Surely, it is not because she is mentally inferior to man. It is some defect in her education or prejudice on the part of society which is responsible.

Having decided to devote herself to this type of work, Mme du Châtelet turns to the English because of her admiration for their vigorous way of thinking, and selects the *Fable of the Bees*. She considers it a work admirably adapted to the needs of humanity and declares it the best book on ethics that has ever been written. In her opinion, Mandeville is the Montaigne of the English, but a Montaigne with more method and a clearer notion of things. None the less, he has his defects: his style is poor and often tedious; his remarks are sometimes extravagant and dangerous for the general reading public. Hence, the translator announces her intention of purifying his style, correcting his exaggerations and even of adding remarks of her own.

To tell the truth, Mme du Châtelet's translation is hardly more than a translation of ideas. Not only have long, tedious passages been abridged, but others, which seem neither long nor tedious, have been suppressed. Even in the rendition of the idea there is sometimes a curious shift in emphasis. For instance, Mandeville had written in his preface (Ed. Kaye I, 6):

For the main Design of the Fable (as it is briefly explained in the Moral) is to shew the Impossibility of enjoying all the most elegant Comforts of Life that are to be met with in an industrious, wealthy and powerful Nation, and at the same time be bless'd with all the Virtue and Innocence that can be wish'd for in a Golden Age. . . .

This passage was rendered by Mme du Châtelet as follows (p. 18):

Mon principal but a été de faire voir combien l'innocence et les vertus du prétendu âge d'or sont incompatibles avec les richesses et la puissance d'un grand état. . . .

It might be added that this particular rendering is close to the intent of Voltaire's *Mondain,* though it is not a faithful rendition of Mandeville. Another trick of Mme du Châtelet as translator is to add an interpretation which is not implied in the original text. Thus when Mandeville states at the end of his introduction (*op. cit.,* I, 40):

. . . I have thought fit to enquire how Man, no better qualified, might yet by his own Imperfections be taught to distinguish between Virtue and Vice. And here I must desire the Reader once for all to take notice, that when I say Men, I mean neither Jews nor Christians; but meer Man, in the State of Nature and Ignorance of the true Deity.

Mme du Châtelet, preoccupied with her own ideas, has added to (and incidently subtracted from) this idea until it is no longer Mandeville's (p. 24):

On y verra d'où le bien et le mal moral ont pris leur naissance, et j'espère convaincre le lecteur, que l'homme ne doit point les idées qu'il en a, à aucune religion. Il est bon d'avertir ici une fois pour toutes que je n'entends parler dans cette recherche ni des Juifs, ni des Chrétiens.

There is no need to dwell upon Mme du Châtelet's mis-translations which are relatively rare. It is true that she thought Mama the name of a girl and Urchin the name of a boy, but on the other hand she comprehended quite correctly such terms as "blackguard" and "scavingers." Her vocabulary is not so rich as

Mandeville's, nor is her expression so vigorous. This difference in style is understandable in a country where classic taste still prevailed.

Of considerably more importance are the conscious additions which Mme du Châtelet made to Mandeville. She makes four of these additions (pp. 21-22, 27-28, 32-34, 43-46) and contradicts twice (p. 43, p. 46) the author of the *Fable*. The first addition occurs in her rendition of his preface. He had just been explaining that the dirty streets of London were necessary concomitants to the wealthy business of the city. Mme du Châtelet evidently felt the need of a more explicit example for his thesis and inserted the following passage:

Tout a des details immenses, auxquels peu de gens font attention. On glisse sur la surface des choses, les gens du monde qui se levent a midy, ignorent les travaux que le disner qu'on leur sert a couté et combien il faut qu'il entre dans la ville de charettes, de bestiaux et de personnes de la campagne pour qu'on puisse a leur reveil, leur servir un repas delicieux. Ils ne voyent dans tout cela qu'une aisance devenüe trop ordinaire pour estre remarquée. Mais le philosophe y voit l'industrie et les travaux de tout un peuple, qui a travaillé a ses plaisirs. Le bourgeois de son costé ne voit que la crote qui luy gâte ses souliers, et ne pense pas que dans les villes ou les rües sont propres on ne joüit d'aucune des commodités que l'abondance de Londres luy procure iusques dans sa mediocrité.

The second passage was inserted just after the opening paragraph in the essay on moral virtue. Mandeville had just presented his paradox in the form of a telescoped syllogism: every animal seeks pleasure; the more passions, the more pleasures; the more passions, the less sociable the animal can be. But Man, the animal with the most passions, is also the most sociable. How explain this situation? Mandeville used the following pages to show how wise legislators appealing to Man's pride tricked him into believing that his merit was greater if he sometimes renounced his personal interest in favor of the community's good. Mme du Châtelet, and apparently Voltaire, were prepared to accept his explanation of the theory of the formation of government, but were interested in knowing how the social group needing this government had been formed. Hence the resourceful Mme du Châtelet inserted her paragraph :

L'amour paroit avoir dû estre le commencement de toute société. L'homme comme tous les autres animaux a un penchant invincible a la propagation de son espece. Un homme estant devenu amoureux d'une femme en aura eü des enfans. Le soin de leur famille aura fait subsister leur union au dela de leur goût. Deux familles auront eu besoin l'une de l'autre des qu'elles auront esté formées, et ces besoins mutuels auront donné naissance a la société. Ainsi Lucrece avoit raison quand il disoit a Venus : nec sine te quicquam dias in luminis oras exoritur. Les besoins mutuels ayant rassemblé les hommes les plus adroits d'entre eux s'aperçûrent que l'homme etoit né avec un orgueil indomptable, et c'est de l'empire que cette passion a sur luy que les premiers legislateurs ont tiré les plus grands secours pour parvenir a civiliser les hommes.

The third passage occurs just after Mandeville has shown how society has arbitrarily labeled as vice, whatever is contrary to its interest and as virtue, whatever is to its advantage. But society is established by pride, hence pride is the source of vice and virtue. Mme du Châtelet, and presumably Voltaire, were willing to accept this theory, for it explained not only the arbitrary character of laws but the relativity of manners and customs. But it had one serious defect. It did not take into consideration the necessity for Moral Law, and neither Voltaire nor Mme du Châtelet approved of this exclusion. Hence, the latter inserted a paragraph in defence of "bienveillance" and the Natural Law :

Voila pour quoy ces noms de *vice* et de *vertu* sont donnés quelques fois a des actions opposées dans differents pays, car les besoins de la société sont differents en differents climats. Mais dans tous les pays on appelle *vertu* ce qui est conforme aux loix etablies, et *vice* ce qui leur est opposé, car aucune société n'a pû subsister sans avoir des loix, de mesme qu'on ne peut ioüer, s'il n'y a des regles du ieu. Mais de mesme que ce qui est une faute au piquet, n'en est pas une au reversi aussi ce qui est vice a Paris, est vertu a Constantinople. Mais tous les hommes s'accordent a observer les loix etablies ches eux, et a regarder les actions comme bonnes ou mauvaises selon leur relation ou leur opposition a ces loix. Il y a une loy universelle pour tous les hommes que Dieu a luy mesme gravée dans leur cœur. Cette loy est, *ne fais pas a autruy ce que tu ne voudrois pas qui te fust fait*, et ie crois que le sage Lock a esté trop loin, quand apres avoir detruit les idées innées, il a avancé qu'il n'y avoit point d'idées de morale universelle. Il n'y a point de peuple, quelque barbare qu'il soit, chés qui, des qu'il y aura une apparence de societé, il soit permis de manquer a sa parolle. Le besoin de la société exige cette loy comme son fondement et les besoins qui sont differents dans les differents pays se reunissent tous dans cette maxime, *ne fais pas a autruy ce que tu ne voudrois pas qui te fust fait*. Le bien de la société est à la verité, le seul *criterium* du vice et de la vertu. Mais cette maxime est non seullement indispensable dans toute societé civilisée, mais tout homme l'a imprimée dans son cœur. Elle est une suitte necessaire de la bienveillance naturelle, que nous avons pour nostre espece : bienveillance que le créateur a mis dans nous et dont nous sentons les effets involontairement, comme la faim et la soif. C'est de quoy ie parlerai bientost plus amplement. Il est vray que sans le secours des loix et des chatimens qu'elles infligent a ceux qui nuisent aux autres, l'interest personel l'emporteroit souvent sur le *dictamen* de la nature. Car l'amour-propre est avec raison plus fort que la bienveillance pour nostre espece, mais quand nostre interest ne nous y porte pas, il n'y a aucun homme a moins qu'il n'ait perdu le sens qui aille assassiner son voisin pour son plaisir.

Mme du Châtelet's preoccupation with Natural Law is responsible also for the fourth insertion which occurs near the end of Mandeville's essay. In Mandeville's paradoxical system where action is guided by interest, there is really no room for altruistic action. And yet there are actions such as saving a child from a fire, or dispensing alms which Mandeville had to consider. His consideration is very summary indeed. He stated that such acts cannot be called altruistic unless the motives prompting them are known and judged, for in these motives a fair degree of pride is ever present. Moreover, he denied that either of the two acts mentioned are necessarily virtuous. To this statement, Mme du Châtelet took violent exception, appending to each case the same note as follows :

Cela est tres faux meme selon les principes de l'auteur, car de sauver un enfant des flames est une action tres utile a la societé et de quelque sens qu'on la regarde c'est une action de vertu et ne le pas faire seroit un tres grand crime.

But contradicting the author does not obviate the difficulty. Hence, she inserted her fourth passage explaining that "mésaise" took its origin in "bienveillance" which had its source in Natural Law:

Ce mesaise involontaire que nous sentons quand nous voyons un de nos semblables dans un danger actuel, est un des traits que le créateur a luy mesme imprimé a son ouvrage. L'homme paroit estre le seul animal qui ait cette bienveillance pour son espece. Les autres animaux ont reçue de l'Etre Supreme l'amour de leur conservation, le desir de la propagation. Plusieurs connoissent l'orgueil et l'emulation, mais aucun ne marque cet amour pour son espece qui est imprimé dans le cœur de l'homme et qui paroit un de ces traits distinctifs qui separent les differents etres. Qu'un chien rencontre un chien expirant, il lechera son sang et continuera son chemin, mais si l'homme rencontre un autre homme son premier mouvement sera de le secourir, et il le secourera surement. Il n'a rien a craindre des marques de sa compassion.

On etouffe ce dictamen de la nature, les hommes malgré cette bienveillance mutuelle, ne laissent pas de s'égorger en bataille rangée, et de s'assasiner mutuellement. La greve est touiours pleine de badauts qui accourent lorsqu'on y fait quelque exécution, mais il n'y a aucun de ces meurtriers payés par le roy, ni de ces badauts dont la curiosité paroit si cruelle qui n'ait eu a surmonter la première fois cette bienveillance naturelle que nous n'effaçons jamais entierement de nostre ame.

Je crois que Mr. de St. Real a bien tort lorsque recherchant quelle peut estre la cause du plaisir barbare que le peuple prend a voir une execution, il l'attribüe au plaisir interieur que nous sentons a estre exempts des mesmes malheurs. La seule source de ce plaisir barbare c'est la curiosité et l'habitude. La curiosité fait surmonter la premiere fois le mesaise involontaire que nous sentons a la veüe des tourments de ces malheureux, et l'habitude ensuite nous y rend insensibles. C'est par la mesme raison qu'un homme qui se voüera a tous les saints et a tous les medecins pour revenir d'une maladie, monte gayement la tranchée, et attaque un chemin couvert. La vanité luy fait surmonter la premiere fois l'eloignement naturel que nous avons du danger, mais il n'y a que l'habitude qui puisse inspirer aux gens de guerre cette gayeté qu'ils portent la plus part dans des endroits dont l'idée seule les feroit fremir en d'autres tems, et il n'y en a aucun quelque brave qu'il soit, qui n'ait senti que nature patissoit en luy au premier coup de canon qu'il a entendu tirer quoiqu'ils finissent par joüer a la boulle avec leurs boulets, c'est ce qui est arrivé au Siège de Philisbourg.

The real significance of Mme du Châtelet's translation of Mandeville can be readily grasped if it is compared with Chapters VIII and IX of the *Traité de métaphysique*. Voltaire accepts Mandeville's theory that pride is the foundation of the State, that wise legislators, dividing mankind into two groups—those willing to sacrifice their interest for the common good, and those unwilling to do so—have persuaded the former group, by appealing to their pride, to organize into a social state. He even goes so far as to accept Mandeville's misanthropic remark to the effect that every one wants to belong to the first group, although in reality every one belongs to the second. He also admits the English philosopher's definition of virtue, as any action which redounds to the common good, and vice as any action which is harmful to that same common good. He confesses that vice and virtue have their origin in the passions. But here his acceptance of the Mandevillian creed ends and throughout Chapters VIII and IX of the *Traité de métaphysique,* his modifications of Mandeville are drawn largely from Mme du Châtelet's four insertions. He avers, for instance, that love first formed families, and families groups, before mutual needs led to the formation of the State. He admits that laws are relative to the climates for which they were made. He emphasizes that irrespective of positive laws, there is in every man a God-given, instinctive love for his kind, "bienveillance." He confesses that this "bienveillance" is not always stronger than self-love. A cursory perusal of the *Traité de métaphysique* will establish beyond all cavil that Voltaire in writing these two chapters was deeply influenced by both Mandeville and Mme du Châtelet.

Another manuscript of Mme du Châtelet now at the Bibliothèque Nationale (F. Fr. 12266-12268) is entitled "Principes mathématiques de la Philosophie naturelle, par M. Newton, traduits en français par Madame la Marquise du Chastellet, avec un commentaire sur les propositions qui ont rapport au sistème du monde." She is supposed to have been occupied with this work when she died, but there are reasons to suspect that she completed it before her death. A note to F. Fr. 12268 reads: "Commentaire sur le livre des principes mathématiques de Mr. Newton, papiers déposés à la bibliothèque du roy par Mᵉ du Chastellet entre les mains de Mr. l'abbé Sallier le 10ᵉ 7ᵇʳᵉ 1749."[18] Furthermore, to Père François Jacquier (1711-1788), a mathematician of some repute, she wrote November 12, 1745:[19]

Je travaille quand j'ay du tems à une traduction de Newton. Si j'avais plus de tems, j'aurois entrepris celle de votre beau comentaire. Mais je me contenterai d'en donner quelques propositions, parce que je crains infiniment d'être prévenue dans mon travail qui est presque fini, et qui est cependant encore un secret que je vous recommande.

The following year, 1746, Clairaut wrote to Jacquier:[20]

Mme du Châtelet a travaillé comme un forçat toute l'année dernière et une partie de celle-ci à la traduction de Newton. Il n'a pas laissé de refluer beaucoup de travail sur moi, et j'ai actuellement sa traduction à revoir. Elle est dans l'intention d'y joindre un comentaire à la fin. Mais, il n'est pas, à vous dire vrai, encore fait. . . .

During the year 1747, or at least during the first half of the year, Mme du Châtelet was still occupied with Newton. On April 13, 1747, she wrote to Jacquier:[21]

Je suis toujours fort occupée à mon Newton. On l'imprime actuellement. Je revois les épreuves ce qui est fort ennuieux, et je travaille au comentaire, ce qui est fort difficile.

[18] Mme du Châtelet died on the 9-10 September, 1749.

[19] Jovy, E., *Quelques lettres inédites de la Mᶦˢᵉ du Châtelet et de la Duchesse de Choiseul (1745-1775)*, Paris, H. Leclerc, 1906, in-8°, p. 10.

[20] *Ibid.*, p. 16.   [21] *Ibid.*, p. 14.

And on July 1, 1747, she announced that the first volume was almost entirely printed :[22]

Je suis, je vous l'avoue, fort occupée de mon Newton. Le premier livre est presque tout imprimé, il y aura quelque comentaire, mais il ne sera pas perpétuel. Il sera dans le second volume à la suite du troisième livre et ne roulera que sur le sistème du monde et les propositions du premier livre qui y ont raport.

In spite of the progress which Mme du Châtelet seemed to be making with her book, it did not appear until 1759, apparently having been seen through the press by Clairaut.[23] Despite Beuchot's opinion to the contrary, it is quite possible that Voltaire had a part in the publication of the work, since, not only did the edition contain his poem "Sur la physique de Newton. A Mme la Marquise du Châtelet," but also his "Préface Historique," which he had already had published in the *Journal étranger* in 1752.[24]

In addition to the translation of Newton's *Principia,* there is also in the second volume Mme du Châtelet's commentary to which she referred in her letter to Jacquier. This commentary is divided into two parts : *Exposition abrégée du système du monde, et explication des principaux phénomènes astronomiques tirée des Principes de M. Newton* (II, 1-116), and *Solution analytique des principaux problêmes qui concernent le systême du monde* (II, 117-286). We are not concerned with the *Solution analytique,* since it is purely mathematical. The *Exposition abrégée* is more interesting, since it is in reality another *Eléments de la philosophie de Newton,* of which Mme du Châtelet did not whole-heartedly approve (*Institutions,* p. 7) The work is divided into six chapters preceded by an introduction as follows:

[22] *Ibid.,* p. 16.
[23] *Principes mathématiques de la philosophie naturelle* [traduits de l'anglais de Newton], par feue Mme la marquise du Chastellet. Paris, Desaint et Saillant, 1759, 2 vols., in-4°. B. N. V 6301-6302.
[24] See Moland XXIII, 515. There are, however, three slight changes. The Moland edition contains three short paragraphs not in the edition of 1759. *Cf.* Moland, p. 519, §1 and §3. The paragraph at the bottom of p. 517 has been slightly rearranged.

A comparison of these chapter headings with some of Voltaire's
in his *Eléments de la philosophie de Newton,* Part III, brings out
a marked similarity:

No one has ever denied that Mme du Châtelet exerted a strong
influence in turning Voltaire from poetry and the theatre to
metaphysics and physics.[25] He himself was the first to recognize
his indebtedness to her. When the *Eléments de la philosophie de
Newton* appeared in 1738, the text was preceded by a poem in
verse, "A Mme du Châtelet," as well as by an "Avant-propos,"
likewise dedicated to Mme la Marquise du Ch******. In the
"Avant-propos," Voltaire did not hesitate to present the work as
exclusively the labor of Mme du Châtelet:

Madame, ce n'est point ici une marquise, ni une philosophie imaginaire. L'étude solide que vous avez faite de plusieurs vérités, et le
fruit d'un travail respectable sont ce que j'offre au public pour
votre gloire, pour celle de votre sexe, et pour l'utilité de quiconque

25 *Cf.* Lanson, *Voltaire,* p. 56: "Elle le tirait vers les besognes moins sca-
breuses, vers les études qu'elle aimait. Elle l'appliquait aux sciences, aux cal-
culs, aux expériences."

voudra cultiver sa raison et jouir sans peine de vos recherches. . . .
Vous vous bornez dans cette étude, dont je rends compte, à vous
faire seulement une idée nette de ces ressorts si déliés et si puissants,
de ces loix primitives de la nature que Newton a découvertes, à
examiner jusqu'où l'on a été avant lui, d'où il est parti, et où il s'est
arrêté. Nous commencerons . . .

It is to be noted that Voltaire spoke in the "Avant-propos" as if
the *Eléments* were the joint production of Mme du Châtelet and
himself, Mme du Châtelet furnishing the explanations and he
transcribing them. In the *Epître dédicatoire de l'édition de 1748*
he not only stressed the collaboration, but also the fact that Mme
du Châtelet had now progressed much further than he in her
studies of Newton:[26]

Madame,

Lorsque je mis pour la première fois votre nom respectable à la
tête de ces Eléments de philosophie, je m'instruisais avec vous. Mais
vous avez pris depuis un vol que je ne peux plus suivre. Je me
trouve à présent dans le cas d'un grammairien qui auroit présenté
un essai de rhétorique ou à Démosthène ou à Cicéron. J'offre de
simples Eléments à celle qui a pénétré toutes les profondeurs de la
géométrie transcendante, et qui seule parmi nous a traduit et commenté le grand Newton.

As a matter of fact, Mme du Châtelet had by 1748 profoundly
entered into Newton's thought. The translation of the *Principia*,
and the *Solution analytique* which she had worked out with the
assistance of Clairaut, were far beyond the comprehension of
Voltaire, who could admire even if he could not follow. For her
part, Mme du Châtelet, better instructed since her translation of
the *Principia* was now in a better position to vulgarize the ideas
of Newton than when she collaborated in writing the *Eléments*.
Apparently discontented with the book of 1738, she wrote the
Exposition abrégée du système du monde and appended it to the
Principes. The *Exposition* is clearer than the third part of Voltaire's work and shows, even on rapid reading, a readier grasp of
the subject.

[26] Moland XXII, 400-402.

Mme du Châtelet, however, did not hesitate to incorporate in her new work what she had undoubtedly contributed to the third part of the *Eléments*. Upon comparing the section of her treatise concerning *Des comètes* with the corresponding passage in the *Eléments,* we can see how closely she and Voltaire had worked together :[27]

Les péripatéticiens prenoient les comètes pour des météores.	Il n'est pas inutile de rappeller ici la pensée d'Aristote et de tous les péripatéticiens sur les comètes.
Tycho reconnut qu'elles étoient par de là la lune.	Tycho-Brahé fut le premier des modernes qui osa dire que les comètes n'étaient point au-dessous de la lune.
Descartes en faisoit des planètes errantes de tourbillons en tourbillons.	Il (Descartes) disait que c'étoient des soleils encroûtés, qui, ayant quitté le centre de leur tourbillon, s'en allaient éternellement et le plus qu'ils pouvaient en ligne directe des confins d'un tourbillon dans les confins d'un autre tourbillon. . . .
Mr. Newton reconnut que les comètes tournoient autour du soleil et étoient soumises aux mêmes lois que les planètes.	Newton embrassa une théorie générale ; il prouve que toute comète doit paraître décrire une parabole autour du soleil, et assigne l'espèce de parabole qu'elle doit paraître décrire dans tous les cas.
Il détermina l'orbite d'une comète quelconque par trois observations.	Or Newton, aidé du célèbre astronome Halley, le Cassini d'Angleterre, ayant suivi dans son cours cette comète de 1680, qui fit tant de bruit inventa une nouvelle théorie par laquelle il détermina la figure de l'orbite que devoit décrire ce comète.

[27] The *Exposition* has printed marginal summaries which I give. For Voltaire, the sentence which corresponds with the summary is given.

Il vérifia son calcul, par les observations d'un grand nombre de comètes.

La durée de leur période ne se peut trouver qu'en trouvant dans l'histoire des apparitions des comètes dans les mêmes circonstances et à intervalles égaux.

Pour s'assurer du cours et du retour des comètes, il faudrait premièrement une longue suite bien conservée d'observations exactes; ensuite, si une comète fait en même temps le même chemin à la même distance, avec la même chevelure et la même queue qu'une comète observée autrefois, on ne sera pas encore absolument certain que cette comète soit la même.

M. Halley a employé la période de celle de 1680 à rectifier l'orbite de cette comète.

La Comète de 1682 doit reparaître en 1758.

[Voltaire says in 500 years]

Différentes opinions sur les queues des comètes.

Descartes s'est mépris dans l'explication de cette queue des comètes.

M. Newton prétend qu'elles ne sont qu'une fumée qui s'exhale du corps de la comète.

Ces trainées de lumière ne sont autre chose que des parties enflammées de la comète même.

Ce qui confirme cette opinion.

Ce qu'il y a de plus surprenant, c'est que Newton a mesuré la ligne que décrit cette fumée de la comète.

Usages de ces queues selon Mr. Newton.

Newton, au contraire, les regarde avec raison comme des effets de la bonté divine, et physiquement nécessaires aux mondes dans le voisinage desquels elles voyagent.

Thus Mme du Châtelet, having contributed material to the *Eléments*, reclaimed and incorporated it in the *Exposition*. It is noteworthy that she followed in her treatise Voltaire's plan of organization in his *Eléments*. That Voltaire, however, recognized the superiority of her treatise over his own, may be gathered from the fact that in later editions he suppressed the chapters which were so largely her work: Chapter XI in 1748, and Chapters XII and XIII in 1756. To the edition of 1756, he added the following note:

On ne poussera pas ici plus loin les recherches sur la gravitation. Cette doctrine étoit encore toute nouvelle quand l'auteur l'exposa en 1736. Elle ne l'est plus, il faut se conformer au temps. Plus les hommes sont devenus éclairés, moins il faut écrire.

A third manuscript of Mme du Châtelet, now at the Bibliothèque Nationale (F. Fr. 13084) contains her *Réflexions sur le bonheur* which were published in 1796 in the *Opuscules philosophiques et littéraires, la pluspart posthumes ou inédits* and again in 1806 in the *Lettres inédites de Mme du Châtelet à M. le Comte D'Argental* along with an essay *Sur l'Existence de Dieu* extracted from the *Institutions de physique*. The *Réflexions sur le bonheur,* analyzed by Maurel in a recent work about the Marquise,[28] not only contain interesting ideas but deal with subject matter which apparently attracted the attention of several of the Cirey habitués. Helvétius, who had already visited Cirey, had sketched his *Epître sur le bonheur.* Voltaire first gave the title of *Epîtres sur le bonheur* to the poems which he later published as *Discours en vers sur l'homme,* and it must be admitted that his former title is really more appropriate than his latter one. La Mettrie also contributed a *Dissertation sur le bonheur.* Mme du Châtelet's position is quite close to Voltaire's, although there is more than a touch also of La Mettrie's physical approach to the problem, intermingled with Helvétius's *Epître sur les plaisirs de l'étude.*

In 1792, there appeared in Paris a *Doutes sur les religions révélées, adressées à Voltaire, Par Emilie du Châtelet, ouvrage posthume,* with the epigraph "quodcumque ostendis mihi sic, in-

---

[28] A. Maurel, *La Marquise du Châtelet,* Paris, 1930, pp. 158-166.

credulus odi." It is, however, not at all certain that Mme du Châtelet was responsible for these *Doutes*[29] which have been attributed to Frederick the Great, Mallet, Boulainvilliers, and many others, although Mme Louise Colet in the *Revue des deux mondes* (1845, p. 1025) has no hesitation in attributing them to the Marquise:

C'est sans doute aussi durant ces studieuses années de retraite passées à Cirey que Mme du Châtelet composa un petit traité qui ne fut publié qu'après sa mort, ayant pour titre *Doutes sur la religion révélée.* Ici, avec ce même style ferme et lucide qui, dans les *Institutions de physique,* lui sert à démontrer l'existence de Dieu, elle exprime ses doutes sur *la révélation, les miracles, l'Ecriture Sainte.* Dans ce rare et curieux écrit, cette intelligence sérieuse et hardie veut soumettre à la raison toutes les propositions de la foi, et souvent elle appelle à son aide l'esprit et la raillerie de Voltaire.

Although there is still reason to question Mme du Châtelet's authorship of the *Doutes,* it is certain that, as well as being interested in moral philosophy, metaphysics and science, she was preoccupied with critical deism. In examining her *Correspondance,* one might well suspect her having this particular interest. Not only does she show herself to be familiar with the *Bible,* quoting from portions of it (Asse, p. 204, p. 221), but she somewhat flippantly uses biblical allusions in discussing every-day matters, as did Voltaire. She writes to Maupertuis (Asse, p. 30) that Voltaire has made of Delilah in his *Samson* "une très honnête personne, malgré ce que vous en conte la Très-Sainte." She assures Algarotti (Asse, p. 26) that Cirey is not situated in a region of thinkers, "mais je pense pouvoir dire, comme le Fils de l'Homme ; mon royaume de Cirey n'est pas de ce monde." She tells D'Argental that his letters have the soothing effect upon her of David's harp (Asse, p. 160). To Algarotti, she writes (Asse, p.

[29] Chamfort is said to have attributed the *Doutes* to Mme du Châtelet. See Mangeot, "Les Réflexions sur le bonheur, etc.," in *Mélanges Lanson,* p. 282: "Après les racontars de Chamfort, de Pougens, de Boisjourdain, etc., on était allé jusqu'à publier, sous le nom de Mme du Châtelet des *Doutes sur les religions révélées, dédiés à Voltaire.*" A fair number of copies in manuscript of the *Doutes* circulated in the eighteenth century.

176) : "Vous êtes comme le royaume des cieux, et violenti rapiunt illud."[30] Maupertuis (Asse, p. 193) is "maître en Israël." To D'Argental, she confesses (Asse, p. 195) : "Nous vivons comme les bons chrétiens, en crainte et en tremblement." She writes to Maupertuis (Asse, p. 202) : "Je suis votre Abbé Trublet, et je vous demanderais volontiers, comme Pilate à Jésus : Quid est veritas?" While to D'Argental, she paraphrases (Asse, p. 358) a famous passage : "In manus tuas, angele, commendo honorem nostrum." Though we should not attach too much importance to these allusions, so common to the writers of the period, it is evident that the Marquise was very familiar with biblical lore and language.

Of more importance is the fact that Mme du Châtelet is known to have evinced an interest in the biblical criticism of her day, both orthodox and unorthodox. In this connection a chance remark from Mme de Graffigny's letters (p. 187) has considerable significance : "Nous lisons Dom Calmet, qui nous fait plus de plaisir que Jacques Massé." The scholarly author of the *Commentaire littéral sur tous les livres de l'Ancien et du Nouveau Testament*, 1720, 28 vols., furnished Voltaire and Mme du Châtelet with more than pleasure, as we shall see presently.[31] Suffice it to say for the present, that he was not the only commentator on the *Bible* who was read at Cirey. The fact that a copy of the *Elie et Enoch,* and another of the *Religion chrétienne analysée* attributed to Dumarsais, are still in one of Mme du Châtelet's manuscripts and that she is credited with having made a copy both of the *Preuves* and *Notes* of the *Religion chrétienne analysée,* indicates that she, and presumably Voltaire, were tremendously interested in unorthodox manuscript commentaries on the *Bible* so numerous in their time.

The Marquise did not limit her activities to reading Dom Calmet and making copies of the *Elie et Enoch,* the *Preuves* and

---

[30] *Cf.* Moland XXXV, 60: "La gloire, en ce métier-ci, est comme le royaume des cieux, et violenti rapiunt illud." (4 Décembre, 1738)

[31] See *infra,* p. 108.

Notes. She is actually credited with having composed one of these unorthodox commentaries herself. At the library of Troyes there is now (2376, 2377) a manuscript commentary in five volumes entitled *Examen de la Genèse.* The title is misleading. In reality, the manuscript contains a thorough examination of all the books of the *Bible*: Volume I examines the Pentateuch; Volume II, the *Bible* from the Book of Joshua to the Maccabees; Volume III, from the Maccabees to the New Testament; Volume IV deals with the Gospels; Volume V, the Epistles and the Book of Revelation. A sixth volume (Troyes 2378) contains the *Notes* and the *Preuves* to Dumarsais's *Religion chrétienne analysée.* A manuscript notation at the beginning of Volume I reads: "Catalogue Auger, vente à l'Institut, adjugé à M^r girout à 50^f 50^c qui me l'a revendu 55^f. Coll. B. No 4, Examen de la Genèse et des livres du N. Testament; Preuves de la religion, en 6 vol. pet. in-8°. M. R. Manuscrit autographe de Mme du Châtelet." Another hand has added on p. 1 of the first volume: "Par Mad^e du Châtelet." The catalogue of manuscripts of the library of Troyes likewise attributes it to Mme du Châtelet. This is not, however, the only manuscript of the *Examen de la Genèse* in existence. Another, an in-4° in two volumes (Tome I, Examen du Nouveau Testament; Tome II, Examen de l'Ancien Testament) marked on the back "Comment. sur la Bible par Voltaire," was put on sale in Paris about three years ago. It is written in an entirely different hand from the manuscript at Troyes, thereby proving that this commentary on the *Bible,* as did so many commentaries of the time, circulated in manuscript form.

L'Examen de la Genèse was not unknown in the eighteenth century, since copies of it were made and circulated. No one,[32]

[32] There is, however, one remark made by Voltaire himself which beyond a doubt, refers to the *Examen de la Genèse.* In a letter to Mme du Deffand, September 17, 1759, Voltaire, referring to the story of Ooliba, wrote: "Enfin, cette naïveté, que j'aime sur toute chose, est incomparable. Il n'y a pas une page qui ne fournisse des réflexions pour un jour entier. Madame du Châtelet l'avait (*i.e.* the *Ancien Testament,* mentioned in a previous paragraph) bien commenté d'un bout à l'autre." Beuchot comments (LVIII, 179): "Le manu-

however, so far as is known, attributed it to Mme du Châtelet. When, in 1776, the *Bible enfin expliquée* appeared, Grimm mentioned in the *Correspondance littéraire* its appearance (Ed. Tourneux, t. XI, p. 348) and thereupon related a curious story:

Le Patriarch de Ferney s'est enfin décidé à nous donner la *Bible expliquée par les aumôniers de sa majesté le Roi de Prusse.* On nous a assuré que cet ouvrage était depuis longtemps dans le portefeuille de M. de Voltaire, et que c'était le fruit des loisirs de Cirey, où on lisait tous les matins, pendant le déjeuner, un chapitre de l'Histoire Sainte, sur lequel chacun faisait ses réflexions à sa manière; et le chantre de la Pucelle s'était chargé d'en être le rédacteur.

It is to be noted that Grimm did not know, or at any rate did not mention, the *Examen de la Genèse*. It was his opinion that the only result of the after breakfast discussions was the *Bible enfin expliquée*. In the nineteenth century, however, the story was slightly changed by Georges Avenel (quoted from Moland XXX, 2, note 1):

Au temps où Voltaire habitait avec la belle Emilie le château de Cirey, on lisait tous les matins pendant le déjeuner, un chapitre de la *Bible,* sur lequel chacun faisait ses réflexions à sa manière. Voltaire et Mme du Châtelet prirent note de ces commentaires impromptus; il en résulta deux manuscrits. Celui de la Marquise est encore inédit; quand à celui de Voltaire, il servit de noyau à la *Bible enfin expliquée,* qui fut publiée au milieu de l'année 1776, c'est-à-dire trente ans après les propos de table du château.

Avenel gave no reference to his source for the story. But Beuchot in the "Avertissement" to the *Bible enfin expliquée* (Moland XXX, 2), from whom Avenel in all probability gathered his information, supplied one more detail, the fact that the autograph manuscript of Mme du Châtelet was still in existence in 1829. This he could say, since, according to the "Coll. B." which I take

scrit autographe était intitulé: *Examen de la Genèse et des livres du Nouveau Testament:* Preuves de la religion; et formait six volumes petit in-8°. Il était dans la bibliothèque de L. S. Auger, et a été vendu le 14 octobre, 1829."

to mean "Collection Beuchot," in the note of Troyes 2376, he possessed it :

Mme du Châtelet s'était aussi exercée sur la *Bible*. Son travail n'a pas vu le jour; mais le manuscrit autographe existait encore en 1829. Il n'y a pas, ce me semble, grande témérité à croire que Voltaire n'avait pas été étranger à cet écrit de Mme du Châtelet: et il ne serait pas étonnant que les deux ouvrages continssent quelquefois les mêmes remarques.

From the combined information of Grimm, Avenel, and Beuchot, supplemented by Mme de Graffigny's remark and Mme du Châtelet's manuscript copies of works on biblical criticism, it is evident that both she and Voltaire had become much interested in critical deism. Whether she was responsible for the writing of the *Examen de la Genèse* is a subject for careful discussion, however. At the outset, several remarks may be made with a fair degree of certainty. It is certain, for instance, that the *Examen de la Genèse* is a product of Cirey. The combined evidence of Grimm, Avenel, and Beuchot supports this. It is likewise fairly certain that the work grew out of a chapter by chapter examination of the *Bible,* since the arrangement of the criticism is not only book by book, but even, except in the case of the short story-books like Jonah, Tobias, etc., chapter by chapter. The only uncertainty is whether Mme du Châtelet or Voltaire transcribed the results of the chapter by chapter examination. Grimm was inclined to attribute the transcription to Voltaire, but he also thought it identical with the *Bible enfin expliquée*. One of the two copies of the *Examen* (that now on sale in Paris) actually ascribes the work to Voltaire. On the other hand, Beuchot and Avenel thought that both Mme du Châtelet and Voltaire made a transcription, that the *Bible enfin expliquée* was Voltaire's, while the *Examen de la Genèse* was Mme du Châtelet's. The two notations in the Troyes manuscript unqualifiedly attribute the work to Mme du Châtelet, probably on the ground that it was thought to be an autograph manuscript. But the objection may be raised that this conclusion, unsupported by other evidence, might lead to error, since the sixth volume of the *Examen* is in the same handwriting, but no one has even suggested that Mme du Châtelet was its author. She may merely have copied the *Examen de la Genèse* just as she is believed to have copied the *Preuves* and the *Notes* of the *Religion chrétienne analysée*. Unless one would care to assume that Mme du Châtelet really did write the *Notes* and the *Preuves,* and even the *Religion chrétienne analysée* itself. It must be confessed that in the light of Beuchot's note upon the *Analyse,* which we have published elsewhere,[33] such an eventuality is far from being impossible.

The manuscript itself offers evidence of being a continuous copy rather than a day by day entry. There are, to be sure, errors —mostly slips in writing. In one place (III, 83), however, a half-page is left blank and a note added to the effect that a passage is to be copied from Pascal. The whole appearance of the manuscript is neat and finished, giving the impression of having been composed from notes already arranged. There are, none the less, introductory passages of a general nature when the author takes up the analysis of a new book of the *Bible*. Even from the beginning, there is no indication of where the breaks occurred day by day. And the stories, for instance, the Books of Tobias, Esther, Jonah, are related as units instead of being subjected to a verse by verse analysis.

Irrespective of the authorship of the *Examen de la Genèse,* which we shall discuss later, there can be no doubt that Voltaire and Mme du Châtelet were interested in the clandestine literature of France dealing with critical deism. Since Voltaire evinced an interest in Meslier as early as 1735 (see letter to Thiériot, 1735, Moland XXXIII, 555), it is to be expected that he then became acquainted with Meslier's work, of which he published, at a later date, the *Extrait*. However, it is impossible to determine whether he knew the *Testament* or the *Extrait* at this time. Since Mme du Châtelet possessed, in a manuscript now in the Voltaire collec-

---

[33] See *The Clandestine Organization and Diffusion of Philosophic Ideas in France from 1700 to 1750,* pp. 170-172.

tion at Leningrad, copies of the *Dissertation sur Elie et Enoch,* the *Preuves de la religion chrétienne analysée,* and presumably the *Notes de la religion chrétienne analysée,* it is reasonable to assume that both she and Voltaire knew those works. But it is rather inconceivable that they should know the *Notes* and the *Preuves* without knowing the *Religion chrétienne analysée,* of which they are a complement, and they could hardly know the *Religion chrétienne analysée* without knowing the *Examen de la religion,* its prototype. Voltaire at a later date also published these two works. Acquaintanceship with the *Examen de la religion* entails a certain knowledge of the *De la conduite d'un honnête homme* which furnished material for the eleventh chapter of the *Examen de la religion.* Moreover, the *Notes* are drawn in large measure from Mirabaud's *Examen critique du Nouveau Testament* which was a portion of the larger *Théophrastus redivivus.* No one can affirm that Voltaire and Mme du Châtelet followed the varied, complicated ramifications of these treatises, nor can one do more than surmise the extent of their knowledge. No one can deny, however, that they were acquainted with some of them, and with portions of other related treatises. Nor can it be denied, after Mme de Graffigny's statement (see *supra*), that they perused at least one orthodox apologist—Dom Calmet. The effect of all this preliminary reading seems quite clearly to have led to the composition of the *Examen de la Genèse* in five volumes.

CHAPTER II

THE EXAMEN DE LA GENÈSE

ANY analysis of the *Examen de la Genèse* within the proportions of a normal chapter is likely to appear tedious because of the necessity of condensing the multiple ideas contained in its seven hundred thirty-eight pages. The inference should not be drawn, however, that the work is necessarily boring. When compared with Voltaire's *Examen important de Milord Bolingbroke* or the *Bible enfin expliquée,* or the hundred odd treatises of a similar nature which were written and circulated at about the same period, the work will be found fully as interesting as any of them. It is true that the *Examen de la Genèse* can hardly be recommended for casual reading today. Times have changed, and the meticulous criticism spread over many pages and interspersed with wit and irony has lost much of its appeal. But it should not be forgotten that its ideas were neither tedious nor insignificant in its day, nor were they without importance to the history of ideas in the eighteenth century, or to the intellectual development of Voltaire.

The work opens with the statement that the portrait of God as jealous, choleric, and subject to repentance, is unworthy of the Deity. This portrait cannot be excused on the ground that it had to be understandable to the Jews in their early barbaric state, for, in the first place, the *Bible* was not written for the Jews alone but for mankind, and, in the second, had it been written only for the Jews, it should not have stooped to their barbarism, nor wrapped its message in impenetrable obscurity. The story of the Creation abounds in contradictions. The apparent contradiction in the two accounts of the creation of man and woman given in Genesis I :27 and II :21-22, lends strength to the argument of the Preadamites. The fact that no distinction is made between the sun and the moon save that one is called "luminare majus" and the other "luminare minus" is ridiculous. Genesis I :24 contains the erroneous statement that the earth produces all living animals when it is a well-known fact that such is not the case. Furthermore, the naming of the animals is a manifest absurdity. The laws of physics are violated where in Genesis I :4, light and darkness are separated. A still more serious error occurs in delaying the sun's creation until the fourth day when it is the sun which causes the distinction between night and day. The passage, I :2, which states that the earth before the creation was empty and bare, is in contradiction with the belief that it was created "ex nihilo." Moreover, the Hebrew text speaks, I :1, of plural gods, a palpable proof that Moses did not believe in the unity of God.

If the story of the Creation is, from the point of view of physics, ludicrous, the story of the Fall is illogically absurd. First of all, there is a confusion between the tree of life and the tree of knowledge. The particular virtue of their fruits is unknown, and it is not clear why they were forbidden to man. The story of the serpent tempter, capable of human speech, is very difficult to explain, so difficult in fact, that it has been deemed an allegory in which the serpent has been likened to the Devil, and a legend of fallen angels has been invented to add likelihood to it. But this legend, first mentioned in the Epistle of Jude, a book of very doubtful authenticity, was invented late. There is no mention of fallen angels in the Genesis version and the word Satan used in Jude is not even Hebrew. Nevertheless, the Fall is consummated and the Deity metes out punishment first to the serpent who is condemned to crawl, to eat earth (which, incidentally, he does not do), and to be crushed by the seed of woman. The Deity then proceeds to the punishment of Adam and Eve, at the same time making them an object of ridicule. There are inexplicable points in this story. Even the

position of Paradise is unknown. The doctrine of Original Sin
derived from the Fall brings out the injustice of the Deity who
up to this point had acted only as a capricious king.

The story of Cain presents an insuperable difficulty. After
having slain Abel, he is marked with a sign and sent forth to
wander on the face of the earth. The mark was given him to
prevent other men from slaying him. But who are the other
men? And what was his sign? A dog? A horn?

The story of the Flood is also fraught with numerous difficulties. The deluge was supposedly sent as a punishment because
the Sons of God had married the daughters of man, but we
do not know who these Sons of God were, demons or angels,
or who the giants issued from the marriage were. Then it is
singular for Noah to have made a distinction between pure and
impure animals, in view of the fact that this distinction was not
known to man until the time of Moses. Another difficulty in
the narrative is, that since America was undiscovered in
Noah's time, he could not possibly have secured animals for his
Ark from that continent, and had he been able to do so he had
no means of sending them back after the Flood. Nor did he
have space in the Ark to house, feed, and care for all these
animals. And why these creatures should be punished for the
sins of man is not clear. The enormous quantity of water
causing the flood is physically impossible. The Jews believed
in cataracts in the sky, but the location of these cataracts is
unknown. Nor is it known where the water was stored after
it withdrew, nor how the damp earth could be habitable after
the flood, nor why the rainbow, which can be explained by
physics as the refraction of light through drops of water, could
be a sign of the Covenant, nor why the Covenant should be
made with both man and animals.

The incident of the Tower of Babel is absurd. To begin
with, God's reason for being offended by the tower is obscure.
The confusion of tongues does not seem to have been a miracle,
since the *Bible* had already stated that the children of Noah

divided the earth, each according to his language. Incidentally, it is to be remarked, that all of the sons of Noah were not chosen as objects of God's favor. Only Shem was chosen, and of Shem's sons, only Abraham, and of Abraham's sons, only Isaac.

There are many events in the history of the Patriarchs which are either absurd, contradictory, immoral, or unjust. The conversations between the Deity and Abraham are interesting. When the order is given to circumcise the Jews, Abraham requests no explanation, a proof that the Jews were not the first to use the rite. His bargaining with the Deity for the salvation of Sodom is most curious. It is to no purpose, however, for Sodom is destroyed, after the peculiar situation in which Lot, Abraham's nephew, and his daughters become embroiled because of the attack of the Sodomites upon the angels. The suite of Lot's adventures is extraordinary: his wife is turned to a pillar of salt, his daughters are seized with a fantastic terror and commit incest. But the story of Abraham is filled with injustice and deceit. The treatment of Hagar is inconsistent and unjust, though commanded according to the Church Fathers by the Deity. The Deity also acts harshly to Abraham in commanding him to slay his son Isaac. Abraham's most reprehensible conduct was in his dealing with the King of Egypt, representing his wife Sarah as his sister, and passing her off as a concubine in order to extort gifts from the king. He practiced this same deceit with Abimelech, although with less dire results to the innocent party. His son Isaac was noted for fraudulent dealings. Jacob continued the family tradition in tricking his brother Esau into selling him his birthright, and his father-in-law Laban in order to have his sheep and his other property. The trickery of Simeon and Levi in the affair of Dinah and Schechem is an "horrible action qui fait frémir la nature"; and the affair of Judah and Tamar rivals it in baseness. The conduct of Jacob's eleven sons toward Joseph, his twelfth, is not only deceitful, but cruel and inhuman. And although Joseph's action toward his brothers is "généreuse" and "touchante," his treatment of the Egyptians is cruel and inhuman. Not only are the Patriarchs famous tricksters, but they practice idolatry, intermarry with idolaters, explain dreams, fight with angels, tell fortunes and prophesy.

The famous prophecy of Jacob at his death is usually interpreted as foretelling the coming of Christ. But the sceptre had many times passed from the tribe of Judah before the coming of Christ, and during His time was held by Herod who was not even a Jew. Moreover, Saul was of the tribe of Benjamin, the Maccabees were of the tribe of Levi. Not much significance can be given this prophecy, since it resembled the speech of a man whose head has been violently disturbed.

The exodus of the Israelites from Egypt was accompanied by many inexplicable events. One puzzle is how the Israelites, of whom the males were cast into the Nile at birth, had grown from sixty-six to a population of six hundred thousand combatants. The murder of the Egyptian by Moses was reprehensible, his flight and marriage with an idolatress of the land of Madian incomprehensible. The episode of the fiery bush needs some clarification. Upon receiving God's command to lead His people, Moses inquires what he shall answer when the Israelites ask who has sent him, and receives the obscure reply "I shall be what I shall be," which has been wrongly translated "I am He who exists." Moreover, God's hardening Pharaoh's heart and then punishing him for resisting the requests of Moses is contrary to the laws of human justice. While the divine order to despoil the Egyptians of their property is contrary to the laws of human morality. The plagues, besides being unjust, are somewhat contradictory. It should be remembered that the Egyptian magicians vied with Moses and Aaron in performing some of them. This competition, it must be admitted, rather discredits all miracles. It is particularly difficult to believe these stories when certain of Moses's miracles and those of the magicians were mutually exclusive. For when Moses turned the

waters into blood, whence came water for the magicians'
duplication of his miracle? And when the fish in the waters
were all killed, whence came the frogs? And if the magicians
could imitate the plague of the frogs, why did they find it
difficult to imitate the plague of the flies? How could the
Egyptians live in the midst of the stench caused by the death
of the fishes and the frogs? And where did the Israelites get
their water? And why were the animals punished with death
in the fifth plague? And if they were dead in the fifth plague,
how were they afflicted with ulcers in the sixth, and with hail
in the seventh, and how could their first-born be slain in the
tenth? More incomprehensible still is Pharaoh's patience in
enduring all these plagues for the mere satisfaction of keeping
the Israelites. However, at the tenth plague, his heart, which
the Deity had hardened, softens, and he sends the Israelites
away laden with the Egyptian booty which they had borrowed,
but only to follow them and to be drowned in the waters of the
Red Sea *ad maiorem gloriam Dei*.

The plagues of Egypt and the miraculous crossing of the Red
Sea lead naturally to an examination of miracles which have
occurred up to this point in the *Bible*. These miracles are either
useless or cruel. For why should an angel be sent to comfort
Hagar after she had been driven out by Abraham, or why
should an angel appear just to change Jacob's name? But the
cruel miracles are more numerous. And they, too, are useless.
For they are performed for a miserable little race which is
constantly ungrateful and discontented, and their only result is
to force this race to wander forty years in the desert when it
could have received the fertile plains of the Nile.

The events which followed the crossing of the Red Sea
require considerable explanation also. We do not know how
the Jews could carry with them sufficient provisions to last
them six weeks. We do not know either what qualities the
manna sent from Heaven possessed, nor even whether it was
miraculous. Probably it was purgative manna which had lost

its purgative qualities. There are also some anachronisms in
this section when the Princes of the people were named before
there were any Princes, and when the Priests were mentioned
before there were any Priests.

When the Jews arrived at Mount Sinai they were given the
Decalogue and their social laws. In the Decalogue, God is represented as a God of vengeance punishing the children of those
who offend Him. This vengeful characteristic is again mani-
fested in the punishment of Achan's family and David's descendants. The laws of the Decalogue are extremely ordinary
and common to all races living in social groups. Certain of the
other laws are peculiar to say the least, for instance, the prohibi-
tion to mount the steps of the altar when this is the only way
of approaching it. The laws concerning slavery are illogical,
and the domestic laws puerile, sometimes revolting, unworthy
of the Deity, and useless to the State. There are some even
which are unjust, for instance, the death penalty for parricide
and thief alike. The "péché d'orgueil" was likewise punishable
by death, although no one knows just what it was. The command
not to work the earth during the seventh year in order that the
poor might live was economically unsound. The laws concerning the building of the tabernacle, the priests' robes, the cov-
erings of the altar are most puerile and detailed.

The God of the Hebrews is not only a God of vengeance,
He is a physical God, having hands, face and feet. But one is
forbidden under pain of death to look upon Him.

While Moses was recording the laws, the people in bore-
dom made a Golden Calf and placed an altar before it. God
informed Moses of what had occurred and threatened to destroy
the whole race. Moses assuaged His anger, but on descending
the mountain, became exceeding wroth and broke the stones
of the law. He took the Golden Calf, reduced it to powder, and
gave it to the Israelites to drink. Just how he did this is not quite
clear, for if he pounded it in a mortar as the Vulgate relates, the
gold being exceedingly malleable would not become powder.

And if he filed it into powder, the operation would have required months, and the powder would not have been soluble in water. These chemical difficulties, however, do not prevent Moses from being the patron of alchemists.

Moses's action was followed by the killing of twenty-three thousand Israelites, an act which has never been explained. The Levites, who had been as guilty as the others, committed it, and Aaron, who had been the leader in the making of the Calf, went unpunished. But the most inexplicable part of the slaughter was why twenty-three thousand Israelites should allow themselves to be slain by a relatively small number of Levites.

The Jewish ceremonies are most elaborately described in Leviticus, and while the Lord requires the fat and the blood of victims, both Isaiah and Jeremiah state that sacrifices are useless and unnecessary. These ceremonies, even in the opinion of Dom Calmet, are not worthy of great respect, if one considers only their external significance. None the less, the Deity was so jealous of this cult that He described it in greatest detail. He has described how a chicken should be prepared for sacrifice, how flour should be mixed with oil, what portion of a sacrificed beast should be preserved for Him, and what should be left for the priests. Sacrifices for sins are prescribed, and ceremonies for the consecration of priests. It is strange that animals should be classified as pure and impure since they were all created by God. And there are some peculiar errors in their classification. The rabbit, for instance, is considered impure, because it was thought to ruminate, although not to have a cloven foot, whereas, in reality, it has a cloven foot, but does not ruminate. The griffon is forbidden when there is no such animal. The manner of purifying women after childbirth, and the purification of lepers and even houses, is prescribed. There is a curious error in maintaining that the effects of the birth of a male child last longer than that of a female. As for the laws accompanying the ceremonies of the cult, some of them are in flat contradiction with the practices of the Jews. For example, it is forbidden to marry one's sister; yet Abraham married Sarah, his sister; it is forbidden to marry the sister of one's first wife, and yet Jacob married Rachel and Leah, two sisters. It is forbidden to pay attention to dreams, and yet the story of Joseph is founded upon dreams, and the *Bible* is filled with them. It is forbidden to marry one's sister-in-law after the death of one's brother, and yet that is precisely what happened in the story of Judah and Tamar, and in another place, in the *Bible* (Deuteronomy XXV:5) it is so ordered. Among the defects which exclude candidates from the priesthood is a nose too long or too short. The most cruel of the ceremonies, however, was human sacrifice. God required that every object, whether beast, field, or man, vowed to Him should be slain. This clearly proves that the Jews practiced human sacrifice, and in one case, that of Jephthah's daughter, we have an example of its execution.

There are many points in the Book of Numbers which are either obscure, contradictory, barbarous or ludicrous. The order to take a census is in itself surprising, for in the Book of Kings, when David proceeded to do likewise without an order from God, a plague was sent upon the whole race. This first census, divinely inspired, is singular in its errors of computation, and especially so in its result, since only one first-born for every fifty-five persons was accounted for in a race where every one was married and celibacy was regarded with scorn. If the order for the census is surprising, the prescribing of a water-test for adultery is ridiculous, particularly in a race which permitted divorce. The Jews themselves must have sensed the absurdity of the test for they never used it.

The story of the Exodus contains many singularities. First of all, it was strange for Moses to request his father-in-law to serve as a guide for the Israelites, since they already had a leader in God Himself, and a guide in the cloud and pillar of fire. The destruction of the Israelites by fire, quails, and serpents of fire was cruel. The constant murmurs of the people none the less prove that they were not so unhappy in Egypt as was said in Exodus, and that the manna sent them did not have a variety of tastes as St. Augustine said. It is noteworthy, also, that on this occasion, Moses, who murmured more than the people, was not punished. This Moses is called by God "le plus doux de tous les hommes" and yet he broke the stones of the Ten Commandments in his wrath, he had twenty-three thousand Israelites slain by the Levites because of the Golden Calf, and he slew the Midianite women and children, preserving only the girls, who had already been spared by Phinehas. The quarrel of Moses the legislator with Mary, and Aaron, the High Priest, followed by the revolt of the latter, and the punishment only of Mary is a curious case of injustice. The sending of spies into Canaan and the subsequent revolt of the Jews is a remarkable story. In the first place, it is absurd to suppose that a group of men could go spying amongst the Canaanites with a bunch of grapes on their backs. In the second, it was useless to send spies, since God had already promised Moses that the land would be flowing with milk and honey. Moreover, there is contradiction in the stories which they told on their return. The punishment decreed the Israelites after their revolt, following the report of the spies, was not executed, since others besides Caleb and Joshua were eventually allowed to enter the Promised Land, according to the statement in Joshua XIV:1. And it was indeed cruel that fourteen thousand seven hundred people should suffer death because of the revolt of Korah, Dathan, and Abiram. The episode of Moses's striking the rock in exasperation at another insurrection of his people is a matter for further comment. It was not unnatural for the Jewish people to have murmured in the wilderness, since they had been led from fertile Egypt into a desert where they lacked food, drink and clothing. And Moses and Aaron were excluded from the Promised Land because of their doubt, when neither this episode of the rock nor any of their experiences in the desert give evidence of doubt on their part. The incident of the plague of fiery serpents resembles tales from the *Arabian Nights,* and the cure imparted by the serpent of bronze is more remarkable still. Moses's mention of the "Livre des Guerres du Seigneur" is a palpable absurdity, because there had been no wars of consequence and there has never been a Book of Wars. If it ever existed, it is lost, an inconceivable thing for an inspired book.

If the Book of Wars is an historical error, the story of Balaam and his ass is a manifest absurdity. In the first place, Balaam was journeying on the animal with the consent of God, and there seemed to be no reason for his encounter with the angel. We do not know why the angel appeared to the ass at first, and not to Balaam, why the ass spoke, why the angel appeared at all, when the sole result of his coming was to administer a reprimand to Balaam. How the animal spoke has never been ascertained. Dom Calmet says that this miracle is no more unlikely than the horse of Achilles, the oak of Dodona, and the elephant of Porus, and one must admit that he is correct. The love affairs of the Jews and Moabites lead to the slaughter of twenty-four thousand Israelites, and the promise that Phinehas and his descendants will retain the office of Grand Sacrificator forever. But there is no such office now among the Jews. As a matter of fact, many of the promises made to the Jews were not kept. They were promised, for instance, the land between the Nile and the Euphrates, and they never possessed this territory.

The Book of Deuteronomy begins with a contradiction in the very first verse in referring to the words uttered by Moses on the other side of the Jordan, when he never crossed the Jordan. Some interpreters claim that the word "Héber" means "on this side of" as well as "on that side of." A funny language, this Hebrew tongue, in which the same word means "yes" and "no." Dom Calmet, however, suggests that the verse was written by Ezra. This explanation is no better than the first, since Ezra must have known that Moses did not cross the Jordan.

The whole Book of Deuteronomy is at variance with events recorded in the four previous books. Here it is written that the people asked Moses to send spies, elsewhere the command was given by God. Here it is said that the Israelites lacked nothing in the desert, elsewhere it is shown that they lacked everything. Here Moses repeats the Decalogue, and it is different from the Decalogue of Exodus. Here God says He will destroy seven races for the Jews, and in Genesis, He says He will destroy ten. Here the order is given to destroy all the vanquished, for fear that the survivors will lead the Jews to idolatry. Elsewhere the Canaanites are allowed to live in the midst of the Jews in order to essay their religious fervor. Here the Jews are forbidden to have foreign alliances or to marry foreign wives, and David, the man after God's own heart, made an alliance with the King of Tyre and married foreigners. Here the encampments of the Israelites are given, and they differ from those given in Numbers. Here Moses says that the bed of Og is still shown in Rabba as a proof of his gigantic stature when he had died only two years previously. The town of Jaïr is mentioned and it is stated that the town still bears that name. The last words of Moses are related in Chapter 33 and his death in 34 when it is supposedly Moses who is talking. But the book is not only full of contradictions and anachronisms. The picture of God, ordering the extermination of the enemies of the Jews, hardening the heart of the Amorrhean King, competing with the gods of neighboring races, ordering the destruction of whole towns in which one or two idolaters are found, is that of a cruel, vindictive Deity, unworthy of the God of Mercy.

The book usually attributed to Joshua was not written by him. It begins by stating, I:II, that the Israelites will pass over the Jordan within three days, while later it is said that they did so after six days. Then Joshua orders them to prepare food for three days, an inconsistent order, considering that manna fell for their use every morning, until after the passage into Canaan. In Chapter II, the prostitute Rahab, guilty of frightful treason toward her ruler and her own people, is alone spared of all the Canaanites and not only adopted by the Jews, but later mentioned as being an ancestor of Christ. Hers is a particularly perfidious example of treason and it is surprising that sovereigns have not denounced this book.

It is singular that Joshua did not ford the Jordan as did his three advance spies, thus sparing God the trouble of performing the miracle. The explanation, III:16, that the waters coming down toward the sea were cut off, and those coming down from above rose in a mountain, is worthy only of the physics of the *Bible*. Furthermore, the people were to follow the Ark at a distance of two thousand cubits, yet the priests stood still with it in the midst of the Jordan which is only forty-five feet wide at its widest. Thus they must have passed by the Ark instead of following. It is further stated that Joshua put twelve stones in the middle of the Jordan to commemorate the event, and later that they are there "to this very day," thus proving that Joshua did not write the book.

In Chapter V we learn that Moses had not circumcised the people during their forty years in the desert but that Joshua, directed by God, ordered it done as soon as they were in a dangerous new land beset by enemies. The taking of Jericho was accomplished by the Israelites merely walking about its walls, an admirable war manœuvre, and when the walls fell, only Rahab's house, which was a part of them, remained intact. The Jews must have desecrated the Sabbath in walking around the walls seven days. The butchery when the city fell was inexcusable. Particularly revolting is the story of Achan who, for his individual sin of theft, brought God's wrath upon the whole band of Israelites. This story offers additional proof that Joshua did not write the book, since it states that the stones on Achan's burned body remain there even to this day. The story of the capture of Haï, a small town, with a brave king and a small garrison, by an army of thirty thousand Israelites in the rear and six thousand in front, has in it many discrepancies. Notably, Joshua held his shield in the air while his men massacred twelve thousand people.

Joshua's command to the sun and moon to stand still twenty-four hours while he was pursuing his enemies is especially absurd. Since the enemy was already routed and it was only ten o'clock in the morning, there was no necessity for such a miracle. According to laws of physics it is extraordinary to have the moon present at ten in the morning, and the sun turning instead of the earth. Furthermore, the Israelites were not affected by the midday sun pouring down upon them for twenty-four hours, and Joshua, to show his gratitude to God for the miracle, killed five captive kings by his own hand. However, we read later that he killed three of these kings over again, when he took their cities, they having been resuscitated for his pleasure. The book continues with Joshua's annihilating the Canaanites, and states that God had hardened the enemies' hearts so that they would fight against Israel. This whole portion is but a mass of contradictions and injustices. Towns mentioned in one verse as being completely destroyed are later listed in the division of Canaan among the tribes.

The Book of Judges begins with an account of the cruelty of the tribe of Judah, in cutting off the hands and feet of a conquered king and offering as justification the excuse that he had done likewise to seventy conquered kings, an unlikely story. It is explained that God left some Canaanites in Canaan so that the Israelites could keep in practice for war. He would have done better to give them perpetual peace. Chapter III contains the story of three judges: Ana, who made an incestuous marriage, Ehud, who murdered the King of Moab through a ruse and was rewarded by being allowed to hold his position as judge for twenty-eight years, and Samgar, who killed a hundred Philistines with a plow share. Chapter IV relates another worthy incident in the murder of Sisera by Jahel, who offered her victim hospitality after his army was defeated, then slew him.

This inspired the prophetess Deborah to write a hymn singing the praises of Jahel.

In Chapter VI, we find the Israelites pursued by the Midianites who in Numbers XXXI:7, were said to have been entirely annihilated by Moses. Gideon, who before accepting the command of the Israelites against this enemy, asks God to perform three miracles, puts an army to rout with three hundred men, kills one hundred twenty thousand of them, pursues and defeats fifteen thousand, pillages two towns, travels eight or ten leagues on foot, all in the space of eight hours. Chapter XI relates the sacrifice of Jephthah's daughter, showing that human sacrifice was permitted by the Deity if it was in execution of a vow to Him. Dom Calmet makes this point in the law of Moses clear, saying that God does not demand these vows, but once made they must be executed. St. Paul mentions Jephthah's act as praiseworthy in his Epistle to the Hebrews. But the story appears to be only a bad imitation of the legend of Iphigenia.

The *Arabian Nights* are surpassed in extravagancy by the story of Samson, whose birth was twice announced by an angel; who, though chosen by God to be a Nazarene, married into the forbidden Philistine race; who killed thirty Philistines not responsible for the guessing of his riddle; who procured three hundred foxes in a country devoid of woods and attaching firebrands to their tails let them free to ravage his enemies' lands; who killed a thousand men with the jawbone of an ass and caused God to miraculously give him drink from the same jawbone; who finally destroyed a large temple by pulling down two of its columns. Though Samson was to deliver his people, he only succeeded after all these miracles in avenging himself. If we may judge from this account of Samson's death, it seems that God at times favors both vengeance and suicide. St. Augustine makes Samson a "figure parlante" of the Christ; Delilah, a symbol of the Church; the jawbone, a symbol of the Cross.

The Book of Ruth deserves scathing criticism. Ruth is a designing creature who wishes to marry Boaz for his money, and as a reward for her perfidy she becomes an ancestor of the Messiah.

The First Book of Kings begins with the story of the priest Eli, his wicked sons, and the boy Samuel. The Ark was stolen by the Philistines and taken to the temple of Dagon, on which occasion God became angry, sending a pest upon them, with the result that they sent the Ark away and it journeyed to several cities, invariably leaving disaster in its wake. Finally, God in His wrath killed fifty thousand and forty people for daring to look upon it. Then it was taken to a private house for twenty years, where apparently it did no harm and was practically forgotten, since Samuel, who in the interval had become a priest, found no necessity for consulting it or sacrificing before it. The Israelites began to demand a king which angered the Deity, since He said that they were rejecting Him. However, the government of the Israelites, from Joshua's death to this period, left much to be desired, giving evidence of the fact that a theocracy is no better than a monarchy. When Samuel anointed Saul, God gave him a list of the powers of a ruler over a people, which proves to be a list of all the injustices of which a king can be capable.

Saul's reign was full of war. Early in his struggles with the Philistines, he incurred God's displeasure because he himself, weary of waiting for Samuel, performed the rite of sacrifice preparatory to going into battle. Thereafter he was pursued by the Deity through His intermediary Samuel, who seems to have been an unusually vengeful agent. Even Dom Calmet finds it difficult to explain the injustice of this heavenly wrath.

When the Israelites went into battle, we make the extraordinary discovery that only Saul and Jonathan, his son, had arms, because their enemies had taken away their blacksmiths who were capable of making weapons. Despite this adverse circumstance, they apparently had been warring just the same, and even winning battles. At the end of this particular battle, Saul was ordered to destroy all the Egyptians since they had displeased God four hundred years previously. When he spared one, King Agag, in the execution, Samuel was sent to tell him that he had disobeyed and that he must cease to rule his people. Saul, in fear, begged Samuel to make a sacrifice with him, on which occasion Samuel cut in pieces the king saved by Saul, in the Lord's presence.

Samuel, directed by God, goes off to find and anoint a new king who happens to be a shepherd boy, David. Saul, not knowing of the subterfuge, receives David in his household as harpist, for God's spirit had departed from him and he was beset by a mysterious, evil, unhappy spirit which found solace only in music. David later gains the king's favor by killing the giant Goliath and is made first squire in the army. Strangely enough Saul does not recognize him as his former harpist.

The story of David's wanderings is one of deceit and trickery. He finally comes out in open revolt against his ruler, but is able to recruit but a few hundred bandits, which goes to show that Saul must have been a popular prince. However, his revolt is approved by the Lord, an approval which may offer a very dangerous example. David, who has been given asylum by the King of Geth, repays his host by making secret sallies upon the king's allies, killing his victims so that they will not disclose his perfidy. He finally joins the king in making war upon the Israelites, his own people. In all this he consults the Lord daily.

Saul, frightened by the Philistine army wishes to consult the Lord, but answered only by silence, consults a magician, asking her to evoke Samuel's spirit for him. And Samuel the prophet of the Lord appears at the behest of a magician who acts in the name of the Devil. There are in this incident many things to be explained. The evocation is useless, since Samuel does not exhort Saul to penitence but predicts disaster for him, saying that he is damned for having wished to save Agag. We have another indication of David's character in Chapter XXIX, when the Philistines fearing treachery on his part beg him to leave their army. He becomes angry, declares his fidelity to Achish their king, and his enmity against the Israelites.

In Chapter I of Second Kings, Saul's death is related differently from Chapter XXXI of First Kings. David becomes king after Saul's son and surrounds himself with a foreign guard, an act which proves that he distrusted his own people. He makes his sons priests, contrary to Jewish law. He falls in love with Bathsheba, Uriah's wife, and has Uriah cold-bloodedly murdered, both a useless and abominable act, since divorce was permissible among the Jews. For this, his guiltless infant son dies, but Bathsheba gives birth to a second son, Solomon, who becomes an ancestor of the Messiah. It may be remarked that Saul had repented before the Lord as well as David, and that though his sin was not to be compared with David's, he was damned while David was pardoned. He makes war upon the Ammonites, descendants of Seth, kills mercilessly the inhabitants of their cities. In all this he receives no reproach.

The conduct of some of David's family is as reprehensible as his own. His son Amnon defiles his sister Tamar, whose honor is avenged by another brother Absalom. The tale concerning the growth of Absalom's hair is an absurdity, but the story of his revolt against David is revealing. It is said that all Israel followed Absalom willingly, giving us to understand that David was not popular with his people. And here, for the first time, David reveals himself a coward, for at the mere rumor of revolt he flees Jerusalem, leaving his ten wives behind. He later shows himself incapable of rendering justice in the affair of Mephibosheth. In Chapter XXI we have an instance of David's cruelty in giving over to the Gibeonites seven survivors of Saul's family whom he had promised Saul to preserve from evil. A little later the Lord becomes very angry with him, not because of any of the crimes he has committed but because he takes a census of the Israelites. The causes of this anger are obscure, but David is given his choice of punishments and chooses the pest, which did not afflict himself who was personally responsible, but seventy thousand of his race. It occurs to him somewhat late to ask the Lord's mercy.

In the second chapter of Kings III, David dies recommending Solomon to kill Joab, to whom he owed his crown, and Shimei, whom he has already pardoned and promised to protect. Solomon begins his reign by first taking personal vengeance on his brother Adonijah under false pretense and killing him, then executing the two murders for his father. Then he marries an Egyptian, which is against the law. God appears to him in a dream bidding him ask for whatever he desires, and though man has no exercise over his reason while sleeping, Solomon is praised for his choice of wisdom, and given riches and glory in the bargain. The details concerning the building of his famous temple abound in exaggerations and discrepancies. As time goes on, Solomon though blessed with heavenly wisdom is influenced by his foreign wives to sacrifice unto idols. However, he is not punished for this except by the threat that his Kingdom will be divided at his death, his son Rehoboam reigning over one of the twelve tribes (he really reigned over two), and he dies in the midst of riches and prosperity. He must have been a cruel ruler because the people come to complain of him to Rehoboam after his death. Rehoboam does not deny his father's cruelty and promises them even more rigid treatment.

The Lord's choice of Jeroboam to reign over the other ten tribes was not a happy one, for no sooner was he king than he made two golden calves as idols for the people, to prevent them from going to Rehoboam's city, Jerusalem, to worship. A prophet was sent to predict for him all manner of evil, and later when his son fell ill and his wife consulted the prophet Ahijah, Ahijah said that Jeroboam's house would end with him and he and all his family would be deprived of the rites of burial. However, Jeroboam was entombed with his ancestors and his son reigned peacefully in his stead. Likewise the account of Asa's reign is a suite of contradictions. Chapter XIV states that Asa of Judah and Baasha of Israel had wars throughout their lives, while Chronicles II :14, records that Asa had a reign of peace, it being God's will, then continues to give an account of his battles.

The miracles performed for and by Elijah were to no purpose. He made certain predictions to Ahab which did not come to pass. Ahab who coveted his neighbor Naboth's vineyard and wanted either to buy it or give him a better one in exchange was not grievously in the wrong. It was Jezebel, Ahab's wife who, unknown to him, had Naboth killed, and yet Ahab was punished for the crime which, indeed, was not so black as David's in murdering the husband of the woman he coveted. There is something inconsistent in the story of Hebrew rulers who had the power of life and death over their subjects, yet dared not seize a vineyard even by paying for it.

Elijah also served as prophet to Ahaziah, son of Ahab, but made strange use of God's power in striking down by heavenly fire a captain and fifty soldiers sent by the king to meet him. When a second captain with fifty men was dispatched, they were treated in the same fashion, but the prophet consented to accompany the third emissary captain to the king. Elijah according to the account of Elisha his successor, who alone saw the miracle, ascended to Heaven in a chariot of fire. One of the first acts of Elisha, blessed with the double spirit of the departed Elijah, was to pray God to avenge the insult he received from some children who called him "bald." A bear came forth and devoured the miscreants. Elisha performed a series of miracles which on examination are decidedly suspicious. There being a famine in Samaria due to a siege by the Syrians, the king suspected Elisha of being the cause of it and sent a man to kill him. He did not accomplish his mission but heard from the prophet's mouth that there would be an abundance of bread on the morrow. The Lord, to accomplish the prediction, frightened the enemy away from the town with a noise of arms and chariots. Elisha indirectly brings about the murder of the Syrian King through the agency of the king's messenger,

Hazaël, who comes to ask him if his master will be cured of a malady. He prophesies that the king will die and be succeeded by Hazaël. Hazaël, on hearing this, promptly does away with his master. Then the prophet proceeds to bring about havoc in Israel also by anointing as king, Jehu, who promptly revolts against Ahaziah, killing him, forty of his brothers and ten sons of Ahab. Thus does the prophet wreak his own personal vengeance on the kings of Syria and Israel. And Jehu the chosen king is but an idolater, murderer and trickster.

The story of Athaliah, though related in Kings IV:12, in a very unlikely fashion, has at least given the subject for Racine's beautiful tragedy. The young Joash who succeeds Athaliah as ruler goes to see the dying Elisha and hears the last of his prophecies. The ruin and dispersion of the tribes of Israel come to pass under the rule of Hosea who, however, had not done evil as the kings who preceded him. When Hezekiah becomes king, he consults a prophet of the Lord named Isaiah to know how he may deliver himself from his enemy Sennacherib. Isaiah says that a spirit will appear to the enemy king and make him return to his country. The spirit proves to be a good or bad angel who kills eighty-five thousand of Sennacherib's men secretly. Hezekiah, suffering from a malady, again consults Isaiah to know if he will recover, and though God has decreed that he will die in three days, at Isaiah's plea He promises that the king will be spared for fifteen years. Hezekiah, reluctant to believe, asks for a sign of assurance. Here, as in the case of Joshua, we have an instance of the Laws of Nature being completely violated, this time for Isaiah's convenience. A shadow on the sundial is made to go back ten degrees instead of proceeding on its normal course forward. This so-called miracle, which has never been mentioned by secular writers, is as useless and absurd as Joshua's. The closing chapters of Kings IV talk of the destruction of Jerusalem by Nebuchadnezzar, making one wonder what has become of God's promises and the Scepter of Judah.

Chronicles should be called the Book of Contradictions instead of the Book of Omissions. It contains practically the same subject matter as Kings with a contradiction in nearly every line. Examples of this in its genealogies are too numerous to mention. Here we are given to understand that it was not Joshua who stopped the sun in its course, that all of Saul's family died with him, that God promised David his throne would be everlasting. David's account of the riches, which he is passing on to Solomon, is indeed fantastic. How could he amass such wealth? His was a poor Kingdom when he became king, he was always at war, his country had no industries, not even artisans, since it is written that Hiram furnished carpenters for the building of Solomon's temple. Solomon could not have spent over twelve billions in the construction of the temple, when Versailles cost only three hundred million. Second Chronicles continues with extravagances. The golden nails for the temple weighed two pounds each; Hiram of Tyre sent boats to Solomon by a route which necessitated their cutting across the Isthmus of Suez; the Ammonites, who apparently were too numerous for their Hebrew opponents, were stricken with dizziness and conveniently killed each other; Jehoiachin who was only eight years old, and who reigned three months and ten days, did evil in the sight of the Lord. Though God did all that He could to bring back the Jews, He did not succeed and seemingly was less powerful in doing good than in doing evil, such as hardening the hearts of his subjects.

It is necessary to make some general observations concerning the Books of Ezra before examining them. They are four in number, two canonical in the Roman Church, the third accepted by the Greek Church, the fourth rejected by everybody. Ezra relates that one day while praying, he heard a voice instructing him to teach his people, and he replied that if God would send him His spirit, he would write His word for future generations. Thus, withdrawing to a quiet spot for forty days, he was inspired to dictate the Word to five helpers who faithfully

transcribed his sayings. At the end of this period, he was ordered
to publish the first things written but to conserve the last. The
fourth book was accepted by the first Church Fathers but
rejected later by the Council of Trent. Certain Church Fathers
believed that it was Ezra who compiled the entire Old Testament from remnants of older books which had been lost during
the captivity. Others believed that he had composed his books
from pure inspiration.

In any event, the Books of Ezra abound in discrepancies.
For instance, the second book is supposed to be written by Nehemiah, for he speaks of himself in the first person, yet in several
places he is spoken of in the third person. Priests are mentioned
up until the reign of Darius, conquered by Alexander, but
Darius lived one hundred twenty years after Nehemiah's arrival
at Jerusalem. Similar inexactitudes prevail throughout the book.

Although there are four Books of the Maccabees, only the
first two are canonical. There was apparently no reason for
accepting the last two since the second book mentioned the Last
Judgment and a future life. The Books of the Maccabees are
more reasonable, and written with more order than other parts
of the *Bible*. They have a different style, a different tone; apparently, relations with the Greeks had a cultivating influence
upon the Jews. To be sure, there are errors in these two books,
too. The statement that Alexander divided his kingdom during
his life-time is "frightfully false." False also is the statement
that the Romans gave to Eumenes the land of the Indians, the
Lydians and the Medes, for at the time of Judas Maccabeus the
Romans had not yet borne arms against the Medes, and had
never penetrated as far as India. It is said further, that each
year the Romans entrusted the magistracy to a single man,
when every one knows that there were two consuls. The books
also contain peculiar contradictions: in one place it is said that
the army of Judas Maccabeus had no sword; then, shortly after,
all his enemies who could not flee were killed at the point of the

sword. His army which fought Nicanor is conflictingly reported as having two thousand and seven thousand men. He returns to sack a camp he has already destroyed. At the end of Maccabees I, Jonathan is killed twice. Antiochus Nicanor ordered that the temple be returned to the Jews when it was already in their possession. The books also contain absurdities, such as the statement that eight hundred men attacked twenty-four thousand in a battle which lasted all day; that three thousand defeated one hundred twenty thousand; that single elephants carried thirty-two men; and that mounted men rode across the sky. From time to time, actions are described which are forbidden by the law, such as Simon Maccabeus's building of pyramids for his family, Simon's observance of dreams, and the election of a High Priest from the tribe of Benjamin. There are cruelties, such as the destruction of Galaad by Judas, and questionable morality, such as the suicide of the venerable old man which is related with approval. Last of all, there are silly remarks. The author (who is considered in this manuscript to be the Holy Spirit) makes a peroration at the end of the work, in which he excuses himself to the reader, by saying that if the stories he has related are not good, he should be blamed, and not the Memoirs which he has consulted. And he adds that he has diversified his style to please his readers, because it is more agreeable to drink successively wine and water than to drink either continuously.

The Book of Job is wrapped in complete obscurity. We do not know who its author was, when it was written, who Job was, when or where he lived. Interpreters are divided in opinion concerning its significance. Some say that it is an allegory; others, that the events took place in a dream. Some claim it to have the form of a drama written in verse, but the verse structure is unrecognizable. It is a "rapsodie" at all events. No one knows whether Job is a Jew or a pagan. He speaks of the Cocytus and names the constellations after the manner of the pagans. His disease is likewise unknown, although Dom Calmet feels justified in saying that it was syphilis and that its cure was not miraculous. Eliphas, one of Job's friends, was a Leibnitzian, since he stated that there is no effect without a cause. Job apparently did not believe in the after-life, although he expressed some obscure ideas concerning the Resurrection, on one occasion denying it, on another affirming it. He complains that God is punishing him unjustly, and maintains that God strikes equally the innocent and the guilty, that He purposely misinterprets the language of sincere people, and deceives the princes of the earth. There is a little of everything in the Book of Job. Fortune-telling is authorized, the Heavens are pictured as solid as bronze, the leviathan is described when we do not even know what a leviathan is. The questions which God addressed to Job concerning the abode of darkness, the manner in which light *descends* to the earth, the movements of the planets, the habits of the doe, are silly or easily answerable. Newton or Kepler could have answered with facility those dealing with astronomy, and a "valet de chien" would be informed about the doe's habits. There are also some ridiculous assertions concerning elephants which carry swords and consume whole rivers. However, the story ends satisfactorily with the restitution of Job's property and the multiplication of his family. It is true that the children of Job were not resuscitated: "ainsi les pauvres enfans moururent à la fleur de leur âge pour une mauvaise plaisanterie entre Dieu et Satan." Still, at the end of this story every one is satisfied.

The customs described in the Book of Tobias are most respectable, but its historical events as recorded are most ridiculous. The manner whereby the elder Tobias became blind is absurd, unless one accepts the fact that he slept with his eyes open. His cure is equally strange, since the fish used for it is not named. Some think that it was a carp, and indeed a carp's bladder will admittedly cure all those who have been blinded by a swallow. There seems no justification for Raphael's lies, and really no reason why Raphael should have accompanied the

younger Tobias, since the latter was already forty years old.
The marriage of young Tobias without the consent of his
parents seems contrary to custom. But it is amazing that the
maiden should have been delivered from the demon Asmodeus
by Tobias's expediency in cooking her the liver of a fish. More
amazing still is Raphael's rapid trip into upper Egypt to chain
Asmodeus, for he went and returned without his absence being
noticed. How he could chain this spirit is incomprehensible, but
Paul Lucas claims to have seen Asmodeus in Egypt, so he must
be there. It is difficult indeed to reconcile the chronological
events of the story. If Tobias married at forty, and died at
ninety-nine, it is hard to understand how he lived to see five
generations of his descendants. And if he died seven or eight
years before his father's death, it is surprising to note that he
closed his father's eyes in death.

The Book of Judith should never have been recognized by
the canon since it is so contrary to the spirit of religion. Apparently, it was accepted by the Council of Trent because it is
mentioned in the New Testament. Its author and the date when
its events occurred are unknown. In one place, there is a reference to the captivity, although Arphaxad certainly lived before
the captivity. The Nebuchadnezzar mentioned in the story cannot
be identified, and its historical events are distorted. According to
its version, Arphaxad built the city of Ecbatana, but history
records that the town was built by his father. Holophernes is
reported as having conquered in three months' time more territory than he could have traversed in that interval. A miserable
village in Judea resists an army of one hundred twenty thousand
infantry and twelve thousand cavalry during a period of two
months. According to the genealogy given in the book, Judith
was descended from Simeon, son of Reuben, but there was no
son of Reuben by that name and Judith herself says that she descended from Simeon, brother of Reuben. And indeed her crime
was as horrible as that of her ancestor, and as unlikely. For what
chance would a widow have to penetrate the enemy's camp of

one hundred thirty thousand or one hundred forty thousand men, cut off the head of the general and return unscathed bearing the head? What chance would the little town of Bethulie, deprived of water and reduced to its last extremity, have of defeating so great an army even if Holophernes, the army's general, had been killed?

The story of Esther, like those of Judith, Tobias, and Job, cannot be placed historically. The author, the period at which the events occurred, the Ahasuerus who is mentioned as King of the Persians, all are unknown. Although considered an allegory by some of the Church Fathers, the book since the Council of Trent has been accepted in the canon. It has a grave imperfection. The last chapters, which incidentally do not appear in the Hebrew version, repeat the story with additional details and contradict on several occasions the first version. For instance, Mordecai, a Jew early in the story, later is called a Macedonian. There are even contradictions in the first part. The children of Haman are recorded in three places respectively as having been hanged the day of their father's death, during the first day's slaughter, and during the second day's slaughter. But these contradictions are no more ludicrous than the actual events related. Ahasuerus marries Esther without knowing that she is a Jewess. He recompenses Mordecai a second time for his fidelity, forgetting his first recompense. Haman announces a Jewish pogrom twelve months in advance, and builds a scaffold to hang Mordecai right at the door of the palace. Ahasuerus, to punish Haman's crime, orders the slaughter of his own people, and when Esther is not satisfied with this carnage, he permits it to continue a second day. The Persians, who vastly outnumber the Jews, permit themselves to be slain by the latter without protest. This whole story is visibly false, but it none the less brings out the essential characteristics of the Jewish race, love of cruelty, and desire for vengeance. One cannot read without horror such barbarous absurdities. Their law inspires the Jews with a constant desire for vengeance, and God always promises them as a reward for their fidelity that they will be avenged. As a result, the Old Testament surpasses all other histories in examples of perfidy, and excels in inspiring loathing and aversion. This accounts for the hatred which surrounding tribes had for the Jews and which Dom Calmet treats with surprised wonder. The surprising thing, however, is that other nations did not unite to exterminate the Hebrews. As a matter of fact, in their whole history, there are only two generous acts: Joseph's generosity toward his brethren and David's clemency toward Saul. All the other stories make humanity shiver with horror, and the worst of it is that crimes not only go unpunished, but are said to be ordered, and even recompensed, by God. And these criminal acts are even extolled by some moderns. This gentle Esther, for instance, is held up as a model to children and Christian princesses. Thus a princess who wishes to acquire fame should exterminate those who do not think as she does in matters of religion.

The opening vision of Ezekiel would resemble the *Arabian Nights* if it were as amusing. The fact that he records seeing wheels filled with eyes and surrounded by the spirit of life, and a book which he ate seemed sweet as honey, give us good reason to believe that he was justly confined by chains. His actions must have been incomprehensible to the Jews. What instruction would they receive from a fool who lay on one side for three hundred eighty days and on the other for forty, and who nourished himself in the most unheard-of manner? How could a man lie for three hundred eighty days on one side? Evidently he had been paralyzed in order to execute this command. And what interpretation can be given these prophecies of the Old Testament? Commentators are baffled trying to guess the meaning of all these "simagrées" which we are brought up to respect and regard as divinely inspired. The Christian Religion is founded upon them, for it was prophets like Ezekiel who announced the coming of Christ. These prophecies have remained notoriously unfulfilled. Ezekiel prophesies, for instance, that the Jews will be reunited to become a single nation, that they will obey a single king, that they will no longer worship idols, that David will reign over them, that they will dwell in the land of their forefathers forever. But the Jews were never reunited after the Captivity, they never had a king of David's race, they have never been able to occupy continuously the land of their forefathers. It may be argued that though these things did not come to pass literally, they were accomplished spiritually. But there is no old wives' tale to which a spiritual interpretation may not be given. The author offers to prove by this method, if one wishes, that everything which has been written in the *Arabian Nights* has been accomplished under Louis XIV. If we rejected the literal interpretation for the allegorical, we should have to abandon all proof founded on the prophecies. The mark of unfulfillment is what distinguishes a false from a true prophet. What can we say then concerning Ezekiel's division of Palestine among the twelve tribes after the Captivity, a division so clear that Dom Calmet has drawn a map to which he has appended: "Plan de la distribution de la terre de Canaan, suivant la vision d'Ezéchiel; laquelle n'a jamais été exécutée." And let it not be said that the literal sense being unfulfilled, the prophecies must have a spiritual sense, and therefore are a proof of the Christian Religion. This subterfuge has been invented by Pascal, "ce grand et beau génie."

The Book of Daniel is less obscure than Ezekiel but hardly more reasonable. Half of it is historical, and most extraordinary. Nebuchadnezzar's dream, which he himself forgot, was interpreted by Daniel although Jewish law forbade the interpretation of dreams. The miracle whereby Daniel's three friends issued unburned from a fiery furnace was useless, since neither the king nor his subjects were converted by it. Daniel interpreted another dream of the king, in which Nebuchadnezzar was transformed into an ox and driven out to roam the fields for seven years. This story has appeared so ridiculous to the Church Fathers that they have regarded it as an allegory. For, in the natural course of events, according to the principle of contradiction, it is impossible to change a man into an ox, even for the Deity. Dom Calmet's explanation that this metamorphosis was merely a lycanthropy is ingenious but contrary to the text. For how could the king roam the fields naked for seven years, resisting the attacks of wild beasts, who would reign in his place, how was he restored suddenly to his faculties, and why do historians who write at length about Nebuchadnezzar never mention the incident? There are many disputes as to whether the king had the power of speech and the use of reason during these seven years. This incident is followed by the story of Belshazzar, who is represented in the *Bible* as Nebuchadnezzar's son, although in profane history there are four generations between the two. An incredible number of events are crowded into one night in the Belshazzar narrative : the feast of the king, the handwriting upon the wall, the calling together of the soothsayers, their vain efforts to read the handwriting, the explanation of Daniel, the honors which were given him, the publication of these honors, the killing of the king, and the capture of Babylon. But Daniel's two miraculous escapes from the lion's den are more incredible still.

Most important in the Book of Daniel, however, is the famous prophecy of the Seventy Weeks, which is supposed to refer to the coming of Christ and is consequently regarded as the keystone of the Christian Religion. When one seeks to interpret it, difficulties begin. In the first place, the weeks cannot be accepted as weeks. According to the most general interpretation, they mean seven years each, that is to say, four hundred ninety years. But how can one determine when the years begin and end, and what chronology should be followed in computing them : Jewish, Roman or modern? Each Church Father, interpreter, and commentator has his system of explanation, but no matter what method of reasoning is followed, the interpretation is false, and the difficulties remain unsolved. Marsham advances the most likely opinion, contending that the seventy weeks begin with Darius the elder, and end with the persecution of Antiochus; that the "Oint du Seigneur" referred to, is either Cyrus or Zorobabel; and that the Christ is none other than Maccabeus. But this

system of reasoning nullifies the theory that the prophecy refers
to the coming of Christ.

The visions of Isaiah were as extravagant as those of the
other prophets. In one place, he prophesied that Judah would
perish at the end of sixty-five years, and yet only twenty-one
years elapsed before the captivity of the ten tribes. His most
famous prophecy, however, was the *Ecce virgo concipiet* which
is now understood to refer to the coming of Christ. But the reference can be in no way proved. To begin with, the word "alma"
in Hebrew does not mean "virgo" as translated by St. Jerome,
but a young woman or a young girl. It cannot therefore refer to
the Virgin Mary. Moreover, the prophecy was made to encour-
age Ahaz, when he was besieged by the Kings of Israel and
Syria. The following chapter proves that the woman to whom
Isaiah referred was his own wife. Jesus was never named Immanuel as Isaiah had predicted. Nor was the land of Judea delivered from its enemies before He knew how to distinguish
good from evil. Even Dom Calmet admits the difficulty of con-
verting the Jews to the Messiah by means of this interpretation.
Thus, when commentators reject literal explanation for mystical,
one mystical interpretation is as good as another, for "c'est
comme dans les nuages." And so it is with all of Isaiah's prophecies: "the Son who is called admirable" of Chapter IX as well
as the "Son of the seed of Jesse" of Chapter XI refer logically
to Hezekiah. Either they refer to unknown events, or they have
never been fulfilled. According to the mystical interpreters the
fifty-third chapter of Isaiah contains the prophecy most clearly
relating to Christ. But there is nothing in this chapter which
could not refer to Isaiah himself, in spite of the vague epithets,
doubtless badly rendered by the Latin. The prophet apparently
deplores his state of humiliation and the fact that the Jews paid
no attention to him. Indeed the chapter might allude to an infinite
number of things which are beyond our slight historical acquaintance of this period. But it is not applicable to the Christ, par-

ticularly the verse which says that He will have a numerous posterity.

Jeremiah lived during the reign of the Kings of Judah when Jerusalem was destroyed. His prophecies are nothing but menacing words mingled with promises, and lamentations over the fall of Jerusalem. His visions of a stick standing guard, a boiling pot turned toward the North, a belt rotting in the soil, and two baskets of figs are most difficult to interpret. But there is no doubt concerning the falsity of his prophecy in which God renews His alliance with the Jews and promises that their happiness after returning from captivity will last as long as the law and order of the world. This promise is so manifestly unfulfilled that Pascal maintains that it has been accomplished in the Christians. "Voilà comme les faiblesses deviennent de la force selon M. Pascal." When Jeremiah foretold that Jehoiakim would have no posterity and would not be buried in his forefather's tomb, he made a grievous mistake, for Jehoiakim was succeeded by his son Coniah, and entombed with his fathers. Similarly, Nebuchadnezzar never overthrew the obelisks of Egypt as was predicted. "C'est une force de plus pour M. Pascal."

The four major prophets are followed by twelve minor ones. Hosea, who lived to be one hundred thirty-seven years old, does not demand much of our attention although one hundred thirty-seven years is a long period for a little prophet to live. He must have been extremely interested in debauched women, for he always treats of them in his prophecies. Joel talks a great deal of a "Jour du Seigneur," which is commonly agreed to mean the Judgment Day. This Judgment is supposed to take place in the valley of Jehoshaphat, of which the exact location is totally unknown. If there is a valley in existence large enough to contain all the men who have ever lived, it is singular that no one even knows of the place. Moreover, Joel, Amos, Micah, and Zephaniah all predict everlasting prosperity for the Jews after the Captivity. The prophecies of Abdias, which referred to the Idumeans rather than to the Jews, are of little interest to us.

The best of the little prophets is the Galilean Jonah. The time of his life is unknown, but undoubtedly it was a jolly good time in which one could live three days and three nights in the belly of a whale. Why Jonah should have been sent to Nineveh, a pagan city, is mysterious. Why he did not want to go, since there was no money in the expedition, is clear. Why it was necessary to resort to a miracle to force Jonah to make the trip, when some one else could have been sent, is inexplicable. He was wrong in becoming irritated when he predicted the destruction of Nineveh and the happy event did not take place, for he should have rejoiced in the city's repentance; but Jonah was a Jew and this race loved destruction.

The Psalms are almost all allegorical. The circumstances of the composition of most of them are unknown, but it is certain that they were hymns sung in the Temple. They are said to be in verse, and that may well be, since Hebrew poetry has neither rime nor measure and consists in a sort of enthusiasm productive of nonsense. David is not the author of all the Psalms, as is commonly believed. They are supposed to have been collected by Ezra and to contain the whole life history of Christ. However, they may just as well be a foreshadowing of events in Mohammed's or Alexander's lives for their figurative language may mean anything. Their inherent obscurity, complicated by the difficulty of translating the Hebrew tongue, which even Dom Calmet admits to be extreme, makes them decidedly unreliable as prophecies. The titles which the Church Fathers believed inspired, sometimes have no connection with the thought of the song, or do not even occur in the Hebrew text, and they are often in contradiction with historical events related in Kings. It is notable that neither Psalms nor any book written before the Captivity contain the slightest trace of belief in a future life. In the translation from the Hebrew to the Vulgate, there are certain peculiarities: Psalms refers to the Kings of Israel as the "Anointed of the Lord," but the Vulgate translates this word "Anointed" by "Christ" and the passages where it occurs are assumed to be prophecies concerning Him. To be sure, certain events related in Psalms may coincidently be analogous to events in the life of Christ, but there are also some which could be interpreted as referring to Louis XIV. Besides, there are mistakes in translation, "Caara" in Hebrew being translated as if it were "caarie," thus altering the text entirely. The Vulgate has added expressions which do not occur in the Hebrew, "et super meam miserunt sortem," for instance.

The authorship of the Book of Proverbs is a subject for dispute. Interpreters generally assign it to Solomon, and indeed the author purports to be Solomon. Some think it, however, a compilation, made either by Ezra or by several persons. Whatever it is, it is far from being the excellent work it is commonly reputed to be, since it abounds in tiresome repetitions of banalities and puerilities. Reason must have been in its infancy at this time. The author charges the sluggard to imitate the ant which diligently puts aside in summer its winter supply of food. But M. de Réaumur has discovered that the ant does not eat during the winter and what is more, it doesn't eat wheat at all. We question the social morality of Proverbs on certain occasions, for instance, when we read that stealing is no great sin if one is hungry. Its comparisons are far from elegant, notably the one in which a fair and foolish maiden is likened unto a gold ring around a trout's snout. We find nothing but pure nonsense in a sentence such as, "The most precious stone is waiting, wherever it turns it understands prudently." And there are contradictions from one verse to another, Verse 4, Chapter XIX, advising not to answer a fool according to his folly, and 5 immediately following, saying just the opposite.

Ecclesiastes, attributed to Solomon, is the most reasonable book of the *Bible*. It is a hymn in praise of happiness, a glorification of pleasure. It contains the strongest statement ever made on the materialism of the Soul; a statement so strong in fact that if one dared write it in the eighteenth century, he would certainly be burned at the stake. Commentators have tried to excuse it by maintaining that Solomon is expressing not his own thoughts, but those of the "libertins" whom he intends to refute. But nowhere does he say that they are not his own beliefs and never does he refute them.

The Songs of Solomon also attributed to him are renowned for their indecency. Obviously written to celebrate the crude rustic love of some Israelite, they contain verses which cause the reader to blush with shame, and which are definitely not translatable in French. The Church Fathers give them a chaste and allegorical interpretation quite at variance with their literal meaning. Grotius has given us a very learned and piquant commentary on the Songs of Solomon.

The Book of Wisdom, the last of the works ascribed to Solomon, is little worthy of its name. In II :13, it states that the just man boasts of being the Son of God. This explains the numerous uses which Christ made of the expression and shows that it did not have the meaning given it by the Christians. Incidents related in this book are not always in accord with accounts of the Pentateuch.

Ecclesiasticus is one of the most reasonable books of the *Bible,* but it is deadly dull. The Vulgate, which was not touched by St. Jerome, is the oldest version and contains numerous passages which do not occur in the Septuagint. The Church refused to accept Ecclesiasticus as canonical for a long time. Some interpreters attribute it to Solomon, but this is absurd, since it was manifestly written after the Captivity by a certain Jesus, son of Sirach, and grandfather of the Greek translator, also named Jesus. Apparently the name Jesus was common among the Jews. The instruction of Ecclesiasticus is sometimes nonsensical, but it contains one of the most philosophical statements ever made: "Melior est mors quam vita amara, et requies eterna quam languor perseverans."

The first difficulty encountered in examining the books of the New Testament is the question of their authenticity. It has never been satisfactorily decided what should determine whether a book is canonical or apocryphal. This is particularly true in the matter of the Gospels. In the early days of Christianity, there was a large number of Gospels, one even by Judas Iscariot. In fact, Dom Calmet has listed thirty-nine, all of them mentioned by the early Christian Fathers as inspired. Why only four have been accepted as canonical is a mystery, since these particular books are certainly no more reasonable than the others.

Very little is known concerning the authorship or the text of these four Gospels as originally constituted. It is very doubtful, as Grotius has already shown, that the Gospel of St. Matthew was written by the apostle Matthew. There existed a Hebrew version of the work, evidently the original, which differed considerably from the Vulgate. St. Jerome confessed being acquainted with this version but disregarded it because of its numerous absurdities. No one knows who St. Mark was, when he wrote his Gospel, or in what language he wrote it. The supposedly original copy now at Venice contains nothing to support its authenticity, being in such a dilapidated state that it is impossible to decipher a single word, or even a single letter in it. Indeed, there is dispute as to whether some of its characters are Greek or Latin. The same uncertainty surrounds the person of St. Luke. It is still not definitely known whether the John who wrote the fourth Gospel was St. John. It is certain, however, that St. John could not have written the twenty-first chapter, because Verse 24 reads: "This is the disciple which testifieth to these things, and wrote these things; and we know that his testimony is true."

The Gospels are often at variance with each other. Matthew and Luke, for example, give different genealogies of the Christ. Matthew talks of two demons which possessed the swine, St. Luke speaks of only one, and gives his name as Legion. In Matthew, Jarius says that his daughter has just died, while in Mark and Luke he says that she is dying. After the multiplication of the loaves and fishes, the disciples embarked on the Sea of Tiberias. Mark says that they started for Bethsaida; St. John, for Capernaum. Matthew speaks of two blind men who were cured at Jericho; Mark mentions only one. Moreover, the Apostles do not all relate the same incidents. The miracle of the paralytic who was lowered through the roof occurs in Mark, the resurrection of Lazarus in John.

In the opening chapter of Matthew we have the genealogy of Jesus, as St. Jerome has given it to us. This genealogy which, curiously enough, is Joseph's, is filled with contradictions: only three generations are attributed to a period of three hundred thirty-six years; Joram is called the father of Ozias when separated from him by five generations. This discrepancy has been explained and defended on the grounds that Matthew was forced for the sake of symmetry to divide his genealogy into three groups of fourteen generations each. But it is absurd to think that there would be only forty-two generations in approximately two thousand years. And, what is more absurd, only forty-one are listed. Jeconias is called the son of Josias when he was his grandson; he is said to have had brothers when he had none, and to have lived at the time of the Captivity, when he died twenty years before. Only four women, all of evil reputation, figure in the genealogy.

In Luke's genealogy of Jesus we find only three names which occur also in Matthew's list. The two disciples do not agree concerning the father of Joseph. Matthew makes Joseph a descendant of David by Solomon; Luke, by Nathan. Some commentators explain that Luke is giving the Virgin's genealogy, but that is impossible because Her father was Joachem and not Heli.

In a discussion of the Immaculate Conception, the question naturally arises as to why a married rather than an unmarried woman should be chosen as the Mother of Christ. The Church Fathers themselves have proposed this question, and suggested various answers. The most ludicrous, given by St. Jerome and others, is that thereby the Devil was fooled. But if the Devil, who is so keen, was unable to recognize Christ, how could the Jews be expected to recognize Him?

The story of the Wise Men presents innumerable difficulties. In the first place, they are assumed to have been kings, but Orientals designate by the term "Magi" all kinds of soothsayers, priests, and philosophers. Their number is unknown, though it is supposed to have been three, in honor of the Trinity probably. Indeed, their bodies are shown at Cologne where they perform miracles daily. The star which they followed is very intriguing. How did they recognize it as the star of Christ? Why does no historian speak of it? Whence did it come and where did it go? Furthermore, why did the Wise Men commit the indiscretion of talking to Herod about the Christ? Why did Herod treat the incident as of scant importance at one moment, and with such suspicion at another that he butchered fourteen thousand children? And, last of all, why was this crime of Herod not mentioned by Josephus who loathed him and would have been only too glad to record it? As for the flight into Egypt, it appears as ludicrous as Mohammed's hegira ridiculed so much by Houtteville. Moreover, though related in Matthew, it is not mentioned in the Gospel of St. Luke who follows the events in Jesus's life very carefully from His birth until Herod's death. In fact, no evangelist except Matthew records this flight. Luke states that after the ceremony of the Circumcision, the Holy Family returned to the town of Nazareth but visited Jerusalem every year at Easter.

On the other hand, Luke speaks of a census which is not recorded in the other Gospels. According to him it was ordered by Augustus and was the first taken under Cyrenius, governor of Syria. Unfortunately, no profane historian of the period mentions this event which would have been of considerable importance, and there has never been a governor of Syria named Cyrenius. Even assuming that the name Quirinus was corrupted into Cyrenius, which is a likely explanation, no Quirinus governed Syria during Herod's reign and consequently no census could have been taken at the time of Christ's birth. Moreover, Luke talks of this first census as if Augustus ordered one to be taken of the whole world every day.

Matthew cites four prophecies in justification of the flight into Egypt and subsequent events. The writers of the four Gospels often make use of Old Testament prophecies either to explain why the event occurred in the New Testament or to show how it was the fulfillment of the prophecy. In either case, discrepancies between prophecy and event can be noted. For instance, Matthew quotes Micah so incorrectly and interprets him so fantastically that St. Jerome thought the Evangelist was making sport of Herod's ignorance. A passage from Hosea, translated "filios" instead of "filium" in the Septuagint, appears to give the right meaning to Micah's words. St. Jerome, however, changed the "filios" to "filium" in order to preserve Matthew's interpretation. He wrongly interprets Jeremiah's prophecy concerning the dispersal of the tribes of Manasseh and Ephraim as referring to the massacre of the innocents in Bethlehem. The fourth prophecy cited by Matthew as justification for the establishment of the Holy Family in Nazareth cannot be found in any prophet's work. Moreover, Matthew assumes that a Nazarene is an inhabitant of the town of Nazareth, thereby giving a false interpretation, since a Nazarene is a member of a religious order observing certain ceremonial laws.

Events surrounding the baptism of Jesus and His temptation by the Devil are not entirely clear. We are not told why Jesus wished to be baptized by John. It is difficult also to understand what is meant by the expression "The Heavens opened," although Dom Calmet has discussed it at length and concluded that the Dove's Descent was accompanied by a little flash of lightning. Christ's temptation in the wilderness after His baptism brings up several puzzling points. The question as to whether the Spirit which drove Him there was the Devil, is of small consequence, although it has been hotly debated by commentators. Fasting for forty days was not a new ceremony, since it had been practiced by both Elijah and Moses. A more serious problem is how the Devil transported Jesus from the desert to the Temple and from the Temple to the mountain. And it is indeed difficult to locate this mountain whence could be seen all the kingdoms of the earth, although the text gives us to understand that it was situated in Judea.

The Sermon on the Mount contains a "morale assez pure," but very trivial and mingled from time to time with the ridiculous. The promise that the poor in spirit shall dwell in Heaven and the meek shall inherit the earth not only gives a poor impression of the Celestial Kingdom but indicates that folly is superior to meekness. The assertion that Christ has come to accomplish, rather than destroy, the law seems to have been belied by the incidents of His life, while the statement that Heaven and earth will not pass away until the whole law is accomplished presupposes that they will last forever. The punishment of death for being in anger against or saying "raca" to one's brother appears severe, and eternal punishment for him who calls his brother a fool is excessive beyond reason. The rule against taking oath is certainly not observed by Christians with the possible exception of the Quakers. And the precept, "Take no thought for the morrow," if followed would be very injurious to society. It is true that monks fare rather well by following this precept, due to the folly of those who support them.

The cures wrought by Jesus were less miraculous than they seem, and attended by incidents which invite criticism. For instance, the touching of the leper was contrary to law. Furthermore, it is said that in effecting these cures Jesus took upon Himself the infirmities of the sick, but this is nowhere confirmed. The explanation sometimes proposed, that this statement refers to the Passion, is contrary to the text. The curing of the woman with the issue of blood has been proved quite possible by the recent case of Mme Lafosse, who, suffering from a similar ill, recovered from her malady because of the violent emotion which she felt at the passing of a religious procession. Mme Lafosse's cure has been pronounced miraculous, although previous remedies had prepared for it, and the patient did not have the ulcer which sometimes accompanies this disease and makes it dangerous. The woman mentioned by Matthew had the ulcer and indeed she died of it shortly afterward, according to tradition. The casting out of the devils into swine, although undoubtedly a miracle, occurred under circumstances which discredit it. In the first place, St. Matthew states that two were possessed of demons, St. Mark says one. It is difficult to explain how one (or two) demons entered two thousand swine, and still more difficult to account for the presence of swine in Judea, since they were held in execration by the Jews, and it was forbidden on pain of death to raise them. Not to mention the fact, that this miraculous cure had economic consequences for the swine's possessors, who must have been ruined by their unjust destruction. The cure of the paralytic who was lowered through the roof gives rise to rational questioning. It is incomprehensible that the people who crowded into the house did not open up a way to let the paralytic in. And no one has explained why those who brought him were so hurried that they removed the roof. Moreover, it must have taken them longer to remove the roof than it would have taken to wait for the crowd to disperse. Furthermore, the danger within the house from falling framework and plaster must have been considerable, and its proprietor must have been in despair at seeing his property ruined. There is a certain inconsequence in the miracle of the blind man related by Mark. When asked what he saw after regaining his sight he replied that he saw men as trees. If he saw men as men, why did he say that he saw them as trees? And if he saw them as trees, who told him that they were men? Of all the cures related in the Gospels, the most puzzling is John's account of the sick at the pool of Bethesda. The legend surrounding the pool is rather incredible in itself, and none of the historians, not even Philo or Josephus, have spoken of this miraculous spot. It is strange that when the pool was surrounded by such crowds of sick, only one was cured after the angel had stirred the waters, and it seems so unfair that the most agile in casting himself therein should have been cured rather than the neediest. There must have been confusion and fighting among the sick to obtain priority in entering the pool and the Magistrates of Jerusalem were certainly very negligent in not establishing order in a place so important. St. Augustine apparently doubted the legend, for he questioned the likelihood of an angel's descending for this purpose. But to return to the sick man, no one yet knows what his malady was. The assumption that he was also a paralytic is purely gratuitous, since he himself says that he could walk to the pool. His execution of the command to take up his bed and walk may thus not have been extraordinary, because he could easily do so if he was not a paralytic. The fact that the order was given on the Sabbath scandalized the Jews, and rightly so, for it was contrary to the law of Moses. Indeed, this miraculous cure has given rise to much comment on the part of the Church Fathers. St. Augustine has asked why Jesus selected this man for healing from all those assembled, but has proposed no answer. St. Chrysostom regarding the story unlikely has chosen to regard it as an allegory or parable. Finally, the Church Fathers have debated as to what would have happened if two sick people had jumped into the pool simultaneously.

The three resurrections recounted in the Gospels are not above suspicion. That of the widow's son related in Luke appears to be the first in date and the most authentic. However, there have been many cases of people who have fallen into a lethargy and been considered dead. If the son had been dead a longer time, some credence might be given this story which, significantly enough, is related only by Luke. The resurrection of Jarius's daughter, on the other hand, is told by both Matthew and Luke, but their versions are somewhat different. Two reflections might be made concerning this event. First, it is not clear why every one was sent from the room during the resurrection. Secondly, it is not understandable why, when Jesus had just brought about the resurrection of the widow's son, Jarius's family should have sent word that their child was dead and therefore His visit to her would be useless. The resurrection of Lazarus gives rise to many questions. Why, for instance, has the event been recounted only by St. John, and not until after the dissolution of the Jewish State, the destruction of the public records, and the death of all those who might have witnessed it? Certain details in the narrative are worthy of attention: we have no way of knowing that Lazarus was really dead, for it is said that his face was covered before the resurrection; and afterwards, although his feet and hands were tied, he walked forth from the tomb. The fact that the command to come forth from the tomb was shouted to Lazarus is also significant. But the most extraordinary part of this story is that Lazarus having been revived did not become an ardent follower of Jesus and a walking testimony of his resurrection. Nowhere in the Gospels or in the Acts of the Apostles do we find that those miraculously cured or resurrected play a further rôle in the establishment of Christianity.

The precepts which Jesus gave His disciples before sending them forth to preach were not always reasonable. The order to provide no clothing for their trips appears very improvident, while the command to wear no shoes is ridiculous. The Apostles are not in complete agreement concerning this order: Matthew states that they were forbidden to wear shoes; Mark, that they were forbidden to have any footwear. The recommendation to exercise the prudence of serpents is queer, since the serpent was an accursed creature. It is more singular still that men should be ordered to speak before thinking. Christ's statement that He came to bring a sword, not peace, is in utter contradiction with His recommendation of meekness in the Sermon on the Mount.

The use of parables is unjustified, but they are probably excusable on the ground that if Jesus had spoken clearly, people would have understood, and become converted, and He would have been obliged to cure their illnesses. But talking seems useless, if the meaning of one's words must be shrouded in obscurity. Moreover, the comparisons employed by Jesus do not portray

a vivid imagination. The parable of the mustard seed is manifestly false, since it is not the smallest of seeds. It has nevertheless given rise to an amusing remark on the part of St. Augustine, who declares that martyrs, like the mustard seed, increase
their talents one hundred fold; virgins, sixty; and married people, thirty. Matthew quoted as from Isaiah a passage prophesying
the use of parables but unfortunately his quotation comes from
Psalms. Porphyry noted this error which has since been rectified.

John's death occurred in an extremely unlikely manner. The
presentation of his head on a charger to a young girl dancer
seems a strange recompense for excellent dancing. The miracle
of the loaves and fishes is a repetition of one of Elisha's miracles.
The miracle of the Transfiguration is both useless and unsub-
stantiated, since there is nothing miraculous in the averred lu-
minous face and person of Christ, and we have no assurance
that the personages accompanying Him were Moses and Elisha.
Interpreters are puzzled to know whether Moses was resuscitated
solely for this appearance and died immediately after. As for
Elisha, it may be presumed that he ascended again to Heaven in
the same chariot in which he departed on the previous occasion,
for apparently he had never died.

Promises made in the Gospels have remained unfulfilled. It is
said that prayers of two or three gathered together will be answered, and yet the prayers of the whole Church for the extirpa-
tion of heresies and the conversion of infidels have not been
granted.

The condemnation of the rich young man because of his riches
is illogical. According to this reasoning the wealth of the Church
is condemnable and half the inhabitants of the earth as well, for
"il faut bien que les richesses soient entre les mains de quelqu'un."

The cleansing of the Temple is surprising to say the least. It
is absurd that one person, alone and without authority, should
drive out a crowd of merchants from the Temple when selling
merchandise in the exterior galleries was not contrary to Jewish

Law. Why should Jesus exhibit such zeal for a religion which He came to destroy? His action is defended on the grounds that He was a devout follower of the Jewish Religion all His life, but if this is true why should Christians, His followers, persecute the followers of the Jewish Law?

The cursing of the fig tree is so ridiculous that several Church Fathers believe it an allegory, Origen stating openly that the incident never happened and St. Augustine remarking that it would have been foolish. There are three embarrassing points for those who accept this miracle as authentic: its absurdity, its uselessness, and its injustice. Its absurdity lies in the fact that it was not the season for figs, and the tree was an insensible thing. It was useless because the dead tree bore no more figs than a living one would have produced at this season; and unjust, for thereby a man's property was destroyed. It is astounding that people do not burst out laughing when ministers gravely read this miracle, drawing from it various beautiful parables, for it has no possible mystic interpretation. It is usually interpreted as referring to the synagogue, but the expression, "it was not the season for figs," precludes this interpretation since good works were encouraged in the synagogue in all seasons. Furthermore, the Apostles do not agree on the time when the tree withered, Matthew saying that it did so immediately; and Mark, the next day. This continual difference in the recorded sequence of events in Christ's life is very embarrassing.

A final miracle worthy of commentary is the turning of water into wine at the Cana marriage feast. It is noteworthy that Jesus showed no respect for His Mother when She informed Him of the lack of wine, addressing Her as "woman" rather than "mother." Some consider His treatment of Mary very harsh on this occasion, while others excuse it by stating that every one at the feast had been drinking. The miracle is inexcusable on those grounds, however, for if the guests were already half drunk, it was not morally right to supply them with more wine. Had the wine appeared magically without the agency of water, only the uselessness and indecency of the miracle would be subject to criticism. As it is, it seems perfectly justifiable to inquire whether Jesus did not make some mixture, punch, for instance, which the half-drunk guests mistook for wine.

The parable of the Wedding Feast is badly told. Its conclusion that many are called but few are chosen is not apparent in the story, since only one man in the group was rejected. And, indeed, he was treated very unjustly in being cast out, merely because he was not dressed for the feast. "On n'a pas toujours sa robe nuptiale dans sa poche." The surprising thing in the parable is that all the others had their wedding garments.

In Matthew XXIII:35, occurs a statement concerning the murder of Zacharias, son of Barachias, which dates the book after the Fall of Jerusalem, for there was no Zacharias, son of Barachias killed under the circumstances described, except the one mentioned by Josephus as being killed during Titus's siege of Jerusalem. This passage is the "écueil des commentateurs" and cannot refer, as they suggest, to Zacharias the High Priest slain by Joash. For this Zacharias was the son of Jehoiada. Then, too, a period of six hundred years elapsed between this Zacharias and Christ, during which time the Jews could slay their prophets with impunity.

Matthew quotes as from Jeremiah a prophecy which is supposed to foretell Judas's casting aside of the thirty pieces of silver, his price of betrayal and the disciples' purchase of a potter's field with this sum. No such passage exists in Jeremiah, but there is one in Zachariah where the prophet has a vision of himself, a shepherd receiving his pay and ordering with it a statue, not a potter's field. This manner of quoting is disconcerting. The Fathers, to excuse it, explain that these prophecies were quoted from memory, but they apparently forgot that the book was inspired.

Matthew also states that at the Crucifixion, darkness covered the earth from the sixth to the ninth hour. No historian, not even Josephus, speaks of this darkness, which cannot be attributed to an eclipse, since we know it to have been the period of the full moon, when eclipses cannot occur. Matthew and Mark differ concerning the time when the Crucifixion took place, Matthew stating that it was at the sixth hour; Mark, at the third hour.

The Resurrection occurred before its appointed hour. Jesus had constantly referred to Jonah's miracle in living three days and three nights in the belly of the whale as a figure of His sojourn in the tomb. But He remained only one day and two nights. Commentators have made every effort to explain this divergence. St. Augustine gives a most peculiar explanation: he agrees that Jesus did not remain in the tomb three days and three nights, but he states that the three days signify the three ages of the world. This Resurrection took place under peculiar circumstances. The descent of an angel to roll away the stone appears unnecessary. Moreover, the event occurred in secrecy when, according to logic, it should have been witnessed before Pilate, the Princes, and the people. Had this been the case, the Resurrection would have possessed all the necessary marks of authenticity. Since it took place in secrecy with only the interested testimony of the Apostles to substantiate it, "on est en droit de conclure qu'il n'est point ressuscité." It is plausible to assume that before the Fall of Jerusalem, written records existed which disclosed the motives for this Crucifixion and exposed the trickery of the Resurrection. Either during the destruction of Jerusalem or during the time when the Christians rose to power, these documents must have been destroyed. Such at least was the fate of Porphyry's writings and we may presume that other records embarrassing to the Christians met a similar fate.

The Acts of the Apostles are attributed to St. Luke because they are addressed to Theophilus as was the Gospel of St. Luke, and because the first verses of the Acts indicate that the same writer was responsible for both works. In the beginning of Christianity there were many Acts of the Apostles but these are the only ones declared canonical. The book in question deals almost exclusively with the acts of St. Peter and St. Paul.

St. Luke begins by stating that he has already told all that Jesus has done and states that others have attempted to do the same, but insinuates that his is the only true version. This was certainly not a compliment to the writers of the other Gospels. Later he speaks of the descent of the Holy Spirit in tongues of fire, giving the gift of foreign tongues and the talent of performing miracles to the Disciples. This gift of interpretation leaves much to conjecture. Was it lasting or limited only to certain times? Peter states that God delivered His Son from the pains of Hell, admitting by this statement that the Devil had his momentary triumph in the damnation of Jesus. He also says that the Jews crucified Christ through ignorance and adds that thus the prophecies concerning Him were fulfilled. If events were thus predestined, why should the Jews be punished for an act which they could not help performing?

Chapter V contains the story of Ananias and Sapphira who, having heard the preaching of St. Peter, sold a piece of their property and brought the proceeds to further his cause as was the common practice among converts. Unfortunately for them, they kept secretly some of the money for themselves. Peter discovered this and they were both stricken and died. This certainly indicates that Peter was indeed cruel and worthy of founding the Roman Church.

St. Stephen in Chapter VII preaches in the synagogue, making many statements in direct contradiction with various parts of the Pentateuch. He says that the Israelites were captives in Egypt four hundred years while the Pentateuch records two hundred fifteen, that they did not sacrifice to God during the forty years in the wilderness. Exodus states quite the contrary and it would have been useless to construct a tabernacle for the Ark if there were not religious services. Stephen continues by upbraiding his listeners, telling them that they had killed all the prophets announcing Christ's birth. This was false, since no prophet with the possible exception of Isaiah had been killed, and the crowd, enraged by Stephen's unjust accusations, stoned him to death.

The conversion of St. Paul recorded in the Acts gives rise to question. Paul, a persecutor of the Christians, while on the road to Damascus saw a great light, which cast him to earth blinding him, and then he heard the voice of Christ calling him. It is singular that those who were with Paul were not blinded at the same time. It is also strange that, though still blind and reduced to being led to Damascus by his friends, he saw Ananias enter the room with the purpose of restoring his sight. Indeed, the scales did not fall from his eyes until he was touched by Ananias.

Another miracle follows, this time to the credit of St. Peter who brought to life St. Tabitha the Christians' dressmaker. This seems useless for she had died a Saint and in resurrecting her he exposed her to the danger of damnation. St. Peter later had a vision on the occasion of a visit from a Roman centurion sent him by an angel. He saw a vessel descending from Heaven containing all manner of beasts and heard a voice saying "kill and eat." This he interpreted to mean that people of every race, rank and faith should be received into the Church without distinction. However, it is to be remarked that Peter was very hungry when he had this particular vision.

In the thirteenth chapter of Acts we find Paul again preaching in the synagogue and making remarks which indicate that he did not know too well his Old Testament. He also says that the Jews, not understanding the prophecies, fulfilled them in condemning Jesus, but why then should they have been punished? Was it merely because the punishment had been predicted? Later Paul and Barnabas give evidence of their belief in predestination when they tell the Jews that all those predestined for life eternal had believed in the coming of Christ.

According to Acts the first council of Christians took place at Jerusalem and the Apostles there abolished all the tenets of the law of Moses beginning with circumcision. Later, however, St. Paul circumcised St. Timothy but would not baptize him, and boasted thereafter that he would circumcise no more, regardless of Jewish edicts. This conduct seems far from logical. Strangely enough, the Jews seemed to know nothing of this first Council, for according to law, they would have exterminated the Christians had they been informed. The story of Paul in prison seeing the jailer in the middle of the night, when there was no light is somewhat suspicious. Strange also is the account of his visit to Athens where he told the Athenians that he had brought them tidings of the Unknown God whose altar he had found in their city. What was this statue, and how could he tell them he brought them this God, whom they served without knowing Him, when the Athenians were idolatrous and consequently condemned by the Christians?

We find later that St. Paul, who had been one of the Council of Jerusalem to abolish the Law, was guilty of the utmost hypocrisy when he returned to that city, for to appease the Jews he went to the Temple, pretended to be a Nazarene and to observe the Law. His trickery was suspected, however, and he would have fared ill had it not been for the interference of the Roman guard who put him in prison. Declaring himself to be a Roman citizen and thus impressing the authorities, he was given trial and appeared before the Sanhedrin. He began by insulting the High Priest, and when reproached protested that he did not know him, but this was untrue since the High Priest wore a special garb. When on the point of being condemned, he very craftily declared himself a Pharisee, knowing that part of the Sanhedrin was Sadducee, that the two sects were bitter enemies, that the Pharisees would take up his cause—which, in fact, was what happened. The court then sent him under guard to Felix, governor of Judea.

The rest of the Book of Acts deals with the case of St. Paul. He remained in prison in Judea, and Festus, successor of Felix, in speaking to King Agrippa of Paul's detention, said that he knew nothing about his crimes, save that he spoke of a certain Jesus, dead, but whom he affirmed to be alive. Evidently neither Felix nor Agrippa had heard of the Messiah. Tried before Agrippa, Paul declared himself a Pharisee, which was singular since this was the sect against which Christ had particularly warned his disciples. When he continued speaking about the Resurrection of Christ, Agrippa believed him mad, but he was allowed to appeal his case to Rome, being sent there under guard.

In Rome his case was neglected two years but he was permitted to go about preaching, chained to a soldier. He continued to assure the Jews that he had done nothing against their Law which was, of course, untrue. Acts records nothing more of his case. In passing, it is significant to note what the book says regarding the sacrament of Baptism. Throughout these chapters, it is said that the disciples baptised only in the name of Jesus, whereas Christ had expressly taught them to baptise in the name of the Father, Son and Holy Ghost.

In the Epistle to the Romans we have St. Paul preaching mainly on two subjects, the law and predestination. He states that no man will be justified before the law because the law has given man knowledge of sin. But what purpose then was this law given man? He goes on to remark that when there is no law, there is no violation of it, a real sophism, for it is just when there is no law that it is violated, for there is a Natural Law which exists for all time. There is definite evidence in St. Paul's words of his belief in predestination. For instance, in speaking of Jacob and Esau he says that it was decreed before their birth that the younger should prevail over the older. Later he states that God through His grace has saved a small number of people whom He has reserved as His own.

The first part of the Epistle to the Corinthians has to do principally with wisdom. St. Paul says that God through Christ has convinced the Sages of the century of the uselessness of their wisdom. This is pure exaggeration, since in Acts it is evident that the majority of people had not even heard of the Christian doctrine. He further remarks that what seems folly in men's eyes is wisdom in God's, and that if one wishes to become wise it is first necessary to become foolish. St. Paul is sometimes vain and insolent. He begs the Corinthians to imitate him as he imitates Christ, and scolds them for letting the judges of their district decide their suits, recommending them to choose instead as judges the least esteemed members of the Church. He holds forth at length on the virtues of continence, disregarding by his precepts God's first commandment after the Creation—increase and multiply. He continues, offering himself as an example, saying that those who are married should remain so, but those who are not should remain in their present state as "I myself live." Yet, he adds that each one has the right to take with him a woman who will be his sister. He goes into detail even concerning the way his converts should wear their hair, calling it glorious for a woman to wear hers long, but shameful for a man to allow his to grow.

Sometimes his statements are utterly absurd. For instance, he affirms that it is written in the Law, "I shall speak to this people a foreign tongue in order that I shall not be understood." In the fourteenth chapter of Corinthians he orders his disciples to follow a procedure in their worship, which has since become the method of the Quakers. He ends his first Epistle with remarks on the Resurrection which are incomprehensible, quoting inaccurately the prophet Hosea on one occasion, and attacking again the Law in saying that the sting of death is sin and the strength of sin is the Law. It is not surprising that he was pursued by the priests for his constant criticism of the Law.

In Second Corinthians St. Paul recounts in detail the persecutions he has undergone, seeming to glory in them. He also digresses concerning false prophets, admitting, in doing so, that the Christian Church from its very origin must have been divided. In one place, he says that if these prophets preach another gospel they should be heeded. This is in contradiction with the teachings of Jesus, and St. Paul later contradicts himself in Galatians when he exhorts his converts to listen to no other Gospel, even though he himself should preach it.

In his Epistle to the Galatians, Paul continues to glorify himself and to digress on the Law. He wants it understood that he owes nothing to the other disciples, that he was chosen by God for his mission from infancy, and that after his conversion he did not go to Jerusalem to see the Apostles. He does not mention Ananias to whom he was sent for baptism and instruction. Later he discusses at great length a quarrel between a certain Cephas (Peter) and himself regarding the doctrine to be taught. This is certainly not flattering to either disciple. St. Paul calls Peter the Apostle of Circumcision and the Jews, and himself the Apostle of the Gentiles. He was evidently jealous of Peter's preeminence. It is singular that the Church often honors jointly these two disciples, since there seems to have been nothing but misunderstanding between them. Indeed, the Church tries in vain to explain the differences of the two. St. Paul explains his hatred of the Law by saying, that if righteousness comes by the Law, Christ is dead in vain. He does not mention the Gentiles, of whom he was the apostle, when he says that Christ came to redeem those under the Law. He ends his Epistle with an exhortation to his followers to assist in every way him who instructs them—a rather useful precaution.

In his letter to the Ephesians Paul falsely attributes to Christ a passage from Psalms; to the Philippians he states that the coming of Christ is at hand and boasts of his connections at Rome; to the Thessalonians he says that he is finishing what Christ has begun, a rather vainglorious remark. He forbids the Thessalonians to refrain from eating certain foods, declaring them essential to the body's nourishment. This is certainly not a good argument for the observation of Lent and the austerity of monastic life. And his later exhortation, that he who does not work shall not eat, is no encouragement for the idleness of monks. He warns the same Thessalonians not to give credence to those preaching that the Kingdom of God is at hand, yet he himself has stated that he expects the Coming of Christ within his lifetime. He makes further reference to this in his letter to Timothy, and Grotius rightly inferred from this passage Paul's belief in an early resurrection.

Paul also writes Timothy that the Law is useful when used properly, but it has been made for malefactors instead of the just; that women will be saved by their children; that a time will come when impostors will forbid marriage and the eating of certain foods. These last two statements respectively condemn the life of nuns and foretell the coming of founders of religious orders. He gives further proof of his modesty in declaring to Timothy that he, Paul, has been established Master of Nations.

There is a verse in Paul's Epistle to Titus which has no doubt attracted the attention of the Jansenists, for he declares that God has saved us not because of our just works but because of His infinite mercy.

The last Epistle given us under the name of St. Paul is addressed to the Hebrews. However, the author of the book is not really known. It seems illogical that he who termed himself the Apostle of the Gentiles should have addressed an Epistle to the Hebrews whom he hated. Church Fathers have attributed it to St. Clement, who has never been considered an inspired writer. Eusebius says that in his time it was not generally attributed to St. Paul, but the Catholic Church finally accepted him as its author. Accepting this attribution, we find St. Paul beginning the Epistle with a long dissertation concerning a certain Melchisedec, affirming that Jesus has been established eternal Pontiff according to the order of Melchisedec, who was created without genealogy, beginning or end to his life, being thus the image of God's Son and forever remaining a priest. The qualities attributed to this personage are so confusing that many interpreters, among them St. Jerome, have given up trying to explain his identity. Some say that it was the Holy Spirit who appeared to Abraham in human form, some that it was Shem or Enoch, some that it was the Son of God. The most likely explanation, however, is that Paul, who wanted to destroy the Law and the priesthood of Aaron, conceived the idea of declaring Jesus eternal Pontiff not according to Aaron's order but according to Melchisedec's which would be previous to Aaron's. He says that the new alliance should have a pontiff who would not be obliged, as the others, to offer daily sacrifices for his own sins, but that he should offer himself as a sacrifice once and for all. Thus he infers in this verse firstly, that Aaron sacrificed every day, which was not the case, and secondly that Jesus offered Himself for His own sins. He also insinuates that there was some defect in the first alliance of God with man, since it became necessary to form a second one. He mentions certain details concerning the Ark which were not at all true according to the Old Testament. Later, wishing to prove the uselessness of continual sacrifice according to the old law he says that if sacrifice had made those who offered it just and perfect, they would have ceased offering it. But, do not people continue daily to offer it in the Mass, and is not regular confession obligatory by order of the Church? According to this reasoning, Jesus's death, source of the Mass and Confession, was useless. St. Paul continues, attributing to Jesus various sayings from Psalms and Jeremiah, quoting them inexactly. He says that Moses left Egypt through faith, when Exodus plainly states that it was through fear of Pharaoh and of having killed an Egyptian. He contradicts Christ's story of the rich man, in which Lazarus and Abraham are shown to be in Paradise, when he states that the holy personages of the Old Testament have not yet received their reward.

The Epistle of St. James has finally been accepted in the canon but it has not been determined which St. James wrote it. It seems that the writer would overthrow the social order, for he says that the poor man should have as honorable a place as the rich. He makes all sins equal in declaring that a person who violates one commandment is guilty of violating the whole Law. He disagrees with St. Paul, who stated that no one will be justified by the works of the Law, when he avers that faith without works does not bring salvation. He, not Jesus, seems to have instituted Extreme Unction, since he orders that the sick man shall call a priest to pray for him and anoint him with oil.

There are three Epistles of St. Peter, of which the first has always passed as canonical. St. Peter gives rise to discussion in affirming God's readiness to judge the living and dead, adding that, for this reason, the Gospel has been preached to the dead. There has never been any reference to an Apostle who went to inform the dead. One of his later statements has been accepted by the Catholic Church as affirming his residence in Rome. He writes that the Church which is in *Babylon* sends greetings to the recipients of the letter. By Babylon, the Church understands Rome. But St. Peter never spoke allegorically, and it is reasonably certain that he had never been to Rome, for none of his letters are dated from that city. His Acts do not speak of a journey there, and St. Paul never mentions him in his letter to the Romans. Furthermore, Paul never liked to continue another's work and if Peter had founded the Roman Church, Paul would not have been willing to instruct it. Then, too, when Paul arrived in Rome, the inhabitants asked him what Christianity was, as if they had never heard of it previously. Peter, the Apostle of the circumcised, would not have chosen Rome as a field of work, since there were only pagans there, Claudius having expelled the Jews. In conclusion, none of the authors who support the belief that Peter was founder of the Roman Church agree as to the date of his journey or the length of his sojourn and the majority of them place the date at a time when it can be proven that he was elsewhere.

The authenticity of St. Peter's Second Epistle has been suspected, but the Council of Trent finally accepted it. In this book, St. Peter speaks of the Transfiguration at which he was present. He affirms having heard the voice of the Holy Spirit addressing Christ, but adds that we have a surer witness of this in the writings of the Prophets. Thus he attaches more im-

portance to the Prophets than to the Voice of God or the Holy
Spirit. He disagrees with the writings of the other Apostles on
eternal punishment and predestination, saying that God wants
no one to perish but desires to save every one through penitence.

There are three Epistles of St. John but the first only is recognized universally as canonical. It contains a famous passage,
of which the authenticity has been discussed no end, for Chapter V, Verse 7, states that there are three in Heaven who bear
witness, The Father, the Word, and the Holy Spirit, and it is
written in Verse 8 that there are also three on earth who bear
witness, the Spirit, the Water, and the Blood. The best critics
agree that Verse 7, referring to the Trinity, has been interpolated, offering as proof that it appeared neither in the ancient
original Greek manuscripts, nor in the Syrian, Arabic or Ethio-
pian versions, nor in several Latin manuscripts. All these manuscripts contain only Verse 8. Furthermore, none of the Church
Fathers or none of the Councils against the heretics cite this
Verse 7. It does not even appear until the seventh or eighth
century and the Arians are accused falsely of deleting it, for
they did not have access to all the manuscripts. And if they
had attempted the deletion the Catholics would have risen immediately in arms against them, but the Catholics never mentioned the verse in their quarrels with the Arians, and in fact,
no one mentioned it before the eighth century. Thus, Verse 7
must be considered a pious fraud.

The Second and Third short Epistles of St. John have been
canonized with difficulty, and contain little of interest. There
was difficulty also in canonizing the Epistle of St. Jude since
it cites the Book of Enoch, declared apocryphal. It is hardly
logical that St. Jude himself should be accepted when he quotes
from apocryphal books, because in doing so he leads the Church
into error.

The most fantastic stories ever invented cannot approach in
extravagance the Book of Revelation. Four interpretations are

given the book. Some say that it depicts the last judgment, some the persecutions of the Roman Emperors, others give it only a moral interpretation, and the Protestants and Newton say that it is concerned with the Pope and the Roman Church. Whatever its meaning may be, it is evident from several allusions that the happenings predicted in it are to arrive soon. However, seventeen hundred years have elapsed and none of them have yet come to pass. The book's much praised description of the Palace of God is surpassed by Ovid's description of the sun palace. The passage concerning the just, who must wait to enjoy their reward, has thrown the Church Fathers and interpreters into a dilemma concerning the state of souls after death who are awaiting judgment.

There are three subjects treated in Revelation which demand special attention: the Antichrist, the end of the world, and the last judgment. The Antichrist is predicted much more clearly by the Apostles than Christ was predicted by the Prophets. He will have his precursors as did Christ. His origin is problematical but he will be a great and powerful lord, working false miracles and practicing seductive wiles. The Scripture is very exact in stating that the world will be ended by fire, but there is dispute over the end being annihilation or change, since there are passages in the *Bible* which support both points of view. The resurrection of the dead, which is one of the main points of the Christian Religion, was considered a prime absurdity by the ancients. This promise of resurrection helps the Christians when in the embarrassing position of trying to answer why the just are persecuted and unfortunate, for they have only to reply that Heaven will recompense those who have been true to the faith. However, they would have done better to preach only the resurrection of the Soul, without adding that of the body, since it would not entail troublesome questions concerning the age, state and sex of the resurrected person. To all of this it is impossible to give a reasonable answer.

Such in brief is the rationalistic criticism of the *Examen de la Genèse*. The criticism offered in these five volumes is not always reasonable or in good taste. The author is neither reverent nor tolerant but extremely witty. Certain of the stories, notably Job, Tobias, Jonah, and Daniel, are told with a verve almost equal to that of Voltaire. Though an acquaintance with Spinoza's critical method in the *Tractatus theologico-politicus* is evident, the author has not imbibed the critical spirit of Spinoza. Nowhere in this treatise is Spinoza's restraint and respect apparent. Everywhere with but few exceptions, the actions and incidents criticized are characterized as absurd, ridiculous, contradictory, barbarous, brutal, unreasonable, or immoral. The two flaws in the *Bible* which are constantly noted and emphasized are its contradictions and its immorality. Underlying this cataloguing of contradictions, absurdities and immorality is the conviction that the *Bible* is not a divinely inspired work and cannot be accepted as a basis for a religion. Once having accepted the validity of this conviction, the author assumes the right to treat the *Bible* as any other book. Hence, a spirit of irreverence and disrespect runs all through the treatise. But allied to this spirit is a spirit of antagonism. The author gives the distinct impression of being amazed that a work which appears so defective should form the basis of the Christian Religion. In a way the treatise discloses a naïve surprise that what has always been accepted on faith appears on examination to be so little worthy of acceptance. Hence, a sudden revolt against the facts as they are recorded and a violent, almost intolerant, condemnation of those facts on grounds of reason or in the name of morality.

This revolt explains the most serious criticism which can be launched against the treatise. Nowhere does the author show the slightest indication of appreciating the *Bible* as a magnificent historical record of a nation's struggle to attain a higher level of morality. Nowhere is there apparent the least comprehension of the underlying search for God implied in the Old Testament stories, a point which had been so neatly appreciated by Spinoza.

And nowhere is the inherent beauty and poetry of certain portions even faintly suggested. One feels in reading the treatise that when the *Bible* ceased to be for the author a divinely inspired work, it ceased to be a human work and became a sort of monster defending a monstrous institution. Hence the author's final attitude: an almost vicious delight in proving that not only the *Bible* is not divinely inspired, but that the Christian Church is not divinely established. Therein lies the explanation of the treatise's rejection of miracles, the attack against the prophecies, negation of the Divinity of Christ, and its constant denunciation of points of dogma, such as transubstantiation, the Trinity, and immortality of the Soul.

CHAPTER III

THE EXAMEN DE LA GENÈSE: SOURCES, AUTHOR, DATE

A. SOURCES AND REFERENCES

THE sources used by the author of the *Examen de la Genèse* are interesting not only in themselves but in that they further reveal the connection between the work and the various pursuits of the Cirey residents. It is at first somewhat surprising to find foremost among these sources the commentaries on the books of the *Bible* made by Dom Calmet, a sincere and learned churchman. As is already known, Voltaire referred on many occasions in his works of the Berlin and Ferney Periods to the opinions of this Benedictine scholar. The general assumption has always been that Voltaire became thoroughly acquainted with these opinions only after his stay at the Abbey of Senones. But there are reasons to believe that this assumption is purely gratuitous. Calmet's two important contributions to biblical criticism, the *Commentaire littéral sur tous les livres de l'ancien et du nouveau Testament* and the *Dictionnaire historique, critique, chronologique, géographique et littéral de la Bible* date respectively from 1720 and 1730. The *Commentaire* was thus contemporary with the *Religion chrétienne prouvée par les faits,* 1722, of Abbé Houtteville, with whom Voltaire was early acquainted, perhaps through Desfontaines's attack upon Houtteville. It is reasonable to assume that at an early date he also became acquainted with Calmet. If such was not the case, however, he could hardly have escaped knowing Calmet's work during the Cirey Period. The eminent scholar was more or less intimately connected with the Du Châtelets, having written a lengthy genealogy of their family. His sincerity, as well as his scholarship, were beyond question. Moreover, in his *Commentaire* he attracted peculiarly the attention of the Cirey coterie in two respects. He was thorough, examining "tous les livres," and he was "littéral." Hence, for anyone wishing to examine the whole *Bible* and to oppose its literal interpretation, Dom Calmet was an opponent worthy of the greatest consideration.

At all events, he is often referred to in the *Examen de la Genèse*. He is quoted (I, 4) as having said that the Hebrew text of Genesis, I:1, reads *dii creaverunt* rather than *Deus creavit* and hence the conclusion that the Hebrews did not recognize the Unity of God. He is mentioned (I, 9) as having given a full discussion of the situation of the Garden of Eden and the Cherubim who defended it. His translation of the *donec veniat Silho* in Jacob's prophecy is given (I, 37) as the most probable of all translations. And in the interpretation of the reducing of the Golden Calf to powder, he is quoted (I, 68) to the effect that the Hebrew corresponds to the Latin *ac in mortario contusit*. His remark that the Jewish ceremonies considered externally do not give one a very exalted idea of their cult is quoted (I, 74) extensively. For a description of the "cuckow," the reader is referred (I, 77) to Dom Calmet. He is cited (I, 82) as authority that there was in Numbers only one first-born for every fifty-five people. He is said (I, 96) to justify the speech of Balaam's ass by stating that such a phenomenon is no more unlikely than Phineas's ram, Achilles's horse, Dodona's Oak, and Porus's elephant. The author agrees whole-heartedly with this justification. In the contradiction concerning the free space surrounding Jewish towns, the reader is referred (I, 101) to him. Dom Calmet is said (I, 108) to excuse the statement in Deuteronomy X where "Moyse paroit perdre entièrement la tête," by saying that we are not permitted to examine the reasons of the Holy Spirit, and that it is sufficient for us that the book is canonical. And his admission that the Jews never occupied all of the Promised Land is quoted (I, 115).

Dom Calmet's defense of Rahab stirs up the ire of the author (II, 2):

> J'aime infiniment la manière dont le Père Calmet deffend cette femme: "Rahab, dit-il, étoit informée des justes prétentions des hébreux, et de l'injuste résistance des Cananéens." Effectivement ces pauvres gens avoient bien tort de combattre contre ces brigands d'Hébreux, *pro aris et focis.* "D'ailleurs, ajoute Dom Calmet, elle savoit que ses concitoyens n'auroient fait que rendre leur condition plus malheureuse en faisant mourir ces espions." Mais que pouvoit-il leur arriver de pire, que d'être tous massacrés comme ils le furent?

And when votive offerings are discussed (II, 30), Dom Calmet is quoted to prove that Jewish Law permitted human sacrifice. He is again referred to in the attempt to confirm that Judges was written after the Captivity (II, 38). The reprobation of Saul appears so unjust that he is said to have stated (II, 49):

> Si on n'étoit pas persuadé de la justice de Dieu, il faudroit ou supposer dans Saül des crimes cachés; ou accuser Dieu de ne pas proportionner ses châtimens aux crimes.

In the discussion of the killing of the prophet by the lion (II, 89), a whole page from Dom Calmet defending the impenetrable ways of Providence is quoted and ridiculed:

> La glose de Dom Calmet sur la mort de ce prophète est inimitable; la voicy: "On ne peut, dit-il, qu'on n'admire ici les secrets impénétrables de la justice de Dieu. Jéroboam se révolte contre son prince légitime; il abandonne le culte du Seigneur, engage tout son peuple dans l'idôlatrie; s'endurcit contre les menaces et les miracles de Dieu. Un faux prophète trompe un innocent par un mensonge, et l'oblige à désobeïr à ses ordres; cependant Jéroboam et le faux prophête séducteur demeurent impunis, tandis que le vrai prophête est mis à mort par un lion, et privé de la sépulture de ses ancêtres. Il faut avouer que les voyes et les vûes de Dieu sont bien différentes des nôtres." C'est toujours Dom Calmet qui parle! "Un Moïse exclus de la terre promise pour un doute supposé; la femme de Loth changée en statuë de sel pour avoir tourné la tête; David puni par la mort de soixante et dix mille de ses Juifs; pour une action qui paroit humainement bonne, et que Dieu avoit lui-même com-

mandée en d'autres rencontres; Ezéchias qu'on verra privé de tous ses biens pour avoir senti un peu de complaisance en les montrant à des ambassadeurs étrangers . . . etc. . . . Si Dieu traite ainsi ses amis et ses serviteurs, que doivent attendre ses ennemis?"

Dom Calmet conclud de là une autre vie; et c'est avoir l'esprit bien fait. Mais Dieu ne disoit rien de cette vie à ceux qui étoient les victimes et les témoins de toutes ces injustices.

Elsewhere (II, 118) he is cited to confirm that a "guerre du Seigneur" is a "guerre très sanglante et très cruelle." He explains the rustling heard in the pear-trees as a celestial army (II,120). When in Chronicles, it is said that the deeds of Jehoshaphat, King of Judah, are inserted in the annals of the Kings of Israel, Dom Calmet is quoted (II, 128) as explaining that "Juda est là pour Israël." And finally, he is cited (II, 132) as having refuted the opinion of the Church Fathers concerning the reconstitution of the *Bible* by Ezra.

Calmet excuses the rebellion of the Maccabees on the grounds that it was inspired by God. But what rebel leader cannot allege a similar excuse (III, 6)? He has placed (III, 18) at the beginning of the Books of the Maccabees a very curious dissertation concerning whether the Ark was found after the Captivity, or whether another Ark was made. He has shown rather conclusively (III, 20) that Job had the pox, although it was contracted, he avers, "très saintement." He has compared the lines of Job (III, 28) to an ode of Pindar. He questions (III, 40) whether angels have digestive organs like men and concludes negatively. He states that when (III, 41) Tobias exclaims, "bénissez le Seigneur parce qu'il a délivré Jérusalem," he was prophesying, since he used the past for the future. He accuses (III, 42) Asmodeus unjustly of being a "démon d'impureté." He admits (III, 79) that the prophecy of Gog and Magog has never been accomplished in history. He confesses (III, 81) that the fountain mentioned in Ezekiel never existed in the Temple. His most curious confession (III, 82), however, concerns Ezekiel's vision of the future repartition of Canaan, for which he has drawn a map and appended to it : *Plan de la distribution de la terre de Canaan, suivant la vision d'Ezéchiel; laquelle n'a jamais été exécutée.* He admits (III, 88) that Nebuchadnezzar was not really changed into an ox, but that the change was a lycanthropy. He avers (III, 95) that the Empire of the Seleucides can with difficulty be proven larger than Alexander's. In his Dissertation on the Seventy Weeks of Daniel (III, 103), he concludes that since the Church has adopted no official opinion, one may adopt any opinion one wishes, and he presents his own to the effect that the prophecy was accomplished literally in Judas Maccabeus, and spiritually in Christ. Then he adds that it would be best to interpret the prophecy as referring literally to Christ, in spite of difficulties. He has confirmed the view that *virgo* (III, 111) means either a young wife or a young girl. As for the famous prophecy of Isaiah, he confesses in his commentary that if one had to convince the Jews of the mission of Christ by means of this prophecy alone, it would be difficult to do so (III, 112). He admits (III, 114) that the natural sense of Isaiah's prophecies has to be somewhat distorted if they are to refer to Christ, and exclaims, "Mais où trouver une prophétie qui cadre dans tous ses points avec l'événement. Si on exigeoit une ressemblance parfaite de l'ancien Testament avec J.C. où en trouveroit-on?" He deplores (III, 115) that some people require a literal accomplishment of Isaiah's prophecy concerning the return of the Jews. He makes an extraordinary dissertation on the subject of Jonah's whale (III, 140). He deplores (III, 149) the commentators' insufficient knowledge of the Hebrew language. He confesses that (III, 152) Psalm 40 may apply to David rather than to the Resurrection. He has proven in his examination of Proverbs that the philosophers (III, 155) have borrowed nothing from the *Bible*. Finally, his pretense that Solomon has refuted his materialism in Ecclesiastes is absurd (III, 161).

Dom Calmet has listed thirty-nine apocryphal gospels which circulated in the early years of the Christian Religion (IV, 1),

giving extracts from one of them, the *Evangile de l'Enfance*
(IV, 2). He has explained the opening of the Heavens on the
occasion of Christ's baptism by John by saying that probably the
baptism was accompanied by a small flash of lightning (IV, 19).
To those who maintain that it was unreasonable for Christ
to have been forced to go into the wilderness by the Devil, he
has replied that it was no more undignified to be driven into
the wilderness than to be tempted by the Devil (IV, 20). Although other interpreters have attempted to affirm that "raca"
is a term much more violent than "fatue," he says that the
words have very much the same meaning (IV, 27). He makes
the observation that Jesus did not present His other cheek to
be smitten when He was struck by Pilate's soldiers (IV, 28).
He avers that the mistake of Matthew, an inspired writer, in
quoting Isaiah for Psalms, has been rectified by some later
writer (IV, 50). He does not accept the explanation that the
withered fig-tree refers to the synagogue (IV, 80). He has
taken considerable pains to prove that Christ's predictions concerning Jerusalem were accomplished when Titus destroyed
the town, although there are many items in these predictions
which cannot be satisfactorily explained (IV, 90). He explains
the darkness which appeared at Christ's death as being caused
by spots upon the sun (IV, 100). His explanation of the "filius
Altissimi vocabitur" of Luke I:32, in which he has recourse to
the Hebrew, is ridiculous, since the Book of Luke was never
written in Hebrew (IV, 137). He has written a dissertation
attempting to conciliate the two genealogies of Christ (IV,
143). He states that Jesus wished to show that the ceremonies
of the Jewish Law were useless, apparently forgetting that
they were God given Laws (IV, 162). He admits the harshness
of Christ's reply to the Virgin in the Wedding Feast at Cana
(IV, 174). And he refuses to believe that St. John is still alive
(IV, 219).

   In contradiction with some early Church Fathers, Dom
Calmet says that Baptism in the name of Jesus alone does not

assure salvation (V, 44). He has contested the opinions concerning the parentage of Melchisedec on the grounds that genealogies contradicting each other cannot be authentic. The same
reasoning, incidentally, could be applied to the two genealogies
of Christ (V, 94). He characterizes Paul's definition of faith
as "mauvaise," adding that it is a description, not a definition
(V, 98). To Paul's explanation for the Crucifixion of Christ
outside of Jerusalem he has added another (V, 100). He admits
that a passage quoted by St. James as coming from the Scriptures is not there (V, 102). His interpretation of the Apocalypse
is nonsensical (V, 120). The meaning of the Palace of God is
obscure to him (V, 122), and he warns that a literal interpretation of the eighth chapter of Revelations is impossible (V, 125).

The above citations will give some idea of the use to which
the author of the *Examen de la Genèse* has put the commentaries
of Dom Calmet. He is quoted as the most representative commentator of the *Bible,* but only his remarks which seemed
ridiculous, naïve or illogical have been cited and all of his
reasonable explanations have been ignored. Any confession on
his part of not understanding the text, any admission of its
being obscure or mutilated has been readily seized upon and
emphasized, and all the time the fact that he is a reliable critic
is stressed. It would seem that the author of the *Examen* takes
a malicious pleasure in quoting Dom Calmet for the very reason
that he was a highly respected and scholarly, earnest commentator of the *Bible,* having won this reputation through his
twenty-eight carefully compiled volumes. He is often spoken
of as "very sensible" or "more sensible than the others," and
then the absurdity of his viewpoint is brought out in sharp
contrast with this characterization of him as a distinguished
scholar. We find an instance of this in V, 120:

Dom Calmet, qui est quelquefois si sensé déraisonne sur l'Apoca-
lipse, il croit en avoir expliqué la plus grande partie, et il dit que
plus il l'a examinée, plus il l'a trouvée remplie de beautés, et
surtout il a admiré, dit-il, l'ordre, le choix des faits, et la lumière

répandue sur certains endroits obscurs. Après l'exemple de Newton, il n'y a rien de si extraordinaire que de voir un tel discours
sortir de la plume de Dom Calmet, qui dans tout le reste de son
commentaire est aussi raisonnable qu'il est permis à un moine de
l'être, et qui l'est même plus quelquefois, même plus qu'on n'oseroit
l'espérer.

There can be no doubt that in the preparation of this manuscript
Dom Calmet was read avidly, though perhaps not wisely. It
should be recalled in this connection that Voltaire and Mme du
Châtelet were reading Dom Calmet even when Mme de Graffigny
was visiting them and she remarks that they found the works
of the Benedictine scholar more entertaining than the adventures of Jacques Massé.[1]

A work utilized even more than Dom Calmet's in the confection of the *Examen de la Genèse* was Thomas Woolston's
Six Discourses on the Miracles of Our Saviour, 1727-29, which
has been shown by Professor Torrey in his *Voltaire and the
English Deists*[2] to have been such an important influence upon
Voltaire. The discourses of Woolston have also been used in
the *Examen de la Genèse* very extensively. Woolston had treated
upon fifteen miracles of Christ: the driving out of the merchants
from the Temple, the casting out of devils, the Transfiguration;
the cure of the woman with the issue of blood, the cure of the
woman with the palsy, the adventure with the Samaritan
woman; the cursing of the fig-tree, the cure of the paralytic
at the Pool of Bethesda; the cure of the man born blind, the
changing of water into wine at the wedding in Cana, the cure
of the paralytic who was let down through the roof; the resurrection of Jarius's daughter, the resurrection of the son of the
widow of Naim, the resurrection of Lazarus; and the Resurrec-

[1] Voltaire's library at Leningrad still contains the *Commentaire littéral sur
tous les livres de l'ancien et du nouveau Testament,* Paris, 1720, 28 vols., in-4°,
as well as the *Dictionnaire historique, critique, chronologique, géographique
et littéral de la Bible,* Paris, 1730, 4 vols., fol. See Havens and Torrey: "Voltaire's Books: A Selected List," in *M. P.,* 1929 (XXVII).

[2] Torrey, N. L., *Voltaire and the English Deists,* New Haven, 1930,
Chap. IV.

tion of Christ. It was his avowed intention to show that these miracles cannot be interpreted literally, that they contain things which are absurd, improbable, and unbelievable. In his opinion they are not a sufficient proof of the Divinity of Christ's mission, but must be interpreted allegorically. Woolston was much concerned with this allegorical interpretation, citing from the allegorizing Fathers to strengthen his own thesis, detailing their allegorical interpretations at length, and adding others of his own making.

The author of the *Examen de la Genèse* was not at all concerned with Woolston's interest in allegory but was much intrigued by his manner of ridiculing the literal events of the *Bible*. Only one of the fifteen miracles treated by the Englishman is not discussed in the *Examen*: that of the woman with the palsy; and with the exception of the miracle of the blind man, all of those discussed contain ideas and even expressions borrowed from Woolston.[3]

In discussing the expulsion of the money-changers from the Temple, both Woolston and the writer of the *Examen de la Genèse* express surprise that a lone man possessing no authority could expel a group of people who were not His disciples and who consequently had no respect for Him. They both inquire why Christ should concern Himself with defending a religious institution which He came to destroy.

The driving out of the demons into the swine produces similar reactions on the part of the two critics. Both profess surprise at the existence of a herd of two thousand swine in a country

---

[3] A list of these miracles with the parallel comments of Woolston and the *Examen de la Genèse* has been placed in the appendix. The edition used is the French *Discours sur les miracles de Jésus-Christ,* traduits de l'Anglais de Woolston, dix-huitième siècle [s. l.]. It should be recalled that manuscript copies of Woolston's *Discourses* (also in French) circulated during the eighteenth century. The Voltaire library at Leningrad possesses both the printed work in French, and a manuscript copy, as well as the work in English. See Torrey, *Voltaire and the English Deists,* p. 72, and Note 55. The French edition is used to bring out the striking similarity between the two works.

where they were held in execration. They note that since the days when Antiochus had defiled the Temple by sacrificing a hog it was forbidden under penalty of death to keep swine. They both revert to a mock expression of pity that the owners of the swine should thus be ruined by their loss. They point out that the inhabitants of the country were so terrified that they begged Jesus to depart immediately. They express the opinion that these inhabitants acted with unaccustomed gentleness in making this request rather than seeking vengeance for their economic losses. And they both conclude significantly that if some eighteenth-century "enthusiast" should dare attempt the same thing, he would be punished by the magistrates.

They can find no reason for the miracle of the Transfiguration, since to their minds it served no purpose. They profess to be baffled by the appearance of Moses and Elijah, and are curious to know whether the two prophets appeared in the flesh or in the spirit. They inquire ingenuously what was the subject of discussion between Christ and the Prophets. They express amazement that this conversation, which to them was the most important part of the miracle, should not have been transmitted to posterity by the Apostles.

They both express themselves to the effect that the cure of the woman with the issue of blood was fatal inasmuch as she died shortly afterward.

The two critics again duplicate each other in their observations concerning Christ's conversation with the woman of Samaria. They assume in discussing this particular miracle that He was a fortune-teller, and remark that the Samaritans apparently awaited a Messiah who had this talent. They both infer from Verse 42 that Jesus also told fortunes for others on this occasion and they express the pious hope that He refrained from making troublesome revelations. They add that present-day fortune-telling is not approved by the priests and that soothsayers are now discredited and persecuted.

Their comments upon the cursing of the fig-tree are strikingly similar. They begin by observing that even the Church Fathers have contested the literal meaning of this miracle, and quote from the same passage of St. Augustine to substantiate this contention. They then comment upon Christ's improvidence in not preparing His food before leaving Bethany. They are astonished at His cursing the tree which was not responsible for His lack of foresight, and both refer to St. Augustine's observations on this point. Citing again St. Augustine, they note that it was not the season for figs and that to all appearances Jesus was unaware of this fact. What would one say of a peasant in Kent, inquires Woolston, who sought apples on his trees at Easter-time? What would one say, echoes the author of the *Examen de la Genèse,* of a peasant who sought peaches in his orchard at Easter-time? They both aver that if the peasant in question should in anger proceed to cut down his fruit-tree, he would be treated like a madman. They wonder why ministers often choose this miracle as a subject for discussion and how the audience refrains from laughing at its being treated seriously. They call attention to the fact that Christ destroyed property not belonging to Him in cursing the fig-tree. They do not fail to recall Mark's statement to the effect that the fig-tree did not wither until the following day, and insinuate that after the curse some of the bark around the roots of the tree was torn away, thus producing the withering.

In discussing the cure of the paralytic at the Pool of Bethesda, the rationalistic imagination of the two writers runs riot. Both presume the sick man to have been more lazy than ill and declare his cure psychological rather than physical, since his illness, if such it was, was only imaginary. They find no foundation for believing the man paralyzed and they point out that not only has no profane historian recorded this incident, but that no mention of this miraculous pool is made elsewhere in chronicles of the time. Both find logical objections to the story. Why, for instance, was the cure given to the most alert rather than to the

sickest? Why should only one be selected for a cure each time
the angel descended? Why did Jesus cure only the paralytic
and not the whole group? Both criticisms call attention to the
fact that St. Augustine has already asked this unanswered question. They also cite St. Chrysostom as authority for saying that
the miracle did not occur literally. And they conclude their
comment by stressing that St. Augustine was skeptical about
the actual appearance of the angel at the pool.

The cure of the man born blind evokes only three similar
remarks on the part of the critics. They express surprise at the
strangeness of the treatment. They suggest that the miracle
would have been better authenticated if Christ had not used
His sputum mixed with mud, since the suggestion might be
made that He had in His mouth some specific which was a cure
for blindness. Finally both quote the passage from St. Chrysostom to the effect that the mud was more efficacious in rendering
a man blind than in curing one of this affliction.

The miracle of the Wedding of Cana elicits further like comment in the two criticisms. Both note St. John's suggestion that
the guests at the wedding feast were already half-drunk. Both
stress that Jesus is said to have spoken disrespectfully to His
Mother, and suggest that He was a model Son. To support
this contention they recall the story of his straying into the
Temple as a boy of twelve. Both mention that Christ's addressing His Mother as "Woman" has caused some people to doubt
Mary's virginity. They both deny that the water was turned into
wine, and suggest that a sort of punch was made which the
guests, being half-drunk, took for excellent wine. They suggest
further that there was some collusion between Jesus and the
master of ceremonies. According to their reasoning, if Jesus
had performed the miracle without the aid of water, the only
objections to it would be its uselessness and its impropriety. But
using the water spoiled everything. They both conclude with
an expression of regret that Christ did not transmit to His
disciples the secret of turning water into wine, for, in their

estimation, this would have been more useful than the power to move mountains which He supposedly gave them.

The two critics propose a similar series of rational objections to the miracle of the cure of the paralytic in Nazareth. Why, they ask, did the people block the door and prevent the sick man from entering when they were present precisely to witness a miracle? Why were the paralytic's attendants so anxious to bring him immediately into Christ's presence when paralysis is not a disease which needs to be treated hurriedly? Why did the attendants not wait a little until the crowd had dispersed? Why should they undertake to demolish the roof, an enterprise requiring fully as much time as waiting for the crowd to disperse? How fortunate Jesus and His disciples were, not to have been struck by some falling tile or scaffolding! Where was the owner of the property during this time? And lastly, why didn't Jesus, in order to prevent the house from being destroyed, cure the paralytic from afar instead of requiring his presence within the house.

In the discussion of the three resurrections brought about by Jesus, the author of the *Examen de la Genèse* and Woolston make many points in common. They agree that the least important of the three was the resurrection of Jarius's daughter, for the Evangelist himself quotes Jesus as saying that she was only asleep. They inquire why a twelve-year-old girl should have been chosen for this miracle when her life was neither important nor necessary. They suggest that it would have been better to resurrect John the Baptist who had rendered such distinguished service to the founding of the Christian Church. In considering the case of the widow's son they agree that he seemed the most truly deceased of the three, but conclude that even in his case there may have been something fraudulent. They recall occasions when so-called corpses have been discovered to be alive. They consider the resurrection of Lazarus the most important of the three, but do not fail to note that it is related only in John's gospel written sixty years after the event when all records of it had been destroyed. They ask why this important event in Christ's life was not related in the other Gospels written immediately after its occurrence when Lazarus himself could have vouched for the authenticity of the miracle. Both note certain circumstances from which it might be rationally inferred that the miracle was a hoax: for instance, Martha pretended that the corpse stank, Lazarus's face was covered so that no one could see whether he was dead or not, and a loud spoken command to come forth was necessary to give Lazarus his cue. They both insinuate that these circumstances are proof of collusion and fraud in the operation of the miracle, and further substantiate this opinion by asserting that a sojourn of four days in the tomb would not have been sufficient to preclude the possibility of fraud. Furthermore, why, they ask, does one hear nothing more of these resurrected people? They should have been the most ardent of Christ's disciples, Lazarus especially, who as His friend, should have been most grateful. They both consider most ridiculous Grotius's statement that Lazarus, being risen, was afraid of the Jews and wandered in secret for the rest of his days in fear of being put to death. For, if he had been raised from the dead by a Superior Power, he would have had confidence in the protection of the same Supreme Power. They suggest that Lazarus really feared the Jews because they were aware of the fraud of the resurrection. They made the additional observation that none of the three persons resurrected by Christ ever made a statement about the hereafter. Moreover, as regards Lazarus's resurrection there is a little logical dilemma. If Lazarus, a friend of Christ, went to Hell after death, it is a reflection upon Christ's choice of His associates, and if he was enjoying the blessings of Paradise, it was unthinkable that he should want to return to this world.

In regard to the Resurrection of Christ, both writers make at various points similar comment. They express surprise that Christ arose before the appointed time and offer the explanation that the Disciples stole His body before this appointed hour because they feared that they would be prevented from taking it later. They express the opinion that the soldier guards at Christ's tomb, being few in number, were either bribed or intoxicated. And they suggest that this conniving was abetted by Pilate who was interested in creating and fostering dissension among the Jews. Both critics find St. Matthew ridiculous when he asserts that the Princes of the People offered bribes to the soldiers to make them swear that the Apostles had stolen Christ's body while they were asleep at their posts. For they argue that if a resurrection had really occurred, no amount of money would have persuaded those who had witnessed it to subscribe to such a lie.

After this formidable list of comparisons there can hardly remain the slightest doubt that the author of the *Examen de la Genèse* had been completely saturated with Woolston's criticism of the miracles of the New Testament. The fact that the two works treat in a similar manner thirteen out of fifteen miracles has its importance. But were these similarities of a general nature, one might still allege coincidence rather than direct influence. However, the specific criticism of the two is so strikingly similar, and so consistently alike, that the possibility of coincidence becomes absurd. The only conclusion which appears valid after an examination of these passages side by side is that the author of the *Examen de la Genèse* either knew Woolston's work by heart or that he presented objections to the miracles (and this is especially true of the driving out of the demons, the cursing of the fig-tree, the cures of the two paralytics, and the three resurrections) with Woolston's text directly before him. Indeed, even the language is so identical at times that there is much justification for believing that the Woolston text used was a French manuscript translation.

There are, in the *Examen de la Genèse,* scattered references to other seventeenth- and eighteenth-century writers. We find, for instance, four references to Pascal (I, 9; III, 83; III, 127; III, 128). The author takes him to task for finding in the story of the Fall a proof of the truth of the Christian Religion and the source of the grandeur and misery of man. In another place, Pascal's defense of the prophecies is attacked:

Cependant lorsque les interprètes donnent des règles pour distinguer un vrai prophête d'un imposteur, ils disent que les prophêties du premier doivent s'accomplir; au lieu que celles de l'autre restent sans accomplissement. Mais quand ils voyent ensuite des prophêties très claires de leurs prophêtes, qui ne sont pas accomplies, ils disent (et qui le croiroit, c'est Pascal, ce grand et beau génie) que c'est cela même qui prouve la vérité de la religion chrétienne, fondée sur ces prophêties: car, dit Paschal, puisqu'elles n'ont pas été exécutées dans le sens littéral, elles avoient donc un sens spirituel, selon lequel elles ont été accomplies. N^a . . citer l'endroit de Paschal (III, 83).

When Jeremiah prophesied (Jeremiah XXXI, 33) to the effect that the Lord would make a new alliance with the Israelites after their return from captivity and that He would abandon them only when one could discover the foundations of the earth and measure the Heavens, Pascal concluded that his prophecy must apply to the Christian Religion, since it was manifestly false for the Jews. The author of the *Examen de la Genèse* has nothing but scorn for this interpretation: "Voilà comme les faiblesses deviennent de la force, selon M. Paschal" (III, 127). And one page further on, when it is remarked that Nebuchadnezzar has never overthrown the obelisks of Egypt, as was predicted, the curt remark is added: "C'est une force de plus pour M. Paschal" (III, 128). There is a short reference to Spinoza, à propos of the miracle of the sun standing still, to the effect that he explains it by a parhelion (II, 14). Richard Simon is mentioned (III, 151) to prove that the translation of Psalm 22: 17-18, "They have pierced my feet" (caarie), is correct while the Vulgate, "surrounded as a lion" (caara), is an error. Richard Simon is mentioned on one other occasion (V, 111) to support the contention that Verse 7, Chapter V, of the First Epistle of St. John referring to the Trinity has been interpolated. A whole page is then devoted to detailing his reasons for that opinion. Grotius is referred to on two occasions: he is cited (III, 163) as having written a very learned and piquant commentary on the Songs of Solomon, and (V, 85) as having been of the opinion that Paul believed the Last Judgment would occur during his lifetime. The Père Hardouin is mentioned as standing alone in the contention (V, 69) that Peter and Cephas, the opponent of Paul, were not one and the same person. And Houtteville is taken to task for making sport of Mohammed's flight when even the Holy Family was forced to flee into Egypt (IV, 13). Bossuet (V, 119) is condemned for trying to explain the Apocalypse.

There are curious references to other works or writers which indicate either a predilection for or an intimate acquaintance with them. Many incidents in the *Bible* are compared with the stories of the *Arabian Nights* (I, 93; II, 35; III, 4; III, 71; III, 79; III, 144; etc.). The cruelty of the Jews is unfavorably compared to that of Nero (II, 17; II, 77). The story of Jephthah is found similar to the Greek legend of Iphigenia (II, 30). The author confesses (II, 108) to a liking for the story of Athaliah because it has furnished the subject of Racine's beautiful tragedy. Versailles is mentioned twice, both times (II, 86; II, 122) in an attempt to compare its cost of construction (300,000 frs.) with that of Solomon's temple (8,000,000). The riches of David are compared to those of Aboulkasem (II, 122. See also *La Bible enfin expliquée,* II, 457). A mistake in Second Chronicles is said to suggest a like error made by Scudéry in one of his novels (II, 124). The walls of the rebuilt Jerusalem (II, 138) are likened to those of Semiramis. Eliphas, the friend of Job, is characterized as (III, 23) Leibnitzian, the only reference to Leibnitz in the whole work. There are on the other hand three (III, 29; V, 119; III, 120) references to Newton. It is stated that he and Kepler could have answered a question which God addressed to Job concerning the order and movements of the Heavens. In another instance the author deplores that Newton has wasted his time trying to find a key to the Apocalypse. In still another instance we find cited Newton's opinion to the effect that the Antichrist of the Apocalypse is the Pope. Réaumur is mentioned as an authority (III, 156) to prove that Solomon was ill-versed in natural history when he spoke of the ant in Proverbs. A chance reference is made to Scarron (IV, 145). And lastly, Voltaire or his works are referred to either directly or indirectly on four occasions. The Canaanites are said (II, 2) to fight "pro aris et focis," a phrase which Voltaire had Charles XII use at Bender. It is stated (III, 6) that Judas Maccabeus ended his life by a deed as rash and unfortunate as that of Charles XII at Bender. In IV, 160, it is admitted that the story of the prodigal son would be delightful in a comedy. And on one occasion where it is impossible to reconcile the events related, the author exclaims (III, 109): "Mais je dirai comme M. de Voltaire, ce n'est pas ma faute."

B.   DATE

A date for the *Examen de la Genèse* can be determined without great difficulty. In discussing the cure of the woman with the issue of blood (IV, 36), the author speaks of a miracle of similar nature, that of Mme Lafosse in 1725, which was said to have occurred in Paris through the intercession of Frère Pâris. These miracles of Frère Pâris, said the author, must have been true, since they were certified by M. de Mongeron in a book which he presented to the King five or six years ago:

> . . . car on ne peut, par exemple, avoir des miracles mieux avérés que ceux de M. Pâris, dont M. de Mongeron présenta il y a cinq ou six ans un recueil au roi; et ce M. de Mongeron auroit volontiers souffert le martyre pour en prouver la vérité.

M. Carré de Mongeron, counsellor in the Paris Parlement was the author of *La Vérité des Miracles opérés à l'intercession de M. de Pâris, et autres appelants,* 1736, in-4°. A sequel to his work was published in 1741, and a third volume in 1748. It was the first volume, however, which Carré carried to Versailles along with a letter on August 29, 1737. As Louis XV passed, the counsellor fell on his knees and presented both book and letter to the King. Incidentally, the event was well-known to Voltaire, who inserted it in the sixty-fifth chapter of the *Histoire du Parlement de Paris.*[4]

According to the phrase, "il y a cinq ou six ans," used by the author of the *Examen de la Genèse,* the date of composition of Volume IV would fall somewhere between 1742-43. But it should be noted that this date is valid only for Volume IV. If the work was composed, as Grimm related, following discussions of a chapter in the *Bible* read after luncheon each day, it must have required a considerable amount of time to assemble material for the first three volumes, and some additional time to compose Volume V. We may assume that the middle portion of the *Examen de la Genèse* was being written in the years 1742-43. How long before 1742 it was begun is very difficult to determine. The sixth volume, however, which was the *Notes* and the *Preuves* to *La Religion chrétienne analysée,* must have been copied, or written, close to 1749, for the *Preuves* usually bear this date in other manuscripts. If it required a six-year period to complete the last three volumes of the six-volume collection, and the first three were assembled at the same slow rate of speed, it would be reasonable to assume that the task of writing the commentary extended roughly over a period of ten to twelve years, that is to say, from 1736-38 to 1746-49.

C. AUTHOR

We are now in a position to discuss the authorship of the *Examen de la Genèse.* From a study of the intellectual atmosphere at Cirey we know that both Voltaire and Mme du Châtelet were addicted to biblical allusions. Voltaire, it is known,

---

[4] Beuchot XX, 319. See also Moland XVI, 78. In Moland XV, 62, Voltaire related the same event but gave the date 1736. As for the miracle of Mme Lafosse, it made a considerable impression upon Voltaire, who mentioned it in XV, 61. Voltaire investigated this miracle personally. See Gazier, "Le Frère de Voltaire" in *R. D. M.,* 1906, pp. 618-620. Carré de Mongeron is mentioned in some manuscripts of *La Religion chrétienne analysée.*

even made several ineffectual attempts at biblical criticism in his works published at this time. It is true that they were effectively suppressed by an over-alert police. From Grimm, we have learned that he and his lady indulged in daily discussions on the text of the *Bible* and that the result of these discussions was the *Bible enfin expliquée* which was not published until considerably later. From Voltaire, himself, we have learned that Mme du Châtelet wrote a complete commentary on the *Old Testament*. From a study of the clandestine biblical movement we have learned that there were being written and circulated between 1720-50, a rather impressive number of manuscripts dealing with the events of the *Bible*. These works furnish an excellent background for the critical deism of the period. Furthermore, we now have good reasons for suspecting that both Mme du Châtelet and Voltaire were impressed and influenced by these manuscripts, some of which they must have known. But they not only knew the unorthodox works; they became acquainted also with the orthodox ones, especially Dom Calmet's. All our information about the intellectual atmosphere at Cirey leads to the conclusion that either Voltaire or Mme du Châtelet could have written the *Examen de la Genèse*.

When we turn from the Cirey atmosphere to the *Examen de la Genèse* itself, we find that internally it bears evidence of belonging to the clandestine biblical current. Indeed, it fits definitely into the Spinozistic tradition of that current and occupies a position in a long line of works written in imitation of or in elaboration of the *Tractatus*. But it also shows a definite relationship to the orthodox treatises influential in the period 1730-50: Pascal, Hardouin, Richard Simon, Houtteville, and especially Dom Calmet. Moreover, the dates of the treatise coincide not only with the Cirey Period, but with the years during which Voltaire and Mme du Châtelet are known to have been interested in biblical criticism, trying their hand at it, acquainting themselves with Dom Calmet and some of the contemporary clandestine critics. In short, a study of the text, sources, references and date of the *Examen de la Genèse* leads inevitably to the conclusion that either one or the other must have written it.

Which of them, then, is the author of the *Examen de la Genèse*? The catalogue of the Troyes Library attributes it without question to Mme du Châtelet, and even goes so far as to state that it was written in the handwriting of that lady. Moreover, a note to Volume I, evidently copied in part from the Catalogue of the sale of the Auger Collection whence came the manuscript, states that it is a "manuscrit autographe de Mme du Châtelet." And on page one of the first volume, a different hand has added "Par Mad^e du Châtelet." In spite of all this testimony, it would seem after a comparison of this handwriting with that of Fonds français 12266-12268 of the Bibliothèque Nationale, which is a manuscript undoubtedly in Mme du Châtelet's hand and dating approximately from the same period as the *Examen de la Genèse,* that this latter manuscript is not in her handwriting. It seems more likely that it is a copy. As a matter of fact, it has the appearance of being professionally copied, executed to order. Moreover, were the handwriting that of Mme du Châtelet, the authorship would not be proved, for the sixth volume (Troyes 2378) which is in the same hand consists of the *Notes* and the *Preuves* to *La Religion chrétienne analysée,* and no one has even remotely suggested that she could have been the author of these *Notes* and *Preuves*.

Was she the author of the *Examen de la Genèse* or is this a copy which she had made for her personal use, as she presumably had a copy made of the *Notes* and *Preuves*? It must be confessed that any first-hand proof of authorship of these deistic treatises is very difficult to secure. They are, as we have seen elsewhere, rarely signed, often ascribed to several people, and seldom definitely attributable to any one individual. The other remaining manuscript of the *Examen de la Genèse,* which was put on sale several years ago, was listed as "Voltaire (inédit), *Commentaire sur la Bible par Voltaire,* 2 volumes in 4°. Maroquin rouge du 18e siècle. Manuscrit." The description of the item suggested, though in a rather indefinite and vague way, that it was the product of the combined efforts of Voltaire and Mme du Châtelet, but the source of this information was not given in the listing. We have examined a part of this manuscript and the handwriting is neither Voltaire's nor Mme du Châtelet's. Nor does the listing indicate that the work was signed.

The attribution of the work to Voltaire is decidedly without foundation, although it must be confessed that portions of it, particularly the stories of Judith, Tobias, Esther, and Job, are not at all unworthy of him. The sentence in III, 119, "Mais je dirai comme Monsieur de Voltaire, ce n'est pas ma faute," suggests that the author was in close relationship with Voltaire but that Voltaire did not write it. Unless, of course, one wishes to have recourse to the argument that the phrase was used in the manuscript as a subterfuge to conceal the writer's identity. But that theory, valid as it is in many instances of Voltaire criticism, seems out of place here. "Ce n'est pas ma faute" is not a phrase commonly used by Voltaire. Nor has it ever been regarded as one of his catch phrases. In all the fifty volumes of his works, I can recall only two places in which it is used, once in the *Examen important de Milord Bolingbroke* (Beuchot XLIII, 114), and again in *Dieu et les hommes* (Beuchot XLVI, 121). Voltaire would hardly have the astuteness to attribute to himself in a clandestine work a remark which the public would with difficulty identify as one of his catch phrases. On the other hand, the phrase is more adapted to conversation than to writing, and it was in talking that presumably he used it often enough to impress the author of the *Examen de la Genèse.*

But, to return to the *Examen de la Genèse,* there is another consideration which would seem to preclude Voltaire from its authorship. It is unnecessary to recall that he wrote many commentaries on the *Bible,* for instance, the *Sermon des cinquante,* the *Questions de Zapata,* the first part of the *Examen important de Milord Bolingbroke,* the *Homélies sur l'interprétation de la Bible,* and the *Bible enfin expliquée.* It is to be observed that in all these works, save in the last-named, he preferred the short condensed form of *Bible* commentary. His masterpiece in this type of writing is the *Sermon des cinquante,* where numerous examples from the *Bible* are chosen to prove his "points," but condensed so aptly that the reader has the definite impression that it is a commentary upon the aspects rather than upon the incidents of the *Bible.* This, of course, is Voltaire's "rogaton" method, considered generally to be characteristic of the Ferney Period. On one occasion, however, he attempted to give a complete commentary of the *Bible,* and that was in *La Bible enfin expliquée.* The result of the attempt is very enlightening for the present discussion. The work begins with a very thorough discussion of Genesis (68 of 302 pp. in Moland), the remainder of the Pentateuch is reviewed in fifty-two pages, Judges and Kings in a hundred twenty-eight pages, the stories and prophecies in thirty-eight, while the whole New Testament is treated in only sixteen. Thus two hundred forty-eight of three hundred two pages comprising the complete work are devoted to the historical books from Genesis through Kings.

The *Bible enfin expliquée* is said by Voltaire to have been written by four almoners. It is not, however, a collaboration. The almoners made their contributions in turn, and an "Avis de l'éditeur" marks the points at which one contribution ends and another begins. The first gave up the task in the middle of Genesis, at the story of Esau; and the editor added the note (p. 73, ed. 1765ff.) :

Ici le commentateur s'est arrêté; et celui qui lui a succédé, voyant que cet ouvrage serait trop volumineux, si on continuait à traduire et à commenter ainsi presque tout l'ancien et le nouveau Testament, s'est restraint à ne donner que les principaux endroits, qui semblent exiger des notes, en liant seulement par des transitions le précis de la Bible, et en conservant le texte, sans jamais l'altérer.

Thus the work is hardly under way when the author realizes that it will never be finished if he continues at the pace he has been going. Hence he determines to cut down the number but

not the length of his notes. It is not long, however, before he
feels the necessity of further simplifying his task. At the end of
Leviticus, he adds a note to explain this new departure:

> On a passé dans le Lévitique tout ce qui ne regarde que les Céré-
> monies: et on s'est attaché principalement à l'historique. C'est ainsi
> qu'on en usera dans tout le reste de cet ouvrage. . . . (p. 167)

Thus, this second change is calculated to cut down the amount
of material piling up on the commentator. Henceforth, he will
concern himself with only the historical aspects of the work.
This method continues halfway through the treatment of
Solomon's reign, where the second commentator relinquishes
his task, the editor explaining that he has been called away to
the court of a great prince:

> Le commentateur, qui avait entrepris de continuer cet ouvrage,
> s'est arrêté ici; ayant été appelé à la cour d'un grand prince pour
> être son aumônier. Un troisième commentateur s'est présenté, et
> a continué avec la même érudition et la même impartialité, mais
> avec trop de véhémence peut-être, et trop de hardiesse. (p. 359)

This third commentator, however, soon finds himself in difficulties, and a "Déclaration" inserted after the story of Jeroboam
excuses the omission of a number of "roitelets" mentioned in
Kings and Chronicles:

> Dans la crainte où je suis que cette histoire et ce commentaire
> ne causent au lecteur un ennui aussi mortel qu'à moi, je passerai
> tous les assassinats des rois de Juda et d'Israël. . . . (p. 380)

Little by little the third commentator changes this method and
in treating the various stories he merges text and commentary
(beginning with Judith). Even after this modification, he aban-
dons his work (at the Maccabees), and a fourth continues it:

> Ici le troisième commentateur s'est arrêté: et un quatrième a
> continué l'histoire Hébraïque d'une manière différente des trois
> autres. (p. 480)

This new method is purely expository and historical. The text is
now omitted completely, the commentary is neglected, the mate-

rial becomes entirely supplementary to an understanding of
Jewish history. When the New Testament is reached, a few
notes on the discrepancies of the Gospels are given and that is
all. The Acts, the Epistles, and the Apocalypse are totally
ignored, while in the Old Testament, no comments are made
upon Job, the Songs of Solomon, the Book of Wisdom, Isaiah,
Jeremiah, the lesser prophets, Psalms and Proverbs.

From this analysis certain conclusions may be drawn. Voltaire, having undertaken a commentary on the complete *Bible,*
soon found himself overwhelmed by the material at hand.
Scarcely was the work well under way than he altered his plan
and continued with some courage until his trip to Potsdam gave
him the excuse for laying it aside, but not before it began to
show signs of fatigue. Sometime after 1750 he picked it up
again, and for a time continued with new vigor and energy, but
the task was overpowering, and moreover, he had no incentive
for it. He became more and more disinterested and never completed it, though it was published in 1776. Thus it becomes evident that he was temperamentally unfitted to complete his commentary. And if he found the task unsuited to him in *La Bible
enfin expliquée,* how could he with reason be suspected of the
authorship of the *Examen de la Genèse* which is complete? And
if he did write the *Examen de la Genèse,* why did he publish in
1776 the incomplete *Bible enfin expliquée?*

It is very improbable that Voltaire wrote the *Examen de la
Genèse.* But the above references to the *Histoire de Charles XII,*
to the *Enfant prodigue,* to the "ce n'est pas ma faute," indicate
that it was written by someone well acquainted with both Voltaire and his work. The author's knowledge of the *Tractatus* and
La Religion chrétienne analysée; the use of Dom Calmet's commentaries; the attack against Pascal, "ce grand et beau génie,"
for his defense of the Christian prophecies; not to mention a
thorough acquaintance with Thomas Woolston's *Discourses*—are
all strongly reminiscent of Voltaire. Voltaire's attitude toward
the *Bible,* namely, that the incidents related therein are cruel,

ridiculous, or contradictory, is fundamentally the attitude of the writer of the *Examen de la Genèse*. His tone, or rather tones, of mockery, gayety, quondam bitterness, have been reproduced at least in part in the *Examen*. Its wit, though not as constant as in Voltaire's works, is decidedly Voltairean. One finds in it at times phrases coined or consecrated by Voltaire. David is "l'homme selon le cœur de Dieu," the fig-tree is cursed "quoique ce ne fût pas le temps des figues," Ezekiel is permitted "par accommodement" to change the spread on his bread. And we shall be able to cite later a large number of passages in the *Examen de la Genèse* which will be reechoed in Voltaire's works published at a considerably later date, sometimes with verbal similarities, sometimes with similarities in ideas, and sometimes even with similar ideas expressed in the same sequence. There can be no doubt that Voltaire, though he did not write the *Examen de la Genèse,* contributed to it by his presence, his conversation, his discussion. And there can be but little doubt that the only associate of Voltaire, sufficiently competent and in a position of propinquity to profit by this presence, conversation, and discussion was Mme du Châtelet. Add to this the fact that on the testimony of Voltaire himself, testimony which is supported in part by Grimm, Beuchot and Avenel, Mme du Châtelet is known to have written a treatise of this nature (see *supra,* p. 45). If one still has a vestige of doubt concerning the authorship, he has only to note the alacrity with which the author pounces upon every biblical incident which is contrary to the laws of science; the creation of light before the sun, the failure to distinguish between the sun and the moon, the command to the sun to stand still, the difficulties of the Flood, Hezekiah's sundial and many others, and he will be ready to admit that only Mme du Châtelet was in a position and adequately equipped to write the book.

Thus in addition to her pursuits in physics, metaphysics, and moral philosophy, at Cirey, it is now quite apparent that Mme du Châtelet was deeply interested in the biblical criticism of the time. The extent of her familiarity with writings of this nature will probably never be known. That she was familiar with the general technique of Spinoza's *Tractatus* and its numerous imitations cannot be denied. She certainly had intimate knowledge of the *Discourses* of Thomas Woolston, and portions, if not all, of the *Religion chrétienne analysée*. In her one work she thus united the extremes of the English Deistic and French movements, while in a curious way she controlled her material by her knowledge of the orthodox treatises of the time, foremost among which were the enormous compilations of Dom Calmet.

CHAPTER IV

THE EXAMEN DE LA GENÈSE
AND VOLTAIRE

IF MME DU CHÂTELET was devoting a considerable portion of
the Cirey Period to biblical criticism, Voltaire was occupying
himself in a similar manner, and the mystery of his seeming lack
of interest in the English Deists after getting acquainted with
them in England (1726-29) and of his seeming lack of acquaintance with the French Deists who were so productive after 1722
becomes immediately clear. He neither ignored the former, nor
failed to know the latter. The informative period of his critical
deism does not begin while he was at Berlin, as M. Lanson would
have us believe, but while he was at Cirey, if not slightly earlier.
Having become interested in the English Deists during his sojourn in England, he became familiar with their works and
learned how to utilize their ideas—and this is especially true of
the most influential of the English Deists, Thomas Woolston—
during the Cirey Period. And if his acquaintance with the
French Deists was superficial before the English journey, he
both broadened and deepened it during the years which followed
his return. Thus, the intellectual atmosphere at Cirey is not
merely full of literature, natural science, metaphysics, and moral
philosophy, but charged, if not supercharged, with the principles of critical deism. Henceforth, the sojourn at Cirey does
not stand as an enigmatic gap in the development of Voltaire's
critical deism. It is a period very necessary for that development.

Indeed, it has always seemed strange that the French and English Deists, having attracted his attention between 1722 and
1735, should have been totally neglected between 1735 and 1762,

that is to say, until the Ferney Period. It has seemed illogical that Voltaire, so alert to the currents of his time, should have waited until the deistic current became crystallized before taking any cognizance of it. As a matter of fact, certain lines of *La Mule du Pape* (1733) or even of *Le Mondain* (1736), his choice of *Samson* (1732) and *L'Enfant prodigue* (1738) as subjects for theatrical representations, not to mention his attitude in *Mahomet* (1742), his letter to Thiériot inquiring about Meslier and his work (1735), his reference to Meslier in the *Sottisier* which apparently dates from 1746, and the date 1742 which appeared upon his published *Extrait de Jean Meslier,* have confirmed the suspicion that he was not entirely unaffected by the deistic movement.

But did Voltaire limit himself to becoming acquainted with Meslier's *Extrait,* the *Discourses* of Woolston, the *Tractatus,* the *Analyse de la religion chrétienne,* the *Notes* and the *Preuves,* while Mme du Châtelet was composing the *Examen de la Genèse* and writing or copying the *Notes* and the *Preuves?* Incidentally, since the *Religion chrétienne analysée* was drawn in part from the *Examen de la religion,* and since the *Notes* contained long passages from the *Examen critique du Nouveau Testament,* he knew also those two works, at least in part. Did he familiarize himself with the arguments of Dom Calmet merely to prepare for some indefinite future time? Did he contribute to the after-lunch discussions merely his verbal wit and his conversation? Or did he also take part in the movement by composing other works upon critical deism? It would be surprising if he did not. Then where is the result of his activity? For at the present stage in Voltaire studies, none of his writings dealing exclusively with critical deism have been assigned to the Cirey Period.

A search for possible early deistic works by Voltaire can lead only in two directions: either he may have written treatises of this nature and never published them under his own name, or he may have published them under his name at a later date. When we begin to examine various treatises which might fall in the first category we are immediately confronted with the *Religion chré-tienne analysée* published in the *Recueil nécessaire* and in the *Evangile de la raison*. Its authorship has never been definitely determined, and although there have been suggestions that Voltaire wrote it, no one has ever proved that he did. The strongest evidence in support of his authorship presents itself in some until recently unpublished notes of Beuchot which I have published elsewhere.[1] It might be added, in partial support of Beuchot's contention, that there is a close parallel[2] between portions of the *Religion chrétienne analysée* and the *Epître à Uranie*. There is an even closer connection between it and Mme du Châtelet's *Examen de la Genèse*. And the fact that the sixth volume of Mme du Châtelet's collection was devoted to the *Notes* and the *Preuves* of the *Religion chrétienne analysée* at least renders plausible the assumption that the whole series, *Analyse, Notes* and *Preuves,* is a product of the Cirey atmosphere. Moreover, it should be noted that the date of composition of the *Religion chrétienne analysée* (1737-42) coincides with that of the first three volumes of Mme du Châtelet's *Examen de la Genèse*. Although there is no conclusive evidence to indicate that Voltaire was not the author of the *Religion chrétienne analysée,* there is still no conclusive evidence that he was its author. And for the time being, it is impossible to say whether the *Religion chrétienne analysée* furnished inspiration for or was a product of the critical deism at Cirey. Voltaire's connection with the work is still problematical save in one respect. It is known that he first published it. Did he prepare *his* draft of it during the Cirey Period? There is no definite proof, although there is a strong presumption that he did so, when the date 1742 which was attached to the *Extrait* of Meslier is recalled. And if he made his draft of the *Analyse,* it

---

[1] See *The Clandestine Organization and Diffusion of Philosophic Ideas in France from 1700 to 1750,* pp. 170-172.

[2] See Wade, "The Epître à Uranie," in *P. M. L. A.,* XLVII, 1081ff. The relationship, however, is the very opposite of what I indicate in this article, since the *Religion chrétienne analysée* is undoubtedly the later work.

becomes more plausible that he made his drafts of the *Examen* and the *Meslier* in and around the same time.

An examination of Voltaire's writings on critical deism published from 1762 to 1776 may be of value in our search for his possible early works of like nature. A list of them with dates of publication, comprises the *Sermon des cinquante* (1762), the *Questions de Zapata* (1767), the *Examen important de Milord Bolingbroke* (1766), *Homélies prononcées à Londres en 1765* (1767), *Dieu et les Hommes* (1769), *La Bible enfin expliquée* (1776). But if these dates of publication are unquestionably late, the dates of composition of some of the items may be earlier than has been commonly supposed. As a matter of fact, three of them, the *Sermon des cinquante,* the *Examen important de Milord Bolingbroke,* and the *Bible enfin expliquée* have been assigned to the Ferney Period without any attempt to distinguish between the time of publication and of composition. And when certain indications such as "vers 1736" on the title-page of the published *Examen important,* or 1749 on the published *Sermon des cinquante,* would lead to the assumption that these works were composed before the Ferney Period and placed in the Voltaire arsenal for future use, these dates have been regarded as a blind or an excellent example of Voltaire's tendency to pre-date his writings. The first rule of Voltaire criticism has been : always regard Voltaire as a prevaricator and dissembler. Now, Voltaire undoubtedly resorted to subterfuges at times. He undoubtedly often distorted the truth until it is barely recognizable. But his efficacy in dealing with the censorship was not due to the fact that he lied continually, but to the fact that he mixed truth with falsehood so ingeniously that the task of separating them appeared hopeless. Thus there was a tendency even in his day to regard all his statements as false, and we who have inherited that tendency have persisted in believing that there is no truth in him. And yet, little by little, certain of his statements assumed to be false have been discovered to be true. For instance, he stated repeatedly that the article "Messie" of the *Dictionnaire philo-*

sophique was written by Polier de Bottens. A falsehood, all critics have said. And yet, after Mr. Naves's recent work on *Voltaire et l'Encyclopédie*,[3] no one can doubt that Polier de Bottens was the author of the "Messie."

However, it is not our purpose here to exculpate Voltaire. We are concerned with investigating whether certain of his deistic works could have been composed wholly or in part in the Cirey Period. The first among them which will bear examination is the *Sermon des cinquante* dated by Voltaire with an enigmatic 1749.[4] It should be noted that if the *Sermon* was published in 1762, it was undoubtedly circulating in manuscript form in 1760. For in August, 1760, Barbier recorded:[5]

Il paraît une pièce manuscrite intitulée *Sermon des cinquante*. On suppose dans le préambule qu'il se tient à Genève une assemblée de cinquante gens de lettres, qui tour à tour font un Sermon, et que celui-ci est de Voltaire à qui ses ennemis prêtent cette pièce dont le style bien différent du sien décèle la méchanceté. Ce Sermon est épouvantable. Les deux premiers points sont une critique affreuse de l'Ancien Testament pour en démontrer la fausseté et l'impiété, et le troisième est de même contre le Nouveau Testament. Si l'auteur était connu, on ne lui ferait pas faire de voyage autre part qu'à la [place de] grève pour être brûlé.

As a matter of fact, it appears that the *Sermon* was circulating in 1759, for on June 11, 1759, Voltaire wrote to Mme de Fontaine who had evidently inquired about it:[6]

Je ne sais ce que c'est que ce *Sermon des cinquante* dont vous me parlez; c'est apparemment le sermon de quelque jésuite qui n'aura eu que cinquante auditeurs: c'est encore beaucoup: les pauvres diables me paraissent actuellement bien grêlés. Mais si c'était quelque sottise anti-chrétienne, et que quelque fripon osât me

---

[3] Naves, R., *Voltaire et l'Encyclopédie*, Paris, 1938.
[4] On the date of the *Sermon des cinquante* see Bengesco, *Bibliographie*, II, 113-116; Champion, E., *Voltaire, Etudes critiques*, Paris, 1893, Chap. XIII; Ritter, E., "Le Sermon des cinquante" in *R. H. L.* (1900), Vol. VII, 315; Pellissier, *Voltaire philosophe*, Paris, 1908, p. 101.
[5] Barbier, *Journal*, Ed. 1856, IV, 360.
[6] Moland XL, 119. Bengesco thinks that the letter is a fusion of two letters.

l'imputer, je demanderais justice au pape, tout net. Je n'entends point raillerie sur cet article : je me suis déclaré hardiment contre Calvin, aux Délices ; et je ne souffrirai jamais que la pureté de ma foi soit attaquée.

Evidently the *Sermon* was one of the clandestine manuscripts which appeared in print only after several years of circulation. Just how many years it circulated before it was printed is problematical. Undeniably Grimm[7] stated that it was read in public at Berlin during the sojourn of Voltaire at Frederick's court. This bit of information is partially confirmed by La Beaumelle who was at Frederick's court in 1752. La Beaumelle, in 1754, published a *Réponse au Supplément du Siècle de Louis XIV*, Colmar, 1754, in which he wrote significantly :[8]

Proscrit ? Dans quel pays ? Et pourquoi ? Serois-je l'Auteur de ce *Sermon de (sic) cinquante*, qui ne peut devenir public que le Prédicateur ne soit mis en pièces par tous les Peuples qui vivent sous la Loi de Christ, de Moyse, ou de Mahomet ?

This was not the only time La Beaumelle referred to the *Sermon*. When he published, in 1763, the *Lettres de Monsieur de la Beaumelle à M. de Voltaire* (Londres, 1763), he mentioned it again :[9]

Je suis dégoûtant pour le public. Et vous qu'êtes-vous à ses yeux ? Qu'est pour les dévots l'auteur de la *Pucelle d'Orléans*, pour les chrétiens l'auteur du *Sermon des cinquante*, pour les rois l'auteur de ce mot à jamais odieux. . . .

The combined testimony of Grimm and La Beaumelle is sufficient to establish the fact that the *Sermon* was known at Potsdam in 1752. Was it composed at that time or had it been brought

---

[7] Grimm, *Correspondance littéraire*, VII, 147 (Octobre, 1766).

[8] Pp. 158-159. Note [N]. This part of the book is dated Paris, 3 mars 1753. See Ritter, E., *op. cit.*

[9] Lettre IX. The letters seem to have been written while Voltaire was at Colmar, since there are passages where he mentions that Voltaire was there. Some of them are dated 1753. Lettre IX, however, does not have the year. The passage given above can be found also in Paillet de Warcy, L., *Histoire de la vie et des ouvrages de Voltaire*, Paris, 1824, I, 101, and Le Pan, *Vie politique, littéraire et morale de Voltaire*. Paris, 1819, p. 117. Lepan dates the twenty-four letters of La Beaumelle from the year 1753.

to Berlin in the baggage of M. de Voltaire? No definite answer can be given this question, although it is to be noted that at the time of his break with Rousseau, Voltaire in a letter to the Maréchale de Luxembourg stated:[10]

Il [Rousseau] dit que je suis l'auteur d'un libelle intitulé *Sermon des cinquante,* libelle le plus violent qu'on ait jamais fait contre la religion chrétienne, libelle imprimé, depuis plus de quinze ans, à la suite de *l'Homme machine,* de la Mettrie.

While no copy of the *Sermon* printed with *l'Homme machine* can be found, there is a copy printed alone and dated 1753.[11] The inclusion of La Mettrie in the title[12] along with mention of the "grand prince très instruit" seems to indicate that the publication of the work was not projected until the Berlin Period. But the reference to the "ville riche et commerçante" on the opening page would seem to apply to Amsterdam with which Voltaire was well acquainted during the Cirey Period, and not to Geneva, as Barbier thought, while the statement in Point I: "lorsque nous avons lu ensemble les écrits des Hébreux" inevitably calls to mind the reading of the *Bible* after luncheon at Cirey.

Enough evidence has been presented to permit us to follow the fortunes of the *Sermon* from its composition to its publication, although there are still some stages in its history which are obscure. Written in 1749, as Voltaire indicated, or certainly by 1752, as Grimm and La Beaumelle would give us reason to believe, it was known to a select circle by 1752. Whether it was printed in Berlin at that time cannot be definitely affirmed. Certain it is that it did not create any stir until 1759 and 1760 when copies circulating in manuscript came to the attention of Mme de Fontaine and Barbier respectively. Two years later it had found its way into print. The significant point, however, is that

---

[10] Moland XLIII, 431 (January 9, 1765).

[11] See Havens and Torrey: "Voltaire's Books, A Selected List" in *M. P.,* XXVII (August, 1929), 20.

[12] *Cf.* the full title: *Sermon des cinquante, 1749. On l'attribue à M. du Martaine ou du Marsay, d'autres à La Métrie; mais il est d'un grand prince très instruit.*

the *Sermon des cinquante* is not a product of Ferney. Nor was it
the product of Berlin, although it is still possible that it was transcribed there. It was a product of the atmosphere at Cirey, and
written in all probability before Mme du Châtelet's death.[13]

Evidence for the validity of this statement can be obtained by
a comparison of the short, rapid, concentrated treatise of Voltaire with the long, rambling, diffuse treatise of Mme du Châtelet. It is not, of course, to be expected that Voltaire's short
Sermon will offer the content of Mme du Châtelet's five volumes.
In the *Sermon*, for instance, Voltaire is inclined to be very brief
and rapid, never thorough. In citing Moses's miracles before
Pharaoh, he mentions only three, whereas Mme du Châtelet
analyses all ten. Voltaire, moreover, is inclined to make comparisons between incidents in the *Bible* and Greek and Roman
legends. This tendency is almost entirely lacking in Mme du
Châtelet who is more inclined to liken the incidents which she
discusses to *Les Fourberies de Scapin* or the *Arabian Nights*.
Finally, the last portion of the *Sermon* which deals with the history of the Church after Christ's Ascension is naturally absent
in the *Examen de la Genèse* which is limited to the *Bible*. On the
other hand, any comment upon Peter's and Paul's activities and
writings, to which Mme du Châtelet devoted a whole volume, is
absent in the *Sermon*. Nor is it to be supposed that Voltaire followed Mme du Châtelet's sequence or made his selection from
her material. It will be remembered that the *Sermon* reviews the
Old Testament twice, once to give examples of the moral perversity of its statements and once again to cite instances of their
falsity.

In spite of dissimilarities between the two treatises, both in
form and content, the *Sermon* shows a definite relationship to the
Examen de la Genèse. Voltaire's two main objections to the

---

[13] As long as the date 1762 was accepted, there were reasons for assuming
that Voltaire pre-dated his work thirteen years. But, if the work was known
in 1752, it seems hardly conceivable that Voltaire would have found any
advantage in pre-dating the work 1749.

Bible, namely, the moral perversity prevalent in its stories and the falsity of its facts, are the two points constantly emphasized by Mme du Châtelet. It is significant that with the exception of three points made by Voltaire (Isaac's falsehood, the absurdity of seventy people becoming two million in two hundred five years, and the disparity between two hundred fifteen and four hundred thirty years recorded for the same period by a chronicler) every incident mentioned in the *Sermon* has been cited by Mme du Châtelet. More significant still is the fact that when discussing the same subject, both take the same point of view. Thus, in treating Eve's temptation by the serpent, both stress the absurdity of the serpent's speaking and the injustice of creating a serpent to tempt Eve. Both deny that Lot's daughters were pure, and express astonishment that they should have become the source of a numerous posterity. They observe with one accord, in speaking of Jacob and Esau, that Esau was dying of hunger or he would not have sold his birthright. They both note that Jacob was a bigamist, decry the cruelty of the Jews in slaying women and children after Dinah's adventures with Schechem, and condemn Joseph as a tyrant for enslaving the Egyptians and treating them unjustly. When the Jews robbed the Egyptians before fleeing into the desert, Voltaire and Mme du Châtelet note that they became robbers at the command of their God. Neither writer forgets that Rahab was a prostitute and a traitor to her country, and they protest with one accord the cruelty of the Jews at the fall of Jericho. In treating the story of the Levite and the tribe of Benjamin, they both comment upon the error which the Jews admitted having made in decreeing the annihilation of one of their tribes. Both remark that Samuel was very angry when the Israelites demanded a king, and express satisfaction that Jonathan was saved by the people when Saul intended to slay him. They concur in condemning David's actions, calling him a bandit and reproaching him for his ingratitude toward Achish, and both remark that his crime toward Uriah was the inaugural incident in the line which extended from David (says Voltaire) or Solomon (says Mme du Châtelet) to the Christ.

The two writers again repeat each other in their comments upon the falsehoods, contradictions, and misstatements in the *Bible*. Both call attention to the existence of days and nights before the formation of the sun. The double creation of Eve does not escape their attention. They jest over the source of the water for the Flood and the belief of the Jews that there were cataracts in the sky. They ridicule in general the unscientific aspects of the whole story of the Deluge, citing particularly the explanation of the appearance of the rainbow as a sign of peace. The incongruity of making Joseph a prime minister just because he could explain a dream is not forgotten by either. Nor do they fail to note that the Jews in their flight from Egypt did not take the shortest route to Palestine. They find nothing extraordinary in the miracles of Moses since the Egyptians could also perform miracles. They both stress this point by showing how the Egyptians could change a rod into a serpent. They repeat each other in expressing surprise that Samson found three hundred foxes so handily when he wished to tie their tails together. They likewise profess astonishment that Samuel should obey the voice of a sorcerer who at Saul's request summoned him from the other world.

The similarity of comment made in the *Sermon des cinquante* and the *Examen de la Genèse* would not necessarily prove the dependence of one work upon the other nor of the two works upon a common atmosphere. This type of comment was not limited to the *Sermon* and the *Examen de la Genèse,* for it is present in the *Religion chrétienne analysée,* the *Examen de la religion,* the *Extrait* of Meslier, even the *Tractatus,* and, as we have shown elsewhere, in many other clandestine works of the time. It is of sufficient evidence to warrant placing the *Sermon* and the *Examen* in the current of deistic criticism existing between 1700 and 1750, but hardly of enough weight to warrant the assertion that one work in any way depended upon the other or even that both sprang from the same milieu. There is, however, another type of similarity which becomes evident when one compares the comments which the two critics made upon certain incidents related in the *Bible*. This resemblance lies not only in point of view, but in verbal expression, and even in some cases in a certain sequence of ideas to form a complete argument. These cases, of which there are eleven in the *Sermon*, are so important in determining the relationship between the two works that we have given them all. In each case, for the sake of brevity, we have listed the biblical incident, and the shortest comment made by Voltaire and Mme du Châtelet, and added a sentence which will bring out, it is hoped, the significance in the similarity of treatment.

1. The sacrifice of human beings.

    Sermon: Il n'est pas étonnant que ce peuple abominable sacrifie des victimes humaines à son Dieu.

    Examen: Or, on dévouait non seulement des ennemis, mais des enfans, des esclaves. . . . (II, 29)

    Sermon: Le vingt-neuvième verset du chapitre XXVII du Lévitique défend expressément de racheter les hommes dévoués à l'anathème du sacrifice.

    Examen: Dieu veut qu'on exécute ces sortes de dévouements quand on les a faits: et c'est dans ce sens qu'il est dit v. 28, et 29, du Lévitique, chapitre 27. . . . (II, 29)

In this case, both critics are speaking of Jephthah's daughter, both agree that the Jews had human sacrifice, and cite the same passage in the *Bible* to substantiate this belief.

2. The murder committed by Ehud.

    Sermon: [Aod] demande à parler tête-à-tête avec le roi de la part de Dieu.

    Examen: . . . et il lui dit qu'il avoit quelque chose à lui communiquer en particulier de la part de Dieu. (II, 23)

    Sermon: . . . et c'est de cet exemple qu'on s'est servi tant de fois chez les chrétiens pour trahir, pour perdre, pour massacrer tant de souverains.

Examen: . . . et ce digne patron des Jacques Clément, et des Ravaillac, jugea le peuple quatre-vingts ans. (II, 23)

In this case, the critics use a similar language, and draw the same conclusion.

3. Samuel dismembers Agag.

Sermon: Mais voici, mes frères, l'action la plus détestable et la plus consacrée.

Examen: Mais voici l'endroit le plus affreux, et le plus révoltant des Livres Saints, et c'est beaucoup dire.

Sermon: . . . ce prêtre boucher coupe Agag par morceaux.

Examen: . . . et le coupe par morceau.

Both critics condemn this crime in similar language.

4. Elisha curses the children who call him bald.

Sermon: . . . il n'y a pas jusqu'au prophète Elisée qui ne soit barbare.

Examen: . . . action assurément bien barbare.

This case, in which the similarity occurs in the word "barbare," is not very impressive.

5. Joshua commands the sun to stand still.

Sermon: . . . le Seigneur Adonaï fait pleuvoir sur les fuyards une grosse pluie de pierres. . . .

Examen: Dieu faisoit pleuvoir sur eux une pluye de pierres.

Sermon: . . . le soleil s'arrête à Gabaon, et la lune sur Aialon.

Examen: . . . il se met à commander au soleil de s'arrêter sur Gabaon, et à la lune de demeurer sur Ajalon.

Sermon: Nous ne comprenons pas trop comment la lune étoit de la partie.

Examen: Au reste on ne sait trop ce que la lune fait là ; ni le besoin que Josué en avoit. . . .

Sermon: . . . et il cite, pour son garant, le livre du Droiturier.

Examen: L'auteur pour faire croire un fait si extraordinaire, dit qu'il est écrit dans le livre des Justes.

Here the criticism and language are rather similar, and the sequence of ideas impressively so. (*Cf.*: *infra,* p. 186)

6. Hezekiah's sundial.

   Sermon: ... supposé que ces misérables eussent des cadrans.
   Examen: Enfin les horloges et la division du jour par heures
   n'ont été connues des Hébreux que depuis le retour
   de la captivité de Babilone, et ces mots d'horloges et
   d'heures ne se trouvent point dans l'hébreu avant la
   captivité. (II, 112-114)
   Sermon: ... recule de dix degrés à la prière d'Ezéchias qui
   demande judicieusement ce signe. Dieu lui donne
   le choix de faire avancer ou reculer l'heure, et le
   docte Ezéchias trouve qu'il n'est pas difficile de
   faire avancer l'ombre, mais bien de la reculer.
   Examen: Ezéchias dit qu'il n'y a rien de si aisé que de faire
   croître l'ombre de dix lignes et qu'il ne veut point de
   ce miracle là, mais qu'il veut qu'elle retourne en
   arrière de dix lignes. (II, 112-114)

Both critics note that the Jews in Hezekiah's time lacked
means of measuring hours. Both stress Hezekiah's astuteness in
demanding a supernatural proof of the verity of the prophecy
rather than a proof in accordance with the laws of nature.

7. Ezekiel's strange vision.

   Sermon: ... ce prophète étoit assurément un homme à lier.
   Examen: Effectivement, il paroit par son livre qu'il avoit
   besoin d'être lié.... (III, 71-73)
   Sermon: ... et Dieu, par accommodement, lui permet de ne
   plus mêler à son pain que de la fiente de vache.
   Examen: ... et Dieu par accomodement lui permit de mettre
   sur son pain de la bousse de vache au lieu de merde.
   (III, 71-73)

In this case, the language is the same, the pun upon the word
"lier" is similar, and the sequence is the same.

8. The date of composition of the Gospels.

   Sermon: ... quoiqu'il soit évident qu'ils l'ont été après la
   ruine de Jérusalem.
   Examen: Ce verset est une preuve que l'évangile de St.
   Mathieu a été écrit depuis la prise de Jérusalem.

Sermon: Il n'est parlé, mes frères, d'un Zacharie, fils de
Baruch, tué entre le temple et l'autel, que dans
l'histoire du siège de Jérusalem, par Flavius
Josèphe.

Examen: ... car il n'y a point de Zacharie fils de Barachie tué
entre le temple et l'autel, que celui dont parle Joseph
dans son histoire, qui fut tué pendant le siège de
Jérusalem par Titus. ...

This case is especially significant since the criticism is historical rather than textual. Both critics make the same point,
refer to the same verse, mention Josephus, and draw the same
conclusion.

9.   The Genealogy of the Christ.

Sermon: ... Matthieu compte quarante-deux générations en
deux mille ans; mais dans son compte, il ne s'en
trouve que quarante et une. ...

Examen: ... car il est absurde qu'en près de deux mille ans
il ne se trouve que quarante-deux générations. Mais
ce nombre de quarante-deux générations que St.
Mathieu a choisi de préférence, il ne le remplit pas,
et il n'en rapporte que quarante et une. ... (IV, 5-6
& IV, 143-144)

Sermon: ... il se trompe ... en donnant Josias pour père à
Jéchonias.

Examen: ... Josias n'a jamais eu de fils appellé Jéchonias. ...

Sermon: ... ces généalogies sont celles de Joseph.

Examen: ... cette généalogie se trouve être celle de Joseph.

In this case, the ideas are similar, both in content and sequence.

10.   The temptation of Christ on the mountain.

Sermon: ... il lui montre de là tous les royaumes de la terre.
Quelle est cette montagne d'où l'on découvre tant
de pays? Nous n'en savons rien.

Examen: ... et mena Jésus ... sur une haute montagne, d'où
il lui montra, v. 8, "tous les royaumes de la
terre. ..." Assurément il faloit qu'elle fût haute,
et que Jésus eût la vue bonne. On ne sait où cette
montagne est placée.

The critics here have the same point of view, take the same oblique method of criticising the story, and employ the same type of irony. This criticism was also made in *La Mule du Pape*. On its origin, see Kellenberger in *M.L.N.*, 1936, 17-21.

11. The cursing of the fig-tree.

> *Sermon:* . . . et le texte ne manque pas d'ajouter prudemment: "car ce n'était pas le temps des figues."
>
> *Examen:* Il n'y a rien assurément de plus absurde que d'aller chercher des figues sur un figuier quand ce n'est pas le temps des figues. . . . (IV, 77-80)

This case is not particularly significant, since the passage in the *Bible* would lead anyone to make a like remark. The point was stressed, however, by Woolston, who admittedly was the source of both Voltaire and Mme du Châtelet.

There can be no doubt that the *Sermon des cinquante,* published in 1762, existed in manuscript form in 1752, and was probably written as the date of the first printed edition indicated in 1749.[14] Then how about the *Examen important de Milord Bolingbroke?* Was it written in the neighborhood of 1766 when it was first published, or was it, too, an earlier work withdrawn from the Voltaire arsenal at the appropriate time for publication? It must be stated at the very beginning that the *Examen important* on first investigation appears to have been written late. One has only to note its masterful smoothness in support of this impression. There can be no doubt that Voltaire was in full possession of all his literary weapons of irony, invective, sarcasm, bitterness and grimness when it was fully completed.

---

[14] I am, to be sure, not certain that this 1749 of Voltaire is an accurate date. I think that Voltaire selected it because it marked a moment in his life which he could not forget. The 1749 would thus indicate even for Voltaire that the work was a product of the Cirey Period. For us, it indicates that in 1749, or thereabout, Voltaire wrote the *Sermon des cinquante*. The "thereabout" could thus be interpreted by the literal-minded as somewhere between 1749 and 1752, and by the broad-minded as somewhere between 1746 and 1749. I do not think it could have been composed before 1746, because, as I shall attempt to show, Voltaire was trying to incorporate the same material in two other works.

Moreover, the sub-title *Le Tombeau du fanatisme* suggests a late approach, although it might be argued that this sub-title was never used until the work was printed and consequently has nothing to do with the date of composition. But particularly, the attack against the crimes of the established Church, which is in large measure very similar to that in *L'Histoire de l'établissement du christianisme,* is certainly a late development in Voltairean technique. And yet it would be prudent to proceed cautiously. It is worthy of note that the defense of Julian, which appeared in late works, was used, as we have seen, in the Cirey Period. Absolutely nothing is known about the composition of the *Examen important.* Voltaire could have composed it (or at any rate, the first thirty-four chapters) at one time. Or, he could have composed a portion of it at one period, laid it aside until a later date when he resumed it, and made additions. Indeed, we know that he actually did make additions, both in the form of chapters as well as somewhat lengthy notes, which were added at various intervals after the first edition. There are some slight indications that some chapters were written long before the first edition and others shortly before its publication. The confusion concerning Chapter IX in the printed edition might be such an indication. But the evident difference in intent between the first part of the work (down to Chapter XIX) and the second is of still greater significance. The first is clearly a critical examination of the *Bible,* while the second is just as clearly an historical examination of the early Christian Church. It is this first part which appears quite in harmony with the movement of ideas of 1722-50, and distinctly out of tone with the period 1750-89, whereas the second part does not seem to belong to the former period, and, on the contrary, is quite typical of the latter.

It seems reasonable, therefore, to give careful consideration to the hypothesis that the *Examen important* was begun in the Cirey Period, that additions were made in 1765 before it was sent to the press, and that further additions, including lengthy notes, were made in subsequent editions. Such an assumption would necessitate reexamination of the phrase "écrit sur la fin de 1736," which has always been assumed to be a totally false date. This "écrit sur la fin de 1736" may have an importance which has never been realized. There is no way of reconciling it with a statement made in the "Avis aux éditeurs" (Beuchot XLIII, 42) : "Ce précis de la doctrine de Milord Bolingbroke, recueillie tout entière dans les six volumes de ses Œuvres posthumes, fut adressé par lui, peu d'années avant sa mort, à Milord Cornsburi." For Bolingbroke died in 1751 and the *Œuvres posthumes,* or rather the *Philosophical Works,* were published by Mallet in 1754-55. Incidentally, these *Philosophical Works* were in five not six volumes. We should note the story concerning the composition of the *Examen important,* namely, that it was extracted not from the published work but from manuscripts of the published work shortly before the death of Bolingbroke. Thus if there is any element of truth in the statement, the *Précis,* that is to say the *Examen important,* could reasonably go back to 1746 or thereabout (*cf.* "peu d'années avant sa mort") but by no stretch of the imagination to 1736. The whole statement, however, has been proved a fiction : the *Examen important* is not a *Précis* of Milord Bolingbroke; it is not, as Professor Torrey[15] has shown, "recueilli tout entière dans les six volumes de ses Œuvres posthumes"; and it was not addressed to Milord Cornsbury "peu d'années avant sa mort." In fact, the only chance of finding some truth in the remark lies in the very slight possibility that the year 1746 or thereabout was associated in some way in Voltaire's memory with the composition of the *Examen important.* But if this association is valid, then the first statement, "écrit sur la fin de 1736," is another fiction, imagined by Voltaire to give a false impression as to the date of composition. And here a very curious problem arises : why give two false dates, 1736 and 1746 or thereabout, for the composition of the

[15] Torrey, N. R., *Voltaire and the English Deists,* New Haven, 1930, Chap. VI.

Examen important? It seems reasonable enough to admit that one of them is false, but it was somewhat excessive on the part of Voltaire to suggest two false dates, ten or so years apart, for the same work.

Obviously, in considering the two dates we are faced with a logical dilemma. Either both are false, or one is false and the other true, or both can be shown to be true. Up to the present, Voltairean critics seem inclined to agree (without examination, it is true, and on the very well-established prejudice that Voltaire could not possibly tell the truth) that any date given by Voltaire for the composition of the *Examen important,* which does not lie within the Ferney Period, is false and invented by him as a smoke screen. But his giving two false dates seems so illogical, and so contrary to his assumed purpose of setting up a smoke screen, that, unless we want to consider him a fool making a stupid blunder, we are forced to the assumption that one of the dates is true and the other false, or that some explanation for the two can be found. But which one is true, and which false? If a choice has to be made on strictly logical lines, I should be inclined to accept the 1736, on the grounds that there are so many falsehoods in Voltaire's statement, which contains the suggestion of the approximate 1746, that I can readily believe the date an additional one, whereas there is no valid reason for rejecting the 1736, and in reality no reason at all except the well-established custom of believing Voltaire incapable of truth. This custom, of late, has been receiving some rude jolts. It had been thought that the *Extrait des sentiments de Jean Meslier* published in 1762 with the date 1742 was a pre-dated work until examination disclosed that some of the manuscripts actually bore the date 1742. It had been thought that Jean Meslier was a pseudonym of Voltaire until the actual discovery of Jean Meslier in documents and in his *Testament* dispelled that suspicion of dissimulation in Voltaire. Until last year, when Mr. Naves published his *Voltaire et l'Encyclopédie,* every one was of the opinion that Voltaire was lying when he said that the article "Messie" of the *Encyclopédie* and the *Dictionnaire philosophique* was written by Polier de Bottens. Now we know that he was not. To be sure, the fact that critics were wrong in their assumptions in these three cases does not prove that he was telling the truth when he wrote on the title-page of the *Examen important* "écrit sur la fin de 1736." It merely justifies more careful examination into the date of composition of the *Examen important*.

There is even the third possibility that Voltaire was truthful in giving the two dates. He may have begun the work in 1736, it may have passed through successive stages from 1736 to 1746 or thereabout, when he regarded a draft of it as completed and possibly laid it aside for future use, or he may have been dissatisfied with his technique and laid it aside for further development. At all events, the draft of 1746 or thereabout must not be considered the final one, for Voltaire as we have seen, kept revising, rearranging, adding chapters and notes even after 1766.

In connection with the dates 1736-46, it should be noted that many of the ideas of the *Examen important* belong specifically to the Cirey Period. This fact may or may not be significant, since it is to be expected that Voltaire would carry over into the Ferney Period some of the intellectual baggage which he had used in the Cirey, as well as any other, Period. It is none the less interesting to note the recurrence of these Cirey ideas in the *Examen important*. In speaking of the effect of milieu upon one's religion, Voltaire here writes (Beuchot XLIII, 43): "A qui soumettrai-je mon âme? Serai-je chrétien, parce que je serai de Londres ou de Madrid? Serai-je musulman, parce que je serai né en Turquie?"[16] There is no need to mention his insistence upon one's examining his religion in the "il faut donc examiner;

---

[16] *Cf.* the passage from *Zaïre, 1732,* Beuchot III, 165:

> Je le vois trop: les soins qu'on prend de notre enfance
> Forment nos sentiments, nos mœurs, notre croyance.
> J'eusse été près du Gange esclave des faux dieux,
> Chrétienne dans Paris, musulmane en ces lieux.

c'est un devoir que personne ne révoque en doute."[17] Of more importance is his reference to Pascal (Beuchot XLIII, 46) : "Pascal commence par révolter ses lecteurs, dans ses pensées informes qu'on a recueillies : 'Que ceux qui combattent la religion chrétienne,' dit-il, 'apprennent à la connaître, etc.' Je vois à ces mots un homme de parti qui veut subjuguer." In another instance he refers (Beuchot XLIII, 100) to Pascal's treatment of the genealogies of the Christ in Matthew and Luke.[18] His reference to Jean Meslier, "mort depuis peu" (Beuchot XLIII, 46), clearly points to the Cirey Period, for Meslier, who died in 1729, first became known to Voltaire in 1735.[19] His subsequent remark concerning the Curate in Dorsetshire, diocese of Bristol, who gave up his two hundred pounds sterling and confessed to his parishioners that his conscience did not permit him to preach the absurd horrors of the Christian sect, is most curious. The only place I have seen this reference elsewhere is in the *Extrait* of Meslier and only in some of the manuscripts.[20] The fact that Meslier and the Curate are put together in the same paragraph in the *Examen important* indicates that Voltaire became acquainted with them at the same time, that is, in the Cirey Period, and in all probability, in the same manuscript.[21] But to these references in the *Examen important,* which go back to the Cirey Period, the mention of Lady Blackacre, a character of the *Plain Dealer* who was utilized by Voltaire in *La Prude* (1740), should be added.[22]

[17] *Cf.* the title of Mme du Châtelet's manuscript. The idea was also stressed in the *Examen de la religion* and the *Analyse de la religion. Cf.* also *Examen critique des apologistes de la religion chrétienne,* and *Examen critique du nouveau testament.*

[18] *Cf.* the twenty-fifth letter of the *Lettres philosophiques,* 1734.

[19] See Voltaire to Thiériot, November 30 [1735]. Voltaire thought that Meslier died in 1733.

[20] *Cf.* Orléans 1115, p. 13, and Arsenal 2559, p. 28. The passage in Arsenal 2559 reads : "Il y a eu un curé en Angleterre, excellent géomètre, qui, en 1722, quitta son bénéfice valant 200 livres sterling pour n'être pas obligé d'enseigner aux hommes des choses si monstrueuses."

[21] Professor Morehouse assumes that Voltaire became acquainted with Meslier in the forties. See *Voltaire and Jean Meslier,* p. 32.

[22] See Beuchot V, 351.

The passage (Beuchot XLIII, 75) which reads: "Mais à la fraude ajoutons encore le fanatisme," gives the subject-matter of *Mahomet* (1742). The reference (Beuchot XLIII, 82) to Fox, "un misérable paysan établit de nos jours la secte des quakers parmi les paysans de nos provinces," recalls the description given of Fox in the *Lettres philosophiques*. The Panther story (Beuchot XLIII, 84) was told also in *La Religion chrétienne analysée*, with which work Voltaire presumably became acquainted between 1742-49. We have already commented upon the "ce n'est pas ma faute" (Beuchot XLIII, 114) which Mme du Châtelet quoted as one of Voltaire's characteristic bons mots. The two lines quoted from the poet Ablavius (Beuchot XLIII, 169):

> Saturni aurea quis requirat?
> Sunt haec gemmea, sed Neroniana.

definitely recall the opening lines of *Le Mondain* (1736).[23] And lastly, the sentence (Beuchot XLIII, 187-188), "Valentinien apprit à tous ceux qui sont nés pour gouverner que si deux sectes déchirent un état, trente sectes tolérées laissent l'état en repos," definitely is an echo of a statement practically similar in the *Lettres philosophiques* (1734).[24]

Now it must be admitted that any one of these references characteristic of the Cirey Period taken by itself does not constitute a valid argument for placing the date of composition of the *Examen important* in that period. But since the work contains a comparatively large number of these references; since, moreover, it deals with a type of critical deism with which Voltaire was preoccupied at Cirey and which was quite prevalent in France in a clandestine way among the elite during the years 1730-50; since, finally, the author himself gives the dates 1736 to 1746 or thereabout as the dates of its composition, and there

---

[23] See Morize, A., *Le Mondain de Voltaire et l'apologie du luxe au XVIIIe siècle.*

[24] *Cf. L. P.* (Lanson edition), I, 74: "S'il n'y avoit en Angleterre qu'une Religion, le despotisme seroit à craindre, s'il y en avoit deux, elles se couperoient la gorge, mais il y en a trente, et elles vivent en paix heureuses."

is no more valid reason for rejecting his statements than an un-
justifiable skepticism—it must be admitted that there is a very
strong presumption that the *Examen important* did take its origin in the intellectual atmosphere of Cirey, and that portions of
it were actually written there between the two given dates.

A comparison of the *Examen important* and the *Examen de
la Genèse* will serve to strengthen this assumption, for many
times passages of one treatise bear a resemblance to passages of
the other. This similarity, of course, does not necessarily indicate
the dependence of one work upon the other, or even the dependence of both upon the same milieu. When both Voltaire (Beuchot XLIII, 68-69) and Mme du Châtelet (II, 39-40) dwell at
great length upon the story of the Levite and his wife who were
attacked by the Benjamites; when they both comment upon the
cruelty of Samuel in slaying Agag (XLIII, 71; II, 52-53);
when both (XLIII, 72; II, 59-75) relate the stories which ex-
emplify David's immorality (the death of Nabal, the usurpation
of Ishbosheth's throne, the assassination of Mephibosheth, the
delivery of Saul's sons and grandsons to the Gibeonites, the assassination of Uriah, and the adultery of Bathsheba) and even
contrast this immoral conduct with the biblical assertion that
David was none the less a man "selon le cœur de Dieu"; when
both note the folly of the Prophets (Ezekiel remaining on one
side for three hundred ninety days and on the other for forty
days, Isaiah walking naked through the streets of Jerusalem,
Ezekiel cutting his beard in three portions, and Jonah remaining
three days in the belly of the whale)—one can conclude from
these similarities that there was merely a similarity of choice
from the original source, and that it is of no particular consequence in establishing the relationship of one of these works to
the other. Still, it is singular that the same biblical events attracted the attention of both writers in so many instances.

Of more consequence is the fact that the reactions of Voltaire
and Mme du Châtelet to certain biblical references are often

similar. Thus both express astonishment that Joshua could write all of Deuteronomy on stones:

> Il est dit dans le livre de Josué que l'on écrivit le Deutéronome sur un autel de pierres brutes enduites de mortier. Comment écrivit-on tout un livre sur du mortier? (XLIII, 49)

> Ensuite Josué v. 30 et 32, écrivit tout le Deutéronome sur des pierres. (II, 10)

Both are frankly amazed that the magicians of Pharaoh could perform miracles to compete with those of Moses:

> Dans quel ridicule roman souffrirait-on un homme qui change toutes les eaux en sang, d'un coup de baguette, au nom d'un dieu inconnu, et des magiciens qui en font autant au nom des dieux du pays? (XLIII, 53)

> Moyse et Aaron voyant que Pharaon ne vouloit point permettre que les Israëlites allassent sacrifier dans le désert, changent toutes les eaux de l'Egipte en sang, les fleuves, les fontaines, les lacs, en un mot toutes les eaux de l'Egipte. Cependant les magiciens en font autant, de savoir où ils prirent de l'eau pour faire leur miracle, c'est ce qu'on ignore. (I, 44)

Both are revolted by the robbery which the Israelites perpetrated upon the Egyptians before their departure:

> C'est de leur aveu, un peuple de brigands qui emportent dans un désert tout ce qu'ils ont volé aux Egyptiens. (XLIII, 66)

> Les Israëlites se disposèrent donc à partir, mais auparavant Moyse eut grand soin d'exécuter ce qu'on a vû que Dieu lui avoit ordonné chap. 3, v. 22, de dépouiller l'Egipte . . . au reste, les Israëlites étoient des voleurs maladroits, d'attendre le jour de leur départ pour emprunter ce qu'ils vouloient emporter. (I, 50-51)

Both are horrified at the slaughter which Joshua ordered at Jericho:

> Josué les (towns) détruit; il livre au fer et aux flammes, vieillards, femmes, enfants, et bestiaux; y a-t-il horreur plus insensée? (XLIII, 66)

> Enfin, ait sonné qui voudra, les murailles tombèrent, et on tua tout, hommes, femmes, enfans, vieillards et animaux. (II, 6)

Both note with an air of amazement that in this slaughter only Rahab the prostitute is spared:

Il ne pardonne qu'à une prostituée qui avait trahi sa patrie. (XLIII, 67)

Ils brûlèrent tout et ne conservèrent que Rahab qui avoit mis un ruban rouge à sa fenêtre pour être reconnue. (II, 6)

Both conclude that Samson must have been a rake:

. . . du débauché Samson. . . . (XLIII, 68)

Samson aimoit beaucoup les filles, c'est ce qui se voit par toute son histoire. (II, 36)

Both stress the faulty philosophy of the Hebrews in having a magician evoke Samuel after his death (XLIII, 71 ; II, 61). And both note with evident glee that David's followers were the malcontents of the Kingdom:

Il (David) ramasse quatre cents malheureux; et, comme dit la Sainte écriture, "tous ceux qui avaient de mauvaises affaires, qui étaient perdus de dettes, et d'un esprit méchant, s'assemblèrent avec lui." (XLIII, 71-72)

Au sortir de chez les Philistins, David se retira dans une caverne au chap. 22, avec tous les mécontens, desquels il tâcha de se faire un parti. (II, 57)

They are revolted by Solomon's first action on becoming king, the slaying of his brother:

Salomon commence par égorger son frère Adonias. (XLIII, 72)

Salomon suivit très bien les ordres cruels de son père; mais il commença par se venger lui-même, et par faire mourir son frère Adonias, auquel il avoit juré au chap. 1er, de ne lui point faire de mal. (II, 81)

They are considerably amused at Jeremiah's action in putting a rope around his neck:

Jérémie, qui prophétisait en faveur de Nabuchodonosor, tyran des Juifs, s'était mis des cordes au cou, . . . car c'était un type; et il devait envoyer ce type aux petits roitelets voisins, pour les inviter à se soumettre à Nabuchodonosor. (XLIII, 76)

Au chap. 27, Dieu ordonne à Jérémie de se mettre des chaînes au cou, et puis de les envoyer à plusieurs rois, dont les ambassadeurs étoient auprès de Sédécias. Je crois qu'ils firent grand cas de ce présent, lequel signifioit que Dieu avoit donné les royaumes de tous ces rois à Nabuchodonosor; et Jérémie devoit charger les ambassadeurs d'annoncer cette nouvelle à leurs maîtres; de quoi, j'imagine qu'ils se gardèrent bien; il leur ordonna d'y ajouter que si ces rois ne se soumettoient pas au roi de Babilone, Dieu les feroit périr par la faim, par la peste, et par l'épée. (III, 125-126)

They are likewise intrigued by the mountain where Satan transported the Saviour and from whence one could see all the kingdoms of the earth:

Le premier qu'il opère, c'est de se faire emporter par le diable sur le haut d'une montagne de Judée d'où l'on découvre tous les royaumes de la terre. (XLIII, 86)

Le Diable . . . mena Jésus, apparemment par la même voiture par laquelle il étoit venu sur le temple, sur une haute montagne, d'où il lui montra "tous les royaumes de la terre et toute la gloire qui les accompagne." Assurément il faloit qu'elle fût haute, et que Jésus eût la vuë bonne. (IV, 22-23)

Both note how useless it was to have the sun stand still when the enemies of Joshua were already crushed by the rain of stones:

. . . et c'est en faveur de ces monstres qu'on fait arrêter le soleil et la lune en plein midi! et pourquoi? pour leur donner le temps de poursuivre et d'égorger de pauvres Amorrhéens déjà écrasés par une pluie de grosses pierres que Dieu avait lancées sur eux du haut des airs pendant cinq grandes lieues de chemin. (XLIII, 67)

. . . et pendant qu'ils fuyoient devant Israël, Dieu fit pleuvoir une pluye de pierres sur eux qui en tua encore plus que n'avoit fait Josué. Qui croiroit après cela que Dieu eut eu encore quelque chose à faire dans cette occasion pour les Israëlites contre les Amorrhéens, cependant Josué ne fut pas encore content, et dans le tems que ses ennemis s'enfuyoient devant lui et que Dieu faisoit pleuvoir sur eux une pluye de pierres, il se met à commander au soleil de s'arrêter sur Gabaon. . . . (II, 11-12)

They pretend not to understand how four hundred thousand from the eleven tribes could not defeat twenty-five thousand from the tribe of Benjamin (XLIII, 69; II, 40). They both condemn Samuel's boldness in asserting that the Jews' desire to have a king was a renunciation of the Lord (XLIII, 70; II, 45). They express amazement that the Lord would permit the Canaanites to capture the Ark and then become irritated at them for having done so:

> ... les Cananéens leur avaient pris leur coffre: Dieu, qui en fut très irrité, l'avait pourtant laissé prendre; mais pour se venger, il avait donné des hémorroïdes aux vainqueurs. ... (XLIII, 70)

> L'arche qui s'étoit laissé prendre se laissa conduire dans le temple de Dagon à Azot, le plus bénignement du monde; mais alors il prit envie à Dieu de se fâcher d'être captif. Il renversa deux fois l'idole de Dagon, et il donna des hémorroïdes à toute la ville. (II, 43)

But they are more amazed still when the Canaanites are forgiven, and yet some fifty thousand Jews are killed for having merely regarded the Ark:

> Il pardonne aux Cananéens, mais il fait mourir cinquante mille et soixante et dix hommes des siens pour avoir regardé son coffre. (XLIII, 70)

> Mais Dieu s'avisa de s'en fâcher, et en vérité, on ne pourroit pas deviner pourquoi, si l'écriture n'avoit soin de dire que ce fut pour avoir regardé l'arche du Seigneur. ... Mais à moins de se crever les yeux ils ne pouvoient s'empêcher de la voir. Enfin, il en mourut cinquante mille soixante et dix. (II, 44)

They condemn the Song of Solomon and blush to quote from it:

> Le Cantique qu'on lui impute est dans le goût de ces livres érotiques qui font rougir la pudeur. Il n'y est parlé que, etc. ... (XLIII, 73)

> Ce livre attribué encore à Salomon est fameux par son indécence. Il a assurément été fait pour célébrer l'amour champêtre et grossier de quelque Israélite. Il y a des versets qui font rougir, et que je n'oserois pas rapporter en françois. (III, 163)

They deny that Herod took forty-six years to rebuild the Temple of Jerusalem (XLIII, 87; IV, 176). They cite with malicious satisfaction the passage from the Galatians where Paul condemns circumcision and recall immediately that Paul himself circumcised his disciple Timothy:

> Il écrit aux Galates: "Je vous dis, moi Paul, que si vous vous faites circoncire, Jésus-Christ ne vous servira de rien." Et ensuite il circoncit son disciple Timothée. . . . (XLIII, 95)

> Au chapitre 5, v. 2, il dit aux Galates que s'ils se font circoncire Jésus ne leur servira de rien. On a vû cependant qu'il a circoncis Timothée son disciple. . . . (V, 75)

When they comment upon Paul's assertion that he has spent twenty-four hours in the bottom of the sea, they recall Jonah's adventure (XLIII, 96; V, 64). They both make sport of the light from Heaven which blinded Paul in the middle of the day (XLIII, 98; V, 14). The fact that the two genealogies of Christ are not similar, although they purport to be the genealogy of Joseph (XLIII, 100; IV, 143), attracts their attention. They stress the contradictions between Matthew and Luke concerning the early years of Christ (XLIII, 100; IV, 141). They assert that the Gospel according to St. Matthew could not have been written until after the fall of Jerusalem, and give the same proof to support their assertion:

> On a une preuve bien sensible dans celui qui est attribué à Mathieu. Ce livre met dans la bouche de Jésus ces paroles aux Juifs: "Vous rendrez compte de tout le sang répandu depuis le juste Abel jusqu'à Zacharie, fils de Barachie, que vous avez tué entre le temple et l'autel." Un faussaire se découvre toujours par quelque endroit. Il y eut, pendant le siège de Jerusalem, un Zacharie, fils d'un Barachie, assassiné entre le temple et l'autel par la faction des zélés. (XLIII, 101)

> (After quoting the same verse) Ce verset est une preuve que l'Évangile de St. Mathieu a été écrit depuis la prise de Jérusalem; et que par conséquent il n'est point de cet apôtre: car il n'y a point de Zacharie fils de Barachie tué entre le temple et l'autel, que celui

dont parle Joseph dans son histoire, qui fut tué pendant le siège de
Jérusalem par Titus. . . . (IV, 88)

Their criticism of the prophecies is analogous. They reject
the prophecy of Isaiah, maintaining that "alma" signifies a ma-
tron as well as a virgin, and that Jesus did not have the name
Immanuel (XLIII, 112; III, 110). According to both writers,
Jacob's prophecy to the effect that the sceptre would always remain in the tribe of Judah had ceased to be true even in the days
of the Levite king, Saul (XLIII, 113; I, 38). They note Matthew's error in referring to a prophecy which cannot be found
in the *Bible* :

"Il s'appellera Nazaréen." Aucun prophète n'avait dit ces paroles;
Matthieu parlait donc au hasard. (XLIII, 114)

Mais ce qu'il y a de surprenant, c'est que cette prophêtie, *il sera
appellé Nazaréen,* qui fit faire à Joseph un voyage exprès à Nazareth pour l'accomplir, ne se trouve dans aucun prophête, de l'aveu
de tous les commentateurs. (IV, 16)

They stress the point that the early Christians expected the world
to come to an end during their lifetime, and both quote from the
same sources to prove it : The First Epistle of Peter, the Second
Epistle of Peter, and the First Epistle of John (XLIII, 116;
and V, 104-105, 110, and 131). Madame du Châtelet, in fact, has
a small chapter at the end of the *Examen de la Genèse* on "La
Fin du Monde." Both finally cite Paul to show that he was of
the opinion of John and Peter :

"Nous qui vivons et qui vous parlons, nous serons emportés dans
les nuées pour aller au-devant du Seigneur au milieu de l'air." Que
chacun s'interroge ici : qu'il voie si l'on peut pousser plus loin l'imposture et la bêtise du fanatisme. (XLIII, 115)

"Mais pour nous qui vivons, et qui avons été laissés ici-bas, nous
serons élévés en même tems avec eux dans les nuées pour aller au-
devant du Seigneur Jésus-Christ avec lequel nous serons toujours."
Peut-on dire plus positivement une chose plus fausse? (V, 81)

Voltaire and Mme du Châtelet stop on occasion to give allegorical interpretations to historical events of the Scriptures.

Three cases of this nature which occur in the *Examen important*
appear again among others in the *Examen de la Genèse*. Both
writers mention the Church Fathers' interpretation of Rahab's
red ribbon, Moses's outstretched arms, and the Shulamite's
kisses:

> Le petit morceau de drap rouge que mettait la paillarde Rahab à
> sa fenêtre pour avertir les espions de Josué, signifie le sang de Jésus
> répandu pour nos péchés. (XLIII, 118)

> Au reste, cette Rahab étoit, selon les Pères, une figure de l'église,
> et il n'y a personne qui ne s'en aperçoive à sa conduite. (II, 7)

> Moïse levant les mains quand il donne la bataille aux Amalécites,
> c'est évidemment la croix, car on a la figure d'une croix quand on
> étend les bras à droite et à gauche. (XLIII, 118)

> Les Hébreux combatirent ensuite et vainquirent les Amalécites,
> parce que Moyse tenoit les mains étendues en l'air, ce qui vouloit
> dire Jésus Christ en croix. (I, 56)

> Les baisers que donne la Sulamite, sur la bouche, etc., dans le
> Cantique des cantiques, sont visiblement le mariage de Jésus-Christ
> avec son église. (XLIII, 118)

> . . . et les amours de l'époux et de l'épouse sont ceux de Jésus-
> Christ et de son église. (III, 163)

Voltaire's treatment of miracles in the *Examen important* and
Mme du Châtelet's in the *Examen de la Genèse* would be expected to show some resemblance, since both writers are known
to have consulted Woolston. In many instances, however, they
have repeated each other both in their choice of miracles taken
from Woolston and in their reactions to them. They deny, for
example, that there was anything miraculous in the whiteness of
Christ's garments at the Transfiguration:

> Ses vêtemens paraissent tout blancs: quel miracle! (XLIII, 86)

> Jésus prit avec lui trois de ses disciples Pierre, Jacques et Jean
> et s'en fut avec eux sur une haute montagne, et quand il y fut arrivé
> son visage parut reluisant comme le soleil, et ses vêtemens blancs
> comme la neige; ce que l'évangéliste v. 2 appelle se transfigurer, et
> à quoi il n'y a rien de bien miraculeux. (IV, 61)

Both note that the guests were already tipsy when water was changed into wine at the Cana wedding:

Il change l'eau en vin dans un repas où tous les convives étaient déjà ivres. (XLIII, 86)

Il est certain, du moins qu'on étoit à la fin du repas, or on ne voit non seulement nulle nécessité de changer l'eau en vin pour des gens qui avoient déjà trop bû, mais on y trouve même de l'indécence. (IV, 174)

They note the passage from Mark to the effect that the fig-tree was cursed at a time when it was not the season for figs:

Il fait sécher un figuier qui ne lui a pas donné de figues à son déjeuner à la fin de février: et l'auteur de ce conte a l'honnêteté du moins de remarquer que ce n'était pas le temps des figues. (XLIII, 86)

Mais le lendemain en revenant de Bethanie à Jérusalem, il eut faim . . . "Il aperçut un figuier sur le chemin, et il s'en approcha pour y prendre des figues, mais n'y en ayant point trouvé, il maudit ce figuier qui sécha dans l'instant." . . . St. Marc, en racontant ce même miracle ajoute une circonstance remarquable: c'est que ce n'étoit point le tems des figues. (IV, 77)

Both are astounded that a large group of merchants would permit themselves to be driven from the Temple by a single individual:

Il entre dans le temple, c'est-à-dire dans cette grande enceinte où demeuraient les prêtres, dans cette cour où de petits marchands étaient autorisés par la loi à vendre des poules, des pigeons, des agneaux, à ceux qui venaient sacrifier. Il prend un grand fouet, en donne sur les épaules de tous les marchands, les chasse à coups de lanières, eux, leurs poules, leurs pigeons, leurs moutons, et leurs bœufs même, jette tout leur argent par terre, et on le laisse faire! (XLIII, 87)

Quand Jésus fut entré à Jérusalem, il alla au temple, et il se mit à chasser les marchands qui étoient dans le parvis, v. 12, à renverser leurs marchandises, et à leur citer les prophêtes. . . . Assurément il n'y a rien de si surprenant que cette action de Jésus et de voir un homme seul, sans autorité, et un homme méprisé chasser cette foule de marchands qui étoient dans les galleries extérieures du temple. (IV, 76)

Finally, both choose the miracle of the swine as the most impossible of the group:

> Le plus beau de tous, à mon gré, est celui par lequel Jésus envoie le diable dans le corps de deux mille cochons, dans un pays où il n'y avait point de cochons. (XLIII, 88)

> Il faut avouer qu'il est plaisant de trouver deux mille cochons dans un pays où ils étoient en horreur, et où il étoit deffendu sous peine de mort d'en avoir, depuis qu'Antiochus Epiphane avoit souillé le temple en y sacrifiant un pourceau. (IV, 33)

Most important of all are the similarities in comment which have not been suggested by the text criticized, or in which the authors try to substantiate their criticisms by the commentary of others, or connect with their discussion some other passage of the *Bible*. Of course, these resemblances taken singly do not necessarily prove the common origin of the two works. We are led to suspect, however, that their frequency of occurrence is not to be attributed to mere coincidence. And when verbal similarity exists as well, the conclusion must be drawn that there is a definite, though probably indirect, connection between the two works. Thus in discussing the first verse of the first chapter of Deuteronomy, both critics find it absurd that Moses, who is supposed to be writing this book, speaks of the words which he pronounced on the other side of the Jordan, when it is a well-known fact that he never crossed the Jordan. They then ridicule the suggestion of Dom Calmet and other reputable critics that the term "heber" means "au-delà" and "en-deça," for, if a word is interpreted thus, as having absolutely contradictory meaning, any standard interpretation of the *Bible* is impossible:

> Ne suffit-il pas du simple sens commun pour juger qu'un livre qui commence par ces mots: "Voici les paroles que prononça Moïse au-delà du Jourdain," ne peut être que d'un faussaire maladroit, puisque le même livre assure que Moïse ne passa jamais le Jourdain? La réponse d'Abbadie, qu'on peut entendre en-deça par au-delà, n'est-elle pas ridicule? (XLIII, 49-50)

> Le premier verset du Deutéronome chap. premier est remarquable et il faut [le] rapporter à cause de la quantité de contradic-

tions qu'il contient. "Voicy les paroles que Moyse dit à tout le peuple d'Israël, au-delà du Jourdain, dans une plaine du désert vis à vis de la mer rouge." Premièrement c'est Moyse qui est censé parler icy et avoir écrit le Deutéronome; or il est certain par les écritures qu'il n'a jamais passé le Jourdain. Comment peut-il donc dire icy que ce sont les paroles qu'il prononça au-delà du Jourdain: On donne à cela deux solutions plus absurdes que la difficulté même. Le mot hébreu héber signifie également dit-on en-delà, et en-deçà: si cela est, quel fond peut-on faire sur un livre écrit dans une langue dont le même mot signifie *oui* et *non*? (I, 102)

In the opinion of Voltaire and Mme du Châtelet, the Israelites should have taken possession of fertile Egypt instead of fleeing from the Egyptians and running into the wilderness:

C'était bien alors que le prétendu Moïse devait s'emparer de ce beau pays (Egypt), au lieu de s'enfuir en lâche et en coquin . . . avec deux ou trois millions d'hommes parmi lesquels il avait, dit-on, six cent trente mille combattants. (XLIII, 54)

Il faut avouer que c'étoit bien la peine de faire tant de miracles et tant de mal aux hommes pour faire sortir les Israëlites d'un beau et bon pays comme l'égipte, pour les faire errer quarante ans dans les déserts de l'Arabie; et qu'il est plaisant de voir plus de six cent mille hommes fuyant devant pharaon, et errans dans les déserts pendant quarante ans, le tout par les soins du Dieu tout puissant. N'étoit-il pas plus court et plus expédient de leur donner tout d'un coup l'Egipte dont Dieu avoit presque détruit tout le peuple à force de miracles. (I, 116-117)

Both remark that Rahab is listed in Christ's genealogy:

Et remarquons en passant que cette femme, nommé Rahab la paillarde, est une des aieules de ce Juif dont nous avons fait depuis un Dieu. (XLIII, 67)

Au reste, cette Rahab eut non seulement l'honneur d'être incorporé au peuple hébreu, mais encore celui d'être ayeule du Messie, et rappellée dans sa généalogie. (II, 2-3)

Both cry out in horror against the blasphemy of attributing to the Deity the carnage committed by Joshua and the Hebrews against the inhabitants of Canaan:

L'auteur, pour ajouter le blasphême au brigandage et à la barbarie ose dire que toutes ces abominations se commettaient au nom de Dieu, par ordre exprès de Dieu, et étaient autant de sacrifices de sang humain offerts à Dieu. (XLIII, 67)

Enfin l'auteur las de raconter tant de meurtres dit au v. 40, "que Josué ravagea tout le pays des montagnes et du midi, et qu'il tua tout ce qui avoit vie, suivant l'ordre qu'il en avoit reçu du Seigneur." Il suffit de ce verset 40 pour faire sentir l'horreur de ce livre qu'on nous donne sous le nom d'écriture Sainte, et quelles abominations il met sur le compte de Dieu. (II, 15-16)

Both are astounded that in one place it is said that the Hebrews had neither sword nor lance and in another that Saul with three thousand soldiers had won a big battle:

Il n'y avait dans leur petit pays ni épée ni lance; les Cananéens ou Philistins ne permettaient pas aux Juifs, leurs esclaves, d'aiguiser seulement les socs de leurs charrues et leurs cognées . . . et cependant on nous conte que le roi Saül eut d'abord une armée de trois cent mille hommes, avec lesquels il gagna une grande bataille. (XLIII, 71)

Il n'y a rien de si extraordinaire que ce qui est marqué au v. 19, "qu'il n'y avoit point de forgerons alors dans Israël; que les Philistins les avoient ôtés aux Hébreux, crainte qu'ils ne se forgeassent des épées et des lances, et qu'il n'y avoit que Saül et Jonathas qui eussent des armes . . . où les Israëlites prenoient-ils donc des armes pour combattre? de quoi les trois mille hommes que Saül choisit au commencement de ce chap. 11, v. 11, avoient secouru Jabès de Galaad. . . . (II, 49-50)

They treat the opening chapter of Hosea in similar fashion, quoting from the Vulgate, stressing that Hosea obeyed with alacrity, and making the same comment about the price he paid for his adulterous woman:

Ici c'est Osée à qui Dieu ordonne de prendre une p . . . et d'avoir des fils de . . . Vade, sume tibi etc. . . . dit la Vulgate. Osée obéit ponctuellement. . . . (XLIII, 77)

Dieu lui ordonne de prendre pour sa femme une prostituée, et d'en avoir des enfans de prostitution. . . . Vade sume tibi etc. . . . On ne sait guères comment des enfants de prostitution sont faits; mais apparemment qu'Osée le savoit, car il obéit. (III, 130)

Cela ne suffit pas au Dieu des Juifs : il veut qu'Osée couche avec une femme qui ait fait déjà son mari cocu : Il n'en coûte au prophête que quinze drachmes et un boisseau et demi d'orge ; c'est assez bon marché pour un adultère. (XLIII, 77)

Dieu lui ordonne au chap. 3, d'aimer une femme adultère, comme le Seigneur aime les enfants d'Israël, quoiqu'ils aiment d'autres Dieux. Osée acheta une femme adultère quinze pièces d'argent et deux mesures de froment, ce qui n'est pas cher, si elle étoit jolie. (III, 131)

They note Luke's exaggeration in stating that Augustus took a census of the whole world:

Je dirais à Luc : Comment oses-tu avancer que Jésus naquit sous le gouvernement de Cyrinus ou Quirinus, tandis qu'il est avéré que Quirinus ne fut gouverneur de Syrie que plus de six ans après ? Comment as-tu le front de dire qu'Auguste avait ordonné *le dénombrement de toute la terre* et que Marie alla à Bethléem pour se faire dénombrer ? Le dénombrement de toute la terre ! Quelle expression ! (XLIII, 105)

Premièrement aucun historien, ne parle de ce dénombrement, qui eut été cependant assés remarquable ; secondement il n'y a jamais eu de Cyrinus gouverneur de Syrie. Mais en supposant que le nom de Cyrinus fut celui de Quirinus corrompu, on n'en est pas plus avancé ; car il n'y eut point de Quirinus gouverneur de Syrie pendant le règne d'Hérode, ni par conséquent du tems de la naissance de Jésus-Christ. Enfin, pour comble de ridicule, St. Luc dit v. 2 que ce dénombrement fut le premier qu'on fit sous le gouvernement de Cyrinus, comme si Auguste avait fait faire tous les jours le dénombrement des habitans *de toute la terre*. (IV, 139)

Finally, both stress the folly of Ananias and Sapphira in giving all their savings to the apostles :

Mais je ne passe point à Simon Pierre Barjone d'avoir fait mourir de mort subite Ananie et sa femme Saphire, deux bonnes créatures, qu'on suppose avoir été assez sottes pour donner tous leurs biens aux apôtres. Leur crime était d'avoir retenu de quoi subvenir à leurs besoins pressants. (XLIII, 158)

Ce chapitre contient l'histoire d'Ananie et de Saphire, qui est assurément très révoltante. Ces pauvres gens sont assés sots pour vendre un petit bien qu'ils avoient, et pour en porter le prix aux apôtres, avec la sage précaution, cependant, d'en garder une partie pour eux, en cas de besoin, et ils sont tous deux unis de mort par St. Pierre. (V, 9)

There seems to be no reason for not believing that the *Sermon des cinquante* was written somewhere around 1749 as Voltaire indicated and that at least a first draft of the *Examen important de Milord Bolingbroke* was composed between 1736 and 1746 as he also indicated.[25] Both works show evident signs of having had their origin in the Cirey Period and a close relationship to the *Examen de la Genèse* of Mme du Châtelet. Then how about the *Bible enfin expliquée*? Was it also inspired by the Cirey atmosphere? Voltaire himself gives absolutely no hint concerning the *Bible enfin expliquée*. When it was published in July 1776 it was not even accompanied by a preface. Grimm, in the *Correspondance littéraire* for September 1776 (Ed. Tourneux II, 348), relates that it was the product of Cirey, where every morning a chapter of the *Bible* was read and commented upon by those present (See *supra*, p. 44). According to Grimm, it was Voltaire who constituted himself the "rédacteur" of these discussions. Grimm's story was repeated, as we have shown above, by George Avenel with some modifications in the *Edition du Siècle* of Voltaire's works. Avenel, however, did not cite Grimm as his source; indeed, he gave no source at all. According to Avenel, Voltaire and Mme du Châtelet made notes of these impromptu discussions, whence came two manuscripts: the unpublished work of Mme du Châtelet, and a manuscript

---

[25] Thus the *Sermon des cinquante* (1746-52) would appear to be a later work than the first draft of the *Examen important* (1736-46). In reality, the former work is a more finished product, more unified and more compact than the latter. On the other hand, the biblical criticism of the latter is more voluminous and closer to that of the *Examen de la Genèse*. The history of the establishment of Christianity, absent from the *Examen de la Genèse,* merely sketched at the end of the *Sermon,* is detailed at considerable length in the *Examen important*. It is this portion of the *Examen important* which makes the date 1766 appear plausible, and which in all probability was added after 1752. The "de Milord Bolingbroke" seems to have been inserted in the title after 1752, probably after the *Défense de Milord Bolingbroke,* or after the publication of the *Philosophical Works* in 1754-55.

which "servit de noyau à la *Bible enfin expliquée.*" Beuchot,
having already told the story related by Avenel, and probably
basing his statement upon Voltaire's letter to Mme du Deffand
and an acquaintance with Mme du Châtelet's manuscript, adds
the remark: "Il n'y a pas, ce me semble, grande témérité à croire
que Voltaire n'avait pas été étranger à cet écrit de Mme du
Châtelet; et il ne serait pas étonnant que les deux ouvrages continssent quelquefois les mêmes remarques" (Beuchot XLIX, 4).
Although these three stories concerning the inception of the
Bible enfin expliquée contain points in common, they are not
sufficiently similar to warrant the belief that they all proceed
from Grimm. It should be noted also that Grimm presented his
account of it as a rumor, not as a fact (*Cf.* On nous a assuré,
etc.). None the less his remark that the work was composed as
"le fruit des loisirs de Cirey" merits some attention. Avenel's
statement that the Cirey draft "servit de noyau" should also be
considered, since there are passages in the *Bible enfin expliquée*
which could not have been written in the Cirey Period.

The full title of the work was *La Bible enfin expliquée par
plusieurs aumôniers de S. M. L. R. D. P.* There has always been
some discussion concerning the meaning of the enigmatic
L. R. D. P. Grimm (Ed. Tourneux II, 327) interpreted the
letters as standing for "le roi de Prusse." So did Condorcet
(Moland L, 98-99), the author of the note in Bachaumont's
Mémoires secrets (IX, 280), and Wagnière (*Mémoires sur
Voltaire,* I, 394). D'Alembert is less precise in his statement
concerning them. On December 30, 1776, he wrote to Frederick
(*Œuvres,* 1805, XVIII, 96-97):

On a imprimé, je ne sais comment, et je ne sais où, un ouvrage
assez curieux intitulé *La Bible enfin expliquée . . . par plusieurs
aumôniers de sa majesté le roi de P.* Vous devinez, Sire, qui est ce
roi-là. . . . Votre majesté, ne pourrait-elle pas lui (Voltaire) rendre le service de faire dire par son ministre au premier président et
aux gens du roi que cet ouvrage maudit est en effet celui de ses
aumôniers, qui se sont amusés à cette besogne, pour soulager
l'oisiveté profonde où V. M. les laisse?

Frederick declined (Moland L, 186) to do this small favor for Voltaire. Whether D'Alembert, however, meant to imply Frederick or Stanislas by the "vous devinez, Sire, qui est ce roi-là" cannot be determined. His letter merely indicates that at one moment Voltaire wished to have the initials interpreted as "le roi de Prusse." Voltaire, however, quickly changed his mind and in the third edition (Londres [Genève] 1777) added an "avertissement," explaining that four scholarly theologians of the palatinate of Sandomir (Poland) composed the work first in Latin at Frankfort-on-the-Oder in 1773 and that a member of the Berlin Academy translated it into French. To this "avertissement" another paragraph was added in the Kehl edition (1784) stating that the four letters did not refer to the "roi de Prusse," as many had thought. Later critics have had divergent opinions upon their interpretation, Beuchot believing them to refer to the "roi de Pologne," and Bengesco, to the "roi de Prusse."

In all probability they mean both the "roi de Pologne" and the "roi de Prusse," and were selected by Voltaire as initials precisely because they could be interpreted both ways. The work being published in 1776, it was perfectly natural for critics of the time, who were very familiar with the relations of Voltaire and Frederick, to interpret them as "le roi de Prusse." This interpretation was abetted by Voltaire who inserted in the commentary the following note:

Le commentateur, qui avait entrepris de continuer cet ouvrage, s'est arrêté ici: ayant été appelé à la cour d'un grand prince pour être son aumônier.

This note, however, did not clarify the title, for if the second commentator became the almoner of Frederick, then obviously both he and the first were almoners of the King of Poland. Voltaire's statement only added confusion to the interpretation, which was exactly what he wished to do, otherwise he would not have used the initials.

But why attribute the work to the almoners of Stanislas? The editors of the Kehl edition (See Moland L, 98) noted the incongruity of ascribing it to an almoner of this pious monarch:

Il n'y aurait eu aucun sel à supposer un commentaire sur la Bible par les aumôniers du roi de Pologne, qui était dévot et avait effectivement des aumôniers ou un aumônier. Pour Frédéric, c'est une autre affaire, et c'est en quoi consiste la plaisanterie de ce titre.

But, there was an element of piquancy in attributing to the almoner of the devout Stanislas a commentary of this nature, for naturally no one would expect it to come from such a source. There is, however, more to the attribution than that. Stanislas in fact, devout as he was, was known to have an almoner reputed to be a free-thinker and even an atheist. Stories even circulated concerning the King's disapproval of him, one of which Desnoiresterres has related (See *Voltaire à la cour,* p. 185). It might be concluded that Voltaire, as usual, was establishing his fiction upon a basis of reality. A conclusion of still more importance might be drawn. In Voltaire's mind there may have been a connection between the inception of the *Bible enfin expliquée* and his experiences at the Court of Lunéville. If the validity of this connection is admitted, the conclusion follows that Voltaire began the *Bible enfin expliquée* in the Cirey Period when he was in close relation with the Court of Stanislas at Lunéville and Commercy, and these logical deductions, in a way, substantiate the reported rumor of Grimm that the published *Bible* was a "fruit des loisirs de Cirey."

The work was begun at Cirey, but was it completed there? One might answer that in reality it was never completed. The unfinished aspect of the *Bible enfin expliquée* was apparent to Condorcet upon its first appearance. On October 6, 1776, he wrote to Voltaire (Moland L, 98-99):

Il m'est tombé entre les mains un commentaire des aumôniers du roi de Prusse, sur un livre fort ancien. C'est dommage que le commentaire ne soit pas complet, et que les aumôniers se soient dégoûtés trop vite.

To this comment, Voltaire (Moland L, 105) replied:

J'ai lu comme vous le commentaire des aumôniers. Je ne m'étonne pas qu'ils se soient dégoûtés de leur travail: car, en vérité, le sujet est horriblement dégoûtant, et ceux que leur intérêt attache au texte sont horriblement fripons.

We have already discussed (See *supra,* p. 132) the inability of Voltaire to complete a treatise of this nature. Our present problem is not to investigate the causes of its general incompleteness but to determine how much of it was completed in the Cirey Period. For it is evident even from a casual perusal of the *Bible enfin expliquée* that certain of its commentaries could not have been written until after 1750. The following remark taken from the first pages is a good case in point:

Il a paru, en 1774, un ouvrage sur les six jours de notre création, par le docteur Chrisander, professeur en théologie. (Moland XXX, 5)

Or the reference to Bolingbroke who died in 1751:

C'est avec douleur que nous rapportons, sur cet événement, les réflexions du Lord Bolingbroke, lesquelles M. Mallet fit imprimer après la mort de ce Lord. (XXX, 125)

Obviously, revision of the original Cirey manuscript was made before publication in 1776. Was this revision, however, limited to a small number of insertions throughout the work or did Voltaire stop at a certain point, lay it aside, and resume it at a later date? The answer to this query is particularly difficult. If Voltaire's own statement quoted above can be taken at its face value, the commentary was discontinued in 1750 in the midst of the discussion upon Solomon and resumed only after his arrival at Potsdam. If this were true, approximately two-thirds of the *Bible enfin expliquée* were written during the Cirey Period. Then it was laid aside until around 1775 when Voltaire, deciding to publish it as a blast against the Abbé Guénée, as Maynard and Beuchot both indicate, made revisions and additions, though probably not very extensively.

Beuchot remarked that it would not be surprising if Voltaire's *Bible enfin expliquée* and Mme du Châtelet's *Examen de la Genèse* sometimes contained the same remarks. And indeed, numerous passages in the two treatises are similar, but this fact should not confuse the issue. Since both set out to give a criticism of events in the *Bible,* it is to be expected that they will often parallel each other in their reactions to the material. It would be almost impossible to comment upon many of these events in a negative way without using the classic arguments adduced by such writers as Spinoza, Fréret, Bayle, Mirabaud, Boulainvilliers, Dumarsais, not to mention a correspondingly large group of English Deists. For example, it is hardly possible to take up the subject of Joshua's command to the sun to stand still without making the classic observation that the sun does not move around the earth. We might cite many other instances of like nature. On the other hand, there are other commentaries more or less personal in nature which would not be anticipated by other critics of the same event. These usually express a curious attitude, or imply a special reaction, or involve a special combination of ideas. For example. a critic in dealing with the passage in Deuteronomy which infers that human sacrifice was practiced by the Hebrews might readily condemn the practice, but would hardly refer to Dom Calmet's defense of the point, unless he had a special interest in Dom Calmet's commentary. For this reason it seems that no especial significance should be attached here to the similarity in viewpoint and attitude of Voltaire and Mme du Châtelet. They both definitely set out to discredit the events of the *Bible,* but so did Meslier, Fréret, the "Militaire philosophe," and many others. To be sure, the general similarity of their successive comments lends support to the assumption that the two works are related. But it should not be accepted as proof that they are.

Nevertheless, *La Bible enfin expliquée* and the *Examen de la Genèse* contain several comments not often made by other critics. Voltaire and Mme du Châtelet assert that the Hebrew text of

Genesis differs from the Vulgate in having "Dei creaverunt" instead of "Deus creavit," Mme du Châtelet citing Dom Calmet as authority for her assertion. They both cite this as evidence that the early Jews were polytheists rather than monotheists, and come back to it again in discussing the serpent's conversation with Eve. They are somewhat unique among eighteenth-century biblical critics in turning their attention to the primitive vulgarity of the *Bible* though each arrives at different conclusions concerning this point. In Voltaire's opinion the author of the Pentateuch related his events in such a way that the Jews might understand them, adapting himself accordingly to the barbarity and vulgarity of a primitive race. Mme du Châtelet, on the other hand, declares that the vulgarity of the Old Testament was inexcusable under any circumstances. Both writers insist upon the physical impossibility of the Flood, a subject previously treated at length in the *Histoire ancienne* of Boulainvilliers, who in all probability took it from Burnet's *Theoria sacra telluris*. But the two Cirey critics concerned themselves particularly with the "cataracts" in the sky, a point to which Voltaire returned in other works like the *Sermon des cinquante* and the *Examen important*. Apparently the study of physics at Cirey had intensified their interest in this explanation of the Flood which was so contrary to laws of science. As a matter of fact, both the *Bible enfin expliquée* and the *Examen de la Genèse* criticise with vigor any incident which occurred contrary to the new physics. The formation of the sun four days after the creation of light, the peculiar separation of light from darkness, the explanation of the rainbow as miraculous, and the stopping of the sun in its course, all violate the rules of physics, and therefore assume for Voltaire and Mme du Châtelet an added importance. Interested as they were in Newton and Leibnitz they probably objected more seriously to these unscientific phenomena than to anything else in the *Bible*.

Both critics note that man and woman were created twice. They recall that the relationship between the Tree of Life and the Tree of Knowledge has been a constant source of embarrassment for commentators. They raise a logical objection to the difficulty that Adam would have in naming the animals. They ask what language the serpent spoke to Eve and, more important still, they reject the allegorical interpretation of the story. They aver that the relationship of Adam to the Deity in the story of the Fall is that of servant to master and stress particularly the irony with which God spoke to Adam. This comment, never made to my knowledge in the criticisms of the time, is especially worthy of notice :

L'ironie amère dont il se sert en leur parlant cette fois, est de la même vérité. Il eût été trop hardi à l'écrivain sacré de mettre dans la bouche de Dieu ces paroles insultantes, si Dieu ne les avait pas effectivement prononcées. (I, 15)

Mais ce qu'il y a surtout de remarquable, c'est la façon dont Dieu parle à Adam et à Eve après leur désobéissance. Il s'abaisse à se moquer d'Adam, et à insulter à son malheur. (I, 8)

More in common with the usual criticism is their mutual remark that serpents don't eat earth. They both express surprise at Cain's fear of being killed when he had no possible adversary except Adam, a point treated at length in the *Preuves* and with which Boulainvilliers also was intrigued. The statement of Lamech they find incomprehensible. They likewise recall that the story of the Fallen Angels was related by St. Jude and incorporated in Jewish tradition at a late date. They condemn as unjust the punishment of animals for the sins of man, Mme du Châtelet dwelling upon this injustice and endeavoring to show that in Jewish philosophy man and beast shared alike. In her discussion concerning the ten plagues of Egypt she returns to this latter point which is very rarely mentioned by the other biblical critics. Unusual also is the comment upon God's making a pact with man and beast alike, which both Voltaire and Mme du Châtelet have noted. They both remark that people had already begun to speak different languages before the episode of the tower of Babel, for the earth had been divided among the sons of Noah on a language basis. They find the account of God descending to the tower of Babel absurd. They pronounce Abraham's conduct in regard to Sarah and the King of Egypt reprehensible, and his treatment of Hagar, cruel, both caustically remarking that there was no purpose in having an angel bring Hagar back a first time just to have her driven out a second. They recall that God's refusal to be seen face to face is contradicted later when Moses is said to have seen Him face to face. They express astonishment that the Jews were not circumcised in the desert, and are amazed that Joshua chose the moment to do so in an unfriendly country when his people might expect an attack at any time. They both speak of the unreasonable fancies of Lot's daughters. They affirm that money was not used by the Jews in Moses's time, although he speaks of Abraham's paying four hundred pieces of silver for Sarah's tomb. They condemn Jacob's action toward Esau. And when Jacob receives the blessing of blind Isaac through trickery, they express surprise that the mere words of Isaac should have the power of bestowing the blessing upon Jacob when it was his desire and intention to give it to Esau. They do not fail to mention that Jacob's wife, Rachel, took with her the idols of her father, inferring from this that she was an idolatress.

Mme du Châtelet and Voltaire make a point concerning the "cuisse" of Jacob, which I have never seen in any other criticism, namely, that the Jews remove the nerve from the flank of animals they eat because Jacob in his struggle with the angel was touched in that particular part of the body. Then both remark significantly that nowhere in the *Bible* is there a law to that effect. They find the crime of Simeon horrible; the fact that Potiphar, a eunuch, was married, ridiculous; and the story of Joseph and his brothers "touchante," although they do not fail to call attention to the fact that Joseph, by consulting the dregs in the cup, was a magician just like the Egyptian sorcerers.

They inquire why the Jews who had an army six hundred thirty thousand strong did not seize Egypt, particularly since it had been weakened by plagues and the death of its first-born, and wonder why they were not given its fertile plains instead of the rocky hills of Palestine. The fact that Pharaoh's magicians could compete in miracles with Moses and Aaron does not escape their attention, and they find strange the wandering of the Jews in the wilderness for forty years after they had been granted the Promised Land. The passage concerning the crossing of the Red Sea recalls to them that Josephus substantiated this miracle by relating Alexander's similar experience at the Sea of Pamphilia. They deny that the manna sent from Heaven was miraculous, identifying it with a purgative plant which still exists in Palestine, and which, on this occasion, had lost from continuous usage its purgative force. The reducing of the Golden Calf to powder appears impossible to Voltaire, difficult to Mme du Châtelet; and the slaying of twenty-four thousand Israelites who refused to defend themselves is met on the part of both with utter skepticism. They find most amazing in the whole procedure the fact that Aaron, who made the Golden Calf, was not punished at all. According to Jewish Law, the rabbit was considered impure because it was thought to ruminate and not to have a cloven hoof, while, as both critics point out, it has a cloven hoof and does not ruminate. They note also that the Jews were forbidden to eat animals which do not exist, Mme du Châtelet maliciously remarking that they would have been very much embarrassed if they had been ordered to eat a griffon. They note the passage in Leviticus where human sacrifice is permitted and recall that Jephthah's daughter was sacrificed in accordance with this law.

The contradictory reports of the spies whom Moses sent into Canaan attract the two critics' attention. Voltaire professes ignorance concerning the nature of the fiery serpents. Mme du Châtelet finds them characteristic of the *Arabian Nights*. To substantiate the miracle of Balaam's ass both cite the same passage from Dom Calmet, Voltaire quoting directly and Mme du Châtelet indirectly. They deny that Aaron's family retained

the highpriesthood *in perpetuo*. They both show that the first
verse in the first chapter of Deuteronomy is manifestly false
and quote Calmet's explanation that "heber" means "en-decà" as
well as "au-delà." Both assert that the clothes of the Jewish
children became larger in proportion to their growth when they
were in the desert and refer to St. Justin to substantiate the
assertion. They note that Joshua did not cross the Jordan on the
day appointed but many days later. They mention Calmet's
defense of Rahab, Voltaire quoting directly, Mme du Châtelet
indirectly. They are revolted by Joshua's cruelty at Jericho and
recall that despite his curse the city was rebuilt and existed in
the days of the Judges as well as during the time of the Romans.
They assert that the mention of the pile of stones which are still
at Achan's tomb is proof that the account was written posterior
to the event related. They point out that Joshua's command to
the Jews to choose between Adonai and the gods which their
forefathers worshipped in Mesopotamia is proof that the
patriarchs were idolaters. And they remark that Samgar is
another Samson. Both mention Iphigenia in connection with
Jephthah's daughter, although differently, Voltaire denying
that the biblical incident was the source of the Greek legend as
Dom Calmet maintained, Mme du Châtelet, on the contrary,
affirming that the biblical incident is a poor imitation of the
Greek legend. Both find Samson's marriage with the Philistine
contrary to Jewish Law. They express surprise that in the story
of Tobias the angel Raphael could carry Asmodeus into upper
Egypt and return so quickly, and they recall that Paul Lucas
saw Asmodeus in Egypt. They consider the cure of Tobias's
blindness no more miraculous than its cause and note the joy
with which Tobias's children are said to have buried him. They
find the story of Judith impossible to date, since it is given in
one place as occurring during the reign of Nebuchadnezzar and
in another as happening after the Captivity. The feast of Judith,
they assert, has never been observed by the Jews. In the story of
Esther, Voltaire stops to explain that the word "adorer" means

"to kiss the hand"; Mme du Châtelet explains that it means to "bow." No one, they remark, has ever been able to explain the meaning of Ezekiel's prophecies.

Throughout the *Bible enfin expliquée,* Voltaire attributes his remarks vicariously to the French or English Deists without paying much attention to relaying accurately what they had said or even to whether they had said it. As Professor Morehouse (*op. cit.,* pp. 76-77) has already demonstrated, there is hardly one accurate reference in the whole *Bible enfin expliquée.* Exception, however, should be made for the references to Dom Calmet. Another curious and frequent trick of Voltaire in the *Bible enfin expliquée* is to refer to an indefinite "les critiques disent" without any specific attribution. Mme du Châtelet not infrequently expresses in the same form as Voltaire what these unknown critics are supposed to have said. For instance, in speaking of Simeon's crime (I, 87), Voltaire states that several critics have remarked with astonishment and pain God's failure to resent the massacre of the Shechemites. Mme du Châtelet (I, 30-31) makes precisely this point:

Dieu . . . ne marqua pas le plus petit ressentiment à Lévi et à Siméon, et choisit même dans la suite parmi tout son peuple la famille de Lévi pour lui être particulièrement conservée par le sacerdoce.

Again on the occasion when Joseph counselled his brethren to tell the Egyptians they were shepherds, Voltaire (I, 109) notes that "les critiques ne cessent de dire" that it was bad advice, since shepherds were despised in Egypt. The point had already been made by Voltaire in *Tanis et Zélide; ou Les Rois pasteurs* (1733). Here, however, the critic in question seems to be Mme du Châtelet who wrote (I, 35):

Le conseil qu'il leur donna (*i.e.* Joseph) en arrivant de se dire des pasteurs paroissoit dangereux, car il étoit très imprudent de se charger de la haine que les Egiptiens avoient pour les pasteurs.

Voltaire notes (I, 112) that Joseph was a very bad minister, a ridiculous and extravagant tyrant, to prevent the Egyptians from sowing wheat, "à ce que disent les critiques." Mme du Châtelet follows him very closely in her observation (I, 36) :

Joseph est très injuste envers les Egiptiens. Il leur prend leur argent, leurs bestiaux, et le cinquième de leur bien à perpétuité. Il n'y a pas de plaisir à être gouverné par les patriarches. Les rois d'Egipte pouvoient être obligés à Joseph, mais pour les Egiptiens, il ne pouvoit les traiter plus durement.

Again (I, 128), Voltaire states that "les critiques disent" that in borrowing things from the Egyptians with no intention of returning them, the Jews committed a manifest robbery. Mme du Châtelet calls the Israelites on this occasion robbers in no uncertain terms (I, 42) :

Voilà donc les Israëlites devenus des voleurs, par l'ordre même de Dieu.

Voltaire attributes to "nos critiques" (I, 131) an attitude of horror that God should harden Pharaoh's heart, then punish him for not obeying. This attitude is a leitmotif which runs through Mme du Châtelet's account of the plagues. In one place, it is particularly strong (I, 43) :

Or certainement cette conduite de Dieu est des plus révoltantes. Que diroit-on d'un homme qui commanderoit à un de ses gens, une chose qu'il le mettroit dans l'impossibilité de faire ; car c'est ce que veut dire *indurabo cor ejus*.

Voltaire notes (I, 133) that "les critiques" are bolder in denouncing that part of the Scripture in which innocent animals are punished by plagues than in any other portion of the *Bible*. Why kill the animals? Mme du Châtelet asks the same question (I, 47) :

Mais qu'avoient fait les pauvres bêtes qu'on fait mourir par la peste et par la grêle?

Voltaire, in commenting (I, 171) upon the story concerning the Israelites, who were punished by death for eating quails sent them by God when they murmured against their fare in the wilderness, quotes the "critiques" as saying that it was a perfectly natural action on their part to eat what was sent them. But Voltaire somewhat ironically accepts the explanation that these deaths were caused by eating to excess after a protracted fast:

Les critiques nous disent qu'il n'est pas étrange que des malheureux, n'ayant pour nourriture que la rosée nommée manne, aient demandé à manger; et qu'il paraîtrait cruel de les faire mourir pour cette faute, et pour avoir mangé des cailles que Dieu même leur envoya. Apparemment qu'ils en mangèrent trop; ce qui arrive presque toujours après un long jeûne.

Mme du Châtelet, who makes this point, does not accept the explanation which Voltaire ironically presents (I, 85):

Aussi les Israëlites étoient en droit de croire que puisque Dieu faisoit ce miracle pour leur donner des cailles, c'étoit pour les manger, mais point du tout. . . . On ne peut pas dire que les Israëlites qui moururent dans cette occasion, moururent d'une mort naturelle causée par l'excès des cailles, comme le voudroient quelques interprètes pour sauver la gloire de Dieu. . . .

In speaking of the thirty-two Midianite maidens who were set aside after the others were all taken captive, Voltaire says that the critics ask what happened to them and even dare to suggest that they were sacrificed (I, 196). Madame du Châtelet dared to make a like assertion (I, 100):

De ces vierges Madianites que Dieu réserva, il y en eut trente-deux pour le Seigneur; l'écriture ne dit point ce qu'on en fit. Je meurs de peur qu'elles n'ayent été immolées.

And when Joshua met the heavenly stranger without anything further happening, the critics are reported as asking why he appeared and, since they can find no explanation, declare this apparition useless (I, 218). This attitude was reflected in the *Examen de la Genèse* (II, 5):

C'étoit bien la peine d'apparoître pour faire déchausser Josué.

When the eleven tribes attacked the tribe of Benjamin after the affair of the Levite and his wife, the critics, says Voltaire (I,

271), are astounded that at first the Lord appeared to favor the cause of the Benjamites. Mme du Châtelet also finds this surprising (II, 39):

> . . . mais ce qu'il y a de singulier, c'est que malgré l'infâme action des Benjamites, le Seigneur parut les favoriser dans le commencement. . . .

The story of Tobias, according to Voltaire (II, 443), has aroused the criticism of these "critiques naturalistes" who contend that blindness would not come from such a cause, and, what is more, the accident could have occurred only in case Tobias had been sleeping with his eyes open. The comment of Mme du Châtelet on this occasion is crudely expressed (III, 34):

> Des hirondelles lui ayant chié sur les yeux, il en devint aveugle; apparemment qu'il dormoit les yeux ouverts.

Further on Voltaire notes that the "critiques obstinés" treat the description of the feast in the story of Esther as a scene from the *Arabian Nights*. This was a favorite comparison, as we have seen, for any event which Mme du Châtelet questioned, and she does not fail to use it on this particular occasion (III, 57). Again, the critics observe, says Voltaire, that Haman was an extraordinary idiot to publish abroad throughout the empire the month and day when the slaughter of the Jews would take place (II, 461). Mme du Châtelet has not failed to note this (III, 60):

> Or je demande aux gens les plus prévenus, s'il est vraisemblable qu'on annonçât un an à l'avance, la ruine de toute la nation, qui pouvoit se mettre en deffense, ou former quelque conspiration.

And the horror attributed to the critics (II, 461) over Esther's cruelty is reflected in the *Examen de la Genèse* (III, 67):

> On ne peut lire sans horreur des absurdités si barbares; car cette histoire quoique visiblement fausse, marque quel étoit le génie du peuple juif.

Practically all of Voltaire's commentary upon Nebuchadnezzar and Belshazzar (II, 465) is presented as coming from "les critiques." They call the story a ridiculous puerility, they make great sport of it, and they declare that Nebuchadnezzar had no son named Belshazzar. Mme du Châtelet, indeed, makes all these comments (III, 84-90). She calls it a story "des plus extraordinaires," uses a whole page to show how ridiculous it is, and finally points out that the scriptural account of Belshazzar's lineage is not in accordance with the records of secular writers:

L'Ecriture est terriblement en contradiction avec les auteurs profanes sur ce Baltazar; car elle dit qu'il étoit fils de Nébuchodonozor . . . et les auteurs profanes marquent quatre princes entre Nébuchodonozor et le prince sous lequel l'empire des Assiriens a été détruit.

It is perhaps hazardous to assume that "les critiques disent" refers constantly to Mme du Châtelet's remarks upon the *Bible*. It would seem more reasonable to believe that "the critics" were the people present at the Cirey "déjeuners," and more reasonable still to infer that they may be identified both with those present in person and those represented by their works. Thus, in the widest sense of the word, the *Bible enfin expliquée* is a product of the Cirey atmosphere. It is even probable that numerous passages which begin "Meslier says," or "Fréret says," or "Milord Bolingbroke says," had their origin in that part of the Cirey atmosphere which was actually composed of what Meslier, Fréret, or Bolingbroke wrote or said. That the references do not fit any particular passage in their works should not be surprising. The group around the table at Cirey did not refer in their sprightly and sparkling conversation to those dry deistic treatises. The important thing was not that Meslier, Fréret, and Bolingbroke actually said what was attributed to them, but that the conversation at Cirey was in the same vein as the treatises of these individuals. Voltaire transmitted the spirit of these meetings even though he did not record the commentaries in stenographic fashion, while Mme du Châtelet seems to have restricted herself more to actual stenographic recording. It is quite possible therefore that the *Examen de la Genèse* has in it much of the spirit of Voltaire, while the *Bible enfin expliquée* probably contains but few of the commentaries of Mme du Châtelet. Thus, when both writers remark that the Maccabees are written in a better style than the other books of the *Bible,* and that it is evident that association with the Greeks had improved the civilization of the Jews, we are dealing with a comment which should once for all establish a relationship between the two works:

Nous nous contentons d'observer, qu'en général ils sont écrits d'un style un peu plus humain que toutes les histoires précédentes, et plus approchant quelquefois (si l'on l'ose dïre) de l'éloquence des Grecs et des Romains. (II, 486)

Malgré les contradictions qu'on trouve dans les livres des Machabées, il est certain cependant qu'ils sont beaucoup plus raisonnables, et écrits avec plus d'ordre que les autres livres de la Bible : on y voit un autre stile, et un ton tout différent ; on sent que le commerce des Grecs successeurs d'Alexandre avoit un peu poli ces barbares. (III, 18)

If one has to choose which of the two contributed this comment, it must be admitted that Voltaire is the more likely. And also he seems to have been the originator of the following remark which both made concerning the account of Alexander's succession, given in Maccabees :

Le romanesque auteur commence ses mensonges par dire, qu'Alexandre partagea ses Etats à ses amis dès son vivant. Cette erreur, qui n'a pas besoin d'être réfutée, fait juger de la science de l'écrivain. (II, 488)

Il est dit au v. 7, qu'Alexandre partagea son royaume de son vivant, aux grands de la cour ce qui est affreusement faux. (III, 1)

But one can never be absolutely certain what is Voltaire and what is Mme du Châtelet. The following passage, which one would attribute to Voltaire in view of the fact that he was better acquainted with history than the lady, seems, on the contrary, to belong to Mme du Châtelet, because she is correct, Voltaire wrong :

L'écrivain des Machabées ajoute que cet Antiochus le grand céda aux Romains les Indes, la Médie et la Lydie. Ceci devient trop fort. Une telle impertinence est inconcevable. (II, 489)

Au chap. 8, v. 8, il est dit que les Romains donnèrent à Eumenes le pays des Indiens, des Lydiens, et des Médes: mais il est prouvé que du tems de Juda Machabée, les Romains n'avoient point encore porté leurs armes contre les Médes; et qu'ils ne sont jamais allés jusqu'aux Indes. (III, 5)

Perhaps the fairer way would be not to try to separate the contributions of the two writers or to prove their mutual dependence upon each other. That there was a definite relationship between them seems after the above comparisons incontestable. That the relationship was a close one can be established by comparing the comments of the *Bible enfin expliquée* and the *Examen de la Genèse* on one point, namely, Joshua's command to the sun. This particular point, as we have already stated, has been chosen for commentary by practically all the biblical critics. But it would be difficult to find another critic who presents his series of objections in the same sequence as those of Mme du Châtelet and Voltaire. Each of these authors makes four comments upon the event in exactly the same order: no need for the miracle after the hail of stones had killed the Amorrheans; no need for the miracle since the sun was in the middle of the sky and there was ample time to complete the rout of the few remaining Amorrheans before nightfall; the miracle could not happen since the sun does not turn around the earth; the Book of the Just, which is mentioned as proof of the miracle, proves on the contrary that Joshua did not write the Book of Joshua:

On remarque seulement ici que ces pierres . . . durent écraser tous les Amorrhéens. . . . C'est ce qui fait que plusieurs savants sont étonnés que Josué ait encore eu recours au grand miracle d'arrêter le soleil et la lune. (I, 225)

Qui croiroit après cela que Dieu eut eu encore quelque chose à faire dans cette occasion pour les Israélites contre les Amorrhéens. . . . (II, 12)

Mais tous les autres commentateurs . . . conviennent tous que le soleil et la lune s'arrêtèrent en plein midi. On auroit eu le temps de tuer tous les fuyards depuis midi jusqu'au soir. (I, 225)

Il étoit selon les interprêtes environ dix heures du matin, et au plus midi, selon le texte *in medio cœli* quand Josué commanda au soleil de s'arrêter pour lui donner le temps de deffaire des ennemis déjà vaincus, il faut avouer qu'il étoit d'une grande précaution. (II, 12)

Les physiciens ont quelque peine à expliquer comment le soleil, qui ne marche pas arrêta son cours, et comment cette journée, qui fut le double des autres journées, put s'accorder avec le mouvement des planettes et la régularité des éclipses. (I, 226)

Je ne parle pas de l'absurdité physique de ce miracle. . . . On est aussi un peu embarrassé à expliquer cet ordre que Josué donne au soleil, depuis qu'il est prouvé que ce n'est pas lui qui tourne, mais la terre. . . . (II, 13)

A l'égard du livre des justes, qui est cité comme garant de la vérité de cette histoire, le Lord Bolingbroke insiste beaucoup sur ce livre. . . . Cela démontre, dit-il, que c'est du livre du droiturier que l'histoire de Josué est prise. (I, 226)

Ce que Josué cite ici du livre des Justes, fait voir évidemment que le livre que j'examine et qui porte son nom n'est pas de lui ; car comment pourroit-il citer un livre où l'événement dont il parle, est marqué comme passé. (II, 14)

Thus, while Mme du Châtelet was assiduously acquainting herself with Dom Calmet's *Commentaries,* Woolston's *Discourses on the Miracles,* and the *Religion chrétienne analysée*; in short, while she was preoccupied with assimilating both the French and English biblical criticism of the time, Voltaire also turned his attention in this direction. His education in the methods of critical deism as well as his absorption of deistic ideas dates therefore from the Cirey Period. But there are many indications that he did not limit himself to using them at some indefinite future date. While Mme du Châtelet was composing her *Examen de la Genèse,* he, too, was busy writing treatises which he published at a much later date. Whether he made his draft of the *Religion chrétienne analysée,* the *Examen de la religion,* and the *Extrait de Meslier* at this time cannot be affirmed with certainty, although it seems entirely reasonable to assume that he did so. It is more reasonable still to assume that he was composing treatises or portions of treatises of his own, of his own accord, upon biblical criticism. A search for these works leads to three, all published in the Ferney Period: the *Bible enfin expliquée,* the *Examen important de Milord Bolingbroke,* and the *Sermon des cinquante.* Whatever evidence can be assembled, external as well as internal, leads to the conclusion that Voltaire attempted, contemporaneously with the *Examen de la Genèse* of Mme du Châtelet, a complete analysis of the *Bible* in the *Bible enfin expliquée.* This attempt, which was his first in the field of critical deism, was not successful and he laid it aside, returning to it at intervals, probably in the Berlin Period, to write the part attributed to the third almoner, and in the Ferney Period for a final, but rather cursory, revision before publication in 1776. Having realized his temperamental unfitness for following detail by detail the events of the *Bible* and having laid aside the first draft of the *Bible enfin expliquée,* Voltaire directed his attention to composing the *Examen important de Milord Bolingbroke.* Here he varied his method, and instead of attempting to imitate the very detailed criticism of Mme du Châtelet he now undertook a synthesis in which he could make a selection of his material to prove his points. He made this tentative effort between 1736 and 1746, as he indicated in his published work. But here also he failed, at least for the time being, since once more there is evidence to indicate that he laid aside the work unfinished. But he continued his biblical criticism, this time changing his method again, cutting down the number of points, selecting more carefully his illustrative material, and reducing the size and scope of the work, but increasing its intensity. This time the finished product was the *Sermon des cinquante,* written sometime between 1746 and

1752. Thus, while Mme du Châtelet was criticising at great length the innumerable events from Genesis to the Apocalypse, Voltaire, profiting by her painstaking but none the less tedious assembling of material, had educated himself in the principles of critical deism, had familiarized himself with deistic literature, and, by trial and error, had evolved his method of presenting the same material which attracted the attention of Mme du Châtelet.

CONCLUSION

I T IS clear that any final evaluation of the intellectual activity which took place at Cirey between 1733-49 will have to await further investigation. However, certain tentative remarks may be ventured. One result of this study is the conviction that the period's importance lies not in the romantic love affair of the poet and his Lady Newton, not in the social glamour which intrigued many of their contemporaries, but in an intense intellectual activity. An understanding of this intellectual activity is imperative, for as our knowledge of it increases, the years 1733-49 appear less and less an amorous interlude in the life of the poet, or a futile social venture into the life of the upper nobility and court, or a period of glorious inactivity. Desnoiresterres's two volumes, devoted to the Cirey Period, are primarily responsible for emphasizing its romantic and social aspects, and even Lanson has fallen into the error of stressing the futility of the years at court. In fact, all those who have become interested in this epoch have magnified the picturesque, the anecdotal, and the superficial at the expense of the intellectual.

For this state of affairs there is, as we have shown, considerable justification. All of the contemporary correspondence which referred to Voltaire and to Mme du Châtelet stressed the picturesque, the anecdotal and the superficial. Either, like Mme de Graffigny, people were overawed by the feverish activity which they witnessed; or, like Mme du Deffand or Mme de Staal, they refused to take Mme du Châtelet and Voltaire seriously; or, finally, like the Abbé Leblanc, they were incompetent to judge the intellectual progress of the two. Voltaire himself must be credited with some responsibility for these contemporary impressions, for in his correspondence as well as in his social conduct he veiled his intellectual activity behind a constant flow of witticisms and superficial clowning. Thus, the public was completely ignorant of certain key works of the period such as the *Traité de métaphysique,* or failed to understand others such as the *Mondain,* which to them was a "badinage," or knew nothing of Voltaire's excursions into new fields of thought such as critical deism. Later biographers have merely interpreted the reports left by contemporaries concerning his life at Cirey and ignored his intellectual preoccupations. Add to this the fact that the picturesque is always more attractive if less interesting than the intellectual, and one can readily understand how Voltaire's biographers would have preferred a superficial interpretation to a more intellectual one, even if they had been in a position to give it. Finally it appears evident that the very complexity of the years 1733-49 precluded any but a superficial interpretation. Properly speaking, there is no Cirey Period, unless one wishes to designate by that name the years 1736-40. Hence, for the years 1733-49, there can be no unity of locale, as at Ferney, and unity of activity is equally difficult to establish because of the diversity of interests involved. In reality, only Mme du Châtelet gives unity to these years; in the final analysis it is not a Cirey, it is a Mme du Châtelet Period. Voltaire's biographers, to be sure, have recognized this, but they have overstressed Mme du Châtelet the mistress and forgotten the intellectual activity of the two.

None the less, it is more and more apparent that the picturesque interpretation is insufficient precisely because it explains nothing. Accepting it, one has difficulty in comprehending how a period so superficial in appearance can be so rich in literary and philosophical works. One understands less how there can be such diversity in Voltaire's intellectual activity. And one fails completely in an attempt to understand how this period unites with the preceding two and the two following to give coherence and unity to Voltaire's life. For until now, it has been somewhat generally accepted that the Cirey Period was an interlude which in no way explained the continuity of Voltaire's thought and interests from the English Period to the Berlin. Indeed, it has been assumed that the years 1733-49 were characterized by a break in the continuity of his development. Hence a whole series of assumptions to explain this discontinuity: the old assumption that Voltaire's life can be divided into a literary epoch (1719-50) and a philosophic epoch (1750-78); Lanson's assumption that it was only at Berlin in the "soirées de Potsdam" that Voltaire's religious impiety and philosophical daring developed; or finally, the assumption that he turned to a systematic consideration of critical deism only in 1762 after his establishment at Ferney.

The present study tends to prove the very opposite of this commonly accepted view. It has attempted to show that the Cirey Period grows logically out of Voltaire's youth and English sojourn and leads just as logically to the Berlin and Ferney years. It is evident from the meager details which we have been able to assemble that the Cirey Period is philosophical as well as literary, that it is replete with religious impiety and philosophical daring, and distinguished in part by biblical criticsm. Moreover it is solidly grounded in the traditional French movement which had been evolving since 1710. It is enriched by English thought which Voltaire brought back from England, as well as by English thought which was already finding its way across the Channel. And it is broadened by the clandestine philosophical movement which was taking place in France. Out of these three movements, represented by numerous writers, philosophers, scientists, and literary works, Voltaire and Mme du Châtelet created an atmosphere which is neither out of harmony with what had gone before nor with what followed. It is characterized by growth, evolution, expansion, but especially by broadened intellectual interests and feverish intellectual activity.

The main lines of this activity are now apparent and the contributions of its two important initiators made more distinct. Only in the drama which Voltaire produced between 1732-49 does the influence of Cirey seem negligible. He received his impetus in this field of activity from Corneille and Racine, from Shakespeare, and to a small extent from Destouches and Nivelle de la Chaussée. The critical assistance which he received came from D'Argental rather than from Mme du Châtelet.

However, credit must be given the lady for turning Voltaire to a serious consideration of metaphysics. Not that he was unfamiliar with metaphysical problems before his liaison with Mme du Châtelet began. But she, by making her own inventory in this realm of thought, encouraged him to make his, and in doing so, he began discussing problems which previously appeared to him of little consequence. Once he had received this impetus, there are reasons to believe that he strongly felt influences other than those of Mme du Châtelet. His interest in Locke, Newton, and Clarke became intensified. And, by a reaction, he was attracted by the materialistic clandestine writers of the time. The central problem became for him, as it was apparently for Mme du Châtelet, the doctrine of free-will. He chose to follow Locke and Clarke in preference to the clandestine materialists. But Frederick precisely at this time preferred the materialists, and a lengthy debate ensued. A field opened for Voltaire by Mme du Châtelet became suddenly enriched by Locke and Clarke, and possibly by Malebranche, and the Cirey interests were broadened and considerably modified by Frederick.

In science, the story was somewhat different. Here Mme du Châtelet's contribution was paramount. Not only did she turn Voltaire to the study of physics, but she guided him in his studies from Leibnitz to Newton. Never did she relinquish the lead in this field. Voltaire, however, though he could but follow, broadened it, and, to some extent, modernized it. To his study of Leibnitz whom he could not understand, and to New-ton whom he only partially understood, he added his contempo-raries Castel, Mairan, and Maupertuis.

In moral philosophy, on the other hand, Voltaire was the leader, Mme du Châtelet, the pupil, though the fundamental equipment of both was the same, a knowledge of Cicero. But Voltaire had had the English experience and was acquainted with Pope, if not Mandeville. Moreover, his interest in moral philosophy was grounded in the experiences of his youth. Out-side influences are also felt here. The central problem is "bon-heur," and Helvétius, La Mettrie, Mme du Châtelet, and Voltaire, not to mention Pope and Mandeville, are all seeking "bonheur." Besides, it was the primary problem of moral phi-losophy in the first half of the eighteenth century, in England as well as in France.

In history, Voltaire has to find his way, encouraged but un-aided by Mme du Châtelet whose interest was purely incidental and whose critical historical sense was negative. Here the influ-ences are all external to Cirey: Bayle, whose position was in the main that of Mme du Châtelet, Lenglet, the Président Hénault, Montesquieu, and perhaps Middleton. And yet, it is unwise at this time to assume that Voltaire had to depend upon purely external influences for his inspiration in history, since our present information concerning his historical activity is very inadequate. If Hénault and others led him to write the history of Louis XIV and Louis XV, it was Mme du Châtelet who reputedly turned him to the philosophic writing of history. And there is some ground for the belief that his philosophy of history was immeasurably influenced by his entrance into the field of critical deism.

In the field of critical deism, there is a strong presumption that Mme du Châtelet is the leader. And yet, one cannot be too sure, for there are also reasons to believe that Voltaire is fur-nishing the criticism and Mme du Châtelet is doing the tran-

scription. At any rate, they are getting acquainted with Woolston, Calmet, Meslier, and the clandestine critics together, and
while she is writing the *Examen de la Genèse,* he is composing
portions of the *Bible enfin expliquée,* at least the first half of the
Examen important, and the *Sermon des cinquante.* To be sure,
there are external influences here: Calmet and Woolston and
Meslier, and a fair number of clandestine manuscripts, among
them the *Examen de la religion,* the *Religion chrétienne analysée,* the *Notes,* the *Preuves,* and portions of the *Examen critique
des apologistes de la religion chrétienne,* and the *Examen critique du Nouveau Testament.* But the one fundamental influence is Mme du Châtelet's *Examen de la Genèse.*

Thus the atmosphere of Cirey is a queer mixture of sudden
enthusiasms, feverish activity, much confusion, and many external influences. The external influences can be easily detected.
In metaphysics, they come from Locke, Newton, Clarke, Malebranche, and Frederick; in physics, from Newton, Leibnitz,
Castel, Mairan, and Maupertuis; in moral philosophy, from
Cicero, Pope, Mandeville, Helvétius, and La Mettrie; in history,
from Bayle, Lenglet, and Hénault; in critical deism, from
Calmet, Woolston, and the clandestine writers. The rôles of
these individuals in the formation of the Cirey atmosphere are
still not too clear, although their general contribution to it is
readily apparent. On the other hand, we should now have a better
acquaintance with the two powerful contributors of sudden
enthusiasm, Voltaire and Mme du Châtelet. Sometimes the
honor for inaugurating an enthusiasm seems to rest with Voltaire, as in the case of drama, moral philosophy, and history;
sometimes with Mme du Châtelet, as in the case of metaphysics,
physics, and biblical criticism. But it is, in the present state of
literary history, difficult to apportion to each his exact share in
this intellectual activity. Nor is it really desirable to do so. No
one would care to prove today that Mme du Châtelet was a great
writer and a great thinker. It is more important to know in what

ways she contributed to making Voltaire a greater writer and a greater thinker. It is significant that by 1749, at the age of fifty-five, Voltaire had completed his education. Never thereafter did he enter new intellectual fields. And when in later years his views on certain particular subjects shifted somewhat, he still based them on the same material which he and Mme du Châtelet had assembled in the Cirey Period.

BIBLIOGRAPHY

BIBLIOGRAPHY

Asse, E., *Lettres de la Marquise du Châtelet,* Paris, s. d.

Audra, L., *L'Influence française dans l'œuvre de Pope,* Paris, 1931.

Ballantyne, A., *Voltaire's Visit to England,* London, 1893.

Barbier, E., *Journal* [Ed. 1856].

Barr, M. M., *A Bibliography of Writings on Voltaire, 1825-1925,* New York, 1929.

Bellessort, A., *Essai sur Voltaire,* Paris, 1925.

Bengesco, G., *Bibliographie des œuvres de Voltaire,* Paris, 1882-90, 4 vols.

Busson, H., *La Pensée religieuse française de Charron à Pascal,* Paris, 1933.

Capefigue, J. B., *La Marquise du Châtelet et les amies des philosophes du XVIIIe siècle,* Paris, 1868.

Caussy, F., *Inventaire des manuscrits de la bibliothèque de Voltaire,* Paris, 1914.

Champion, E., *Voltaire, Etudes critiques,* Paris, 1893.

Colet, L., "Mme du Châtelet," in *R. D. M.,* 1845.

Collé, C., *Journal et mémoires,* Paris, 1868, 3 vols.

D'Argenson, M., *Journal et mémoires,* Paris, 1859-67, 9 vols.

Desnoiresterres, G., *Voltaire et la société française au XVIIIe siècle,* Paris, 1871-76, 8 vols.

Du Châtelet, E., *Examen de la Genèse* etc., [Troyes 2376, 2377, 2378]

Du Châtelet, E., *Institutions de physique,* Paris, 1740.

Du Châtelet, E., *Principes mathématiques de la philosophie naturelle* [traduits de l'anglais de Newton], Paris, 1759, 2 vols.

Graffigny, Mme de, *Vie privée de Voltaire et de Mme du Châtelet,* Paris, 1820.

Grimm, F., *Correspondance littéraire* [Ed. Tourneux].

Hamel, F., *An Eighteenth-century Marquise,* New York, 1911.

Havard, J. A., *Voltaire et Mme du Châtelet,* Paris, 1873.

Havens, G. R., & Torrey, N. L., "Voltaire's Books: A Selected List," in *M. P.,* 1929 (XXVII).

Hénault, C., *Mémoires*, Paris, 1854.

Hoffman, A., *Voltaires stellung zu Pope*, Königsberg, 1913.

Jovy, E., *Quelques lettres inédites de la M*ᵗˢᵉ *du Châtelet et de la Duchesse de Choiseul*, Paris, 1906.

La Beaumelle, A., *Réponse au supplément du Siècle de Louis XIV*, Colmar, 1754.

La Beaumelle, A., *Lettres de Monsieur de la Beaumelle à M. de Voltaire*, Londres, 1763.

Lanson, G., *Voltaire*, Paris, 1910.

Lanson, G., "Questions diverses sur l'histoire de l'esprit philosophique en France avant 1750," in *R. H. L.*, 1912.

Ledeuil d'Enquin, J., *La Marquise du Châtelet et le passage de Voltaire*, Semur, 1892.

Lepan, E., *Vie politique, littéraire et morale de Voltaire*, Paris, 1819.

Libby, M., *The Attitude of Voltaire to Magic and the Sciences*, New York, 1935.

Longchamp, S. G., [& Wagnière] : *Mémoires sur Voltaire et sur ses ouvrages*, Paris, 1826.

Lounsbury, T., *Shakespeare and Voltaire*, New York, 1922.

Mangeot, G., "Les Réflexions sur le bonheur" in *Mélanges Lanson*, Paris, 1922.

Maurel, A., *La Marquise du Châtelet*, Paris, 1930.

Morehouse, A., *Voltaire and Jean Meslier*, New Haven, 1936.

Morize, A., *Le Mondain et l'apologie du luxe au XVIIIᵉ siècle*, Paris, 1909.

Naves, R., *Voltaire et l'Encyclopédie*, Paris, 1938.

Paillet de Warcy, L., *Histoire de la vie et des ouvrages de Voltaire*, Paris 1824.

Patterson, H. T., "Voltaire's 'Traité de métaphysique'," *M. L. R.*, 1938, pp. 261-266.

Pellissier, G., *Voltaire philosophe*, Paris, 1906.

Piot, C., *Cirey-le-château*, Paris, 1894.

Ritter, E., "Le Sermon des cinquante" in *R. H. L.*, 1900 (VII), 315.

Sonet, E., *Voltaire et l'influence anglaise*, Rennes, 1926.

Torrey, N. L., *Voltaire and the English Deists*, New Haven, 1929.

Voisenon, C., *Œuvres complètes*, Paris, 1781, 5 vols.

Voltaire, F. M. A. de, *Œuvres complètes*, Paris, 1882 ff., 52 vols.

Wade, I., "The Epître à Uranie," in *P. M. L. A.,* 1932 (XLVII).

Wade, I., *The Clandestine Organization and Diffusion of Philosophic Ideas in France from 1700 to 1750,* Princeton, 1938.

Woolston, T., *Discours sur les miracles de Jésus Christ,* s. d. [dix-huitième siècle] n. l.

APPENDICES

APPENDIX I

(1)

Works with which Voltaire was familiar during the Cirey Period as seen in his *Correspondance*:

Adlerfelt: *Histoire militaire de Charles XII.* 1740. (XXXV, 506)

Algarotti: *Il Neutonismo per le dame.* (XXXIV, 487)

Anson: *Voyage.* (XXXVII, 8)

Aubert de la Chesnaie: *Lettre à Mme la Comtesse D***.* 1734. (XXXV, 245)

Banier: *La Mythologie et les fables expliquées par l'histoire.* (XXXIV, 410)

Banières, J.: *Examen et réfutation des Eléments de la philosophie de Newton.* (XXXV, 323)

Bayer: *Histoire de la Bactriane.* (XXXVI, 94)

Beausobre: *Dissertation.* (XXXIV, 295)

Boerhaave: *Chimie.* (XXXIV, 253, 272)

Boerhaave: *Institutions.* (XXXV, 58)

Bonneval: *Lettre de M. de B. sur la critique des Lettres Philosophiques.* (XXXV, 22)

Bougeant: *L'Amusement philosophique sur le langage des bêtes.* (XXXV, 226, 235)

Bouhier: *Poème de Pétrone sur la guerre civile.* (XXXV, 269)

Boulainvilliers: *Vie de Mahomet.* (XXXV, 560)

Boullier: *Défense de Pascal.* (XXXVI, 62)

Bourzeis: *Traité des droits de la reine.* (XXXV, 207)

Boyle: *De Ratione inter ignem et flammam.* (XXXIV, 292)

Bremond (Trans.): *Transactions philosophiques.* (XXXV, 260)

Buffon. *Histoire naturelle.* (XXXVII, 37)

Cantemir: *Histoire ottomane.* (XXXV, 210)

Cassini: *Histoire de l'astronomie.* (XXXIV, 62)

Castel: *Traité de la pesanteur.* (XXXIV, 170)

Castel: *Mathématique universelle abrégée.* (XXXIV, 282)

Castel: *Traité de la pesanteur universelle.* 1724, 2 vols. (XXXIV, 439)

Castel: *Lettres philosophiques sur la fin du monde.* 1736. (XXXIV, 440)
Castel: *Lettre sur le vide.* (XXXV, 258)
Castel: *Optique des couleurs.* 1740. (XXXV, 401)
Caylus: *Frétillon.* (XXXVI, 533)
Choisy, Abbé de: *Comtesse des Barres.* (XXXIV, 138)
Cicero: *De Divinatione.* (XXXIV, 435)
Clairaut: *Eléments de géométrie.* (XXXV, 346)
Clément (à Dreux): *Conte.* (XXXVI, 313)
Corneille, T.: *Comte d'Essex.* (XXXIV, 375)
Crébillon: *L'Histoire japonaise.* 1734. (XXXIII, 472)
Crébillon: *Catilina.* (XXXVII, 3)
Crébillon: *Rhadamiste.* (*id.*)
Crébillon: *Electre.* (*id.*)
Crébillon: *Sémiramis.* (*id.*)
Crébillon, fils: *L'Ecumoire.* 1734. 2 vols., in-12. (XXXIII, 475)
D'Alembert: *Réflexions sur la cause générale des vents.* (XXXVI, 473)
Dampierre: *Histoire des vents.* (XXXIV, 467)
Dangeau: *Mémoires.* 40 vols. (XXXV, 30)
D'Argens: *Lettres juives.* (XXXIV, 204, 281)
D'Argens: *La Philosophie du bon sens.* (XXXV, 501)
D'Argens: *Le Mentor Cavalier.* (XXXIV, 138)
D'Argenson: *Considérations sur le gouvernement ancien et présent de la France.* (XXXV, 272)
D'Arnaud: *Coligny.* (XXXV, 423)
Daudet: *Géométrie.* (XXXV, 58)
De Belloy: *Le Siège de Calais.* (XXXV, 306)
De Boissy: *Les Dehors trompeurs.* (XXXV, 423)
Deidier: *Mesure des surfaces et des solides.* 1739. (XXXVI, 32)
De la Chapelle: *Téléphonte.* (XXXIV, 378)
De la Fautrière: *Examen du vide.* 1739. (XXXV, 245)
De la Fayette: *Zaïde.* (XXXV, 334)
De la Martinière: *Introduction à l'histoire générale et politique de l'univers.* (Puffendorf) (XXXVI, 273)
De la Place: *Venise sauvée.* (XXXVI, 472)
Delisle: *Histoire de la mer.* (XXXIV, 467)
De Longue: *Les Princesses Malabares.* 1734. (XXXIII, 475)
Démosthène (grec et latin). (XXXV, 235)
Descartes: *Dioptrique.* (XXXIV, 112)

Desfontaines: *Observations sur les écrits modernes.* (XXXIV, 427, 468, 489)

Desfontaines: *Racine vengé.* (XXXV, 199)

Desmolets: *Mémoires de littérature.* (XXXIII, 513)

Destouches: *Théâtre.* (XXXVI, 360)

D'Herbelot: *Bibliothèque orientale.* (XXXVI, 182)

Diderot: *Lettre sur les aveugles.* (XXXVII, 22)

D'Olivet: *Pensées de Cicéron.* 1744. (XXXVI, 292)

D'Olivet: *Cicéron.* (XXXVI, 577)

Drivetière: *Essai sur l'amour-propre.* (XXXIV, 436)

Dryden, C. (Trans.): *Mémoires du Roi Jacques.* 2 vols., in-4°. (XXXIII, 501)

Dubos: *Réflexions sur la peinture.* (XXXIV, 155)

Dubos: *Réflexions critiques.* (XXXIV, 504)

Du Châtelet: *Institutions physiques.* (XXXV, 29)

Duclos: *Confessions du comte de ***.* (XXXVI, 111)

Duclos: *Histoire de Louis XI.* (XXXVI, 352)

Dufresny: *Le Double veuvage.* (XXXVI, 522)

Duguet: *L'Institution d'un Prince.* (XXXV, 489)

Durand, D.: *Vie de Vanini.* (XXXIV, 2)

Dutot: *Réflexions politiques.* (XXXIV, 487)

Duvaure: *Le Faux savant.* (XXXVII, 51)

Euclide (grec et latin). (XXXV, 235)

Ferrand: *Recueil du Sieur Ferrand.* (XXXIV, 441)

Fontenelle: *Discours.* (XXXVI, 104)

Frederick II. *Titus.* (XXXVI, 259)

Frederick II. *L'Anti-Machiavel.* (XXXV, 354)

Frederick II. *Considérations sur l'état présent de l'Europe.* (XXXIV, 544)

Gamaches: *L'Astronomie physique.* (XXXV, 462)

Gordon: *Discours politiques.* (Introduction to Tacitus). (XXXV. 321)

Gresset: *Edouard III.* (XXXV, 373)

Helvétius: *Epître sur l'amour de l'étude.* (XXXV, 224)

Hénault: *Nouvel abrégé chronologique de l'histoire de France* 1744. (XXXVI, 298)

Hénault: *François II.* (XXXVII, 48)

Hermann: *De Viribus et mortibus corporum.* 1716. (XXXVI, 35)

Horace (Latin). (XXXVI, 422)

Kahle, M.: *Examen du livre intitulé la Métaphysique de Newton, ou Parallèle des sentiments de Newton et de Leibnitz.* 1744. Translator Gauthier de Saint-Blancard. (XXXVI, 309)
Keil: *La Physique.* (XXXIV, 467)
Keil: *Introductio ad veram physicam.* (XXXIV, 380)
La Bletterie: *Vie de l'Empereur Julien.* 1734. (XXXIII, 484)
La Bruère: *Dardanus.* (XXXV, 41)
La Chaussée: *Mélanide.* (XXXVI, 68)
La Chaussée: *Paméla.* (XXXVII, 34)
La Chaussée: *Maximien.* (XXXIV, 445)
La Chaussée: *L'Ecole des maris.* (XXXIV, 282)
La Chaussée: *L'Ecole des mères.* (XXXVI, 291)
Lagrange-Chancel: *Amasis.* (XXXIV, 375)
Languet de Gergy: *Visions de Marie Alacoque.* (XXXIV, 281)
La Noue: *Mahomet II.* (XXXV, 201)
Le Blanc: *Aben-Saïd.* (XXXIV, 31)
Le Febvre: *Bayle en petit.* 1737. (XXXV, 289)
Le Franc: *Lettre de M. Le Franc, avocat général de la cour des aides de Montauban, à M. l'abbé Desfontaines.* (XXXV, 27)
Legendre: *Traité de l'opinion.* (XXXV, 56)
Leibnitz: *Mélanges.* (XXXVI, 63)
Lemery: *Chimie.* (XXXIV, 277)
Lenglet: *Tables chronologiques.* (XXXVI, 228)
Lenglet: *De la méthode pour étudier l'histoire.* (XXXVI, 228)
Linant: *Les Accroissements de la Bibliothèque du Roi.* 1739. (XXXVI, 104)
Mably: *Parallèle des romains et des français.* 1740. (XXXV, 392)
Mairan: *Dissertation sur les phosphores.* 1717. (XXXIV, 380)
Mairan: *Mémoires sur les forces motrices.* (XXXIV, 154)
Mairan: *Mémoire.* (XXXIV, 161)
Mairan: *Lettre de M. de Mairan à Mme du Châtelet.* 1741. (XXXVI, 31)
Mairan: *Mémoire de 1728.* (XXXVI, 32)
Mairan: *Traité physique et historique de l'aurore boréale.* 1733. (XXXIII, 407)
Mairan: *Eloges des académiciens de l'Académie royale des sciences, morts dans les années 1741, 1742, et 1743.* 1747, in-12. (XXXVI, 502)
Malebranche: *Recherche de la vérité.* (XXXIV, 523)
Malésieu: *Eléments de géométrie.* (XXXIV, 14)

Mariotte : *De la Nature de l'air.* (XXXIV, 292)
Mariotte : *Du froid et du chaud.* (XXXIV, 293)
Marmontel : *Aristomène.* (XXXVII, 15)
Marmontel : *Denis le Tyran.* 1748. (XXXVI, 503)
Maupertuis : *La Figure de la terre.* (XXXIV, 483)
Maupertuis : *La Figure des astres.* (XXXIV, 524)
Maupertuis : *Discours à l'Académie.* (XXXVI, 222)
Melon : *Mahmoud le Gasnevide.* 1729. in-8°. (XXXIII, 476)
Melon : *L'Essai sur le commerce.* (XXXIV, 155)
Mermet : *De la Corruption du goût dans la musique française.* 1746.
 (XXXVI, 462)
Milletot : *L'Homme du Pape et du Roi.* (XXXV, 244)
Molières : *Leçons de physique.* 1739. (XXXV, 401)
Moncrif : *Zélindor.* (XXXVI, 377)
Montesquieu : *Lettres persanes.* (XXXVI, 204)
Montesquieu : *Considérations sur les causes de la grandeur et de la
 décadence des Romains.* 1734. (XXXIII, 466)
Morand : *Childéric.* (XXXIV, 282)
Moréri : *Dictionnaire.* 1740. (XXXV, 455)
Musschenbroeck : *Physique.* (XXXIV, 96)
Nadal : *Œuvres.* (XXXV, 121)
Newton : *Optics.* (XXXIV, 126)
Nicéron : *Histoire des hommes illustres.* (XXXIV, 298)
Nicéron : *Mémoires pour servir à l'histoire des hommes illustres de
 la République des lettres.* 1727-45. 43 vols. (XXXIII, 513)
Nordberg : *Histoire de Charles XII.* (XXXV, 510)
Pancirole : *Nova Reperta et Antigua deperdita.* (XXXVI, 83)
Pardies : *Géométrie.* (XXXV, 219)
Pemberton, H. : *A View of Sir Isaac Newton's philosophy.* 1728.
 (XXXIII, 320)
Piron : *La Métromanie.* (XXXIV, 436)
Piron : *Ode sur les miracles.* (XXXIV, 67)
Polinière : *Livre des expériences.* (XXXIV, 302)
Poniatowski : *Remarques d'un Seigneur Polonais.* (XXXVI, 30)
Pont-de-Veyle : *Le Fat puni.* (XXXIV, 465)
Pope : *Poème sur les richesses.* (XXXIII, 341)
Pope : *Essay on Man.* 1732. (XXXIII, 339)
Pope : *Lettres de Pope.* (XXXIV, 16)
Pope : *Satires.* (XXXV, 226)
Pope : *Epîtres.* (XXXV, 198)

Prévost: *Le Pour et contre*. (XXXIV, 468, 520)
Prévost: *Vie de Cicéron*. (Middleton). (XXXVI, 292)
Rameau: *Les Indes galantes*. (XXXVI, 324)
Ramsay: *Histoire de Turenne*. 1735. 2 vols. (XXXIII, 499)
Réaumur: *Mémoire pour servir à l'histoire des insectes*. 1734-42.
    6 vols., in-4°. (XXXIII, 312)
Regnault: *Entretiens physiques*. (XXXIV, 281)
Regnault: *Lettre d'un physicien sur la philosophie de Newton*.
    (XXXIV, 522)
Roi: *Nirée*. (XXXVI, 312)
Rousseau, J. B.: *Lettres*. (XXXVII, 37)
Rousseau, J. B.: *L'Allégorie de Pluton*. (XXXV, 180)
St. Hyacinthe: *Recueil de divers écrits sur l'amour*. (XXXIV, 67)
St. Hyacinthe: *Mathanasius et la vie d'Aristarchus*. 1714. 6th ed.
    1732. (XXXIII, 485)
St. Réal: *Conjuration des Espagnols contre Venise*. 1674, in-12°.
    (XXXIV, 2)
Savari: *Dictionnaire du commerce*. (XXXVI, 411)
Scarron: *L'Héritier ridicule*. (XXXV, 309)
Schulenbourg: *Journal of Campaigns of 1703, 1704*. (XXXV,
    506)
Sirmond: *Le Coup d'état*. (XXXV, 244)
Smith: *Cours complet d'optique*. 1747. (XXXVII, 61)
Spon: *Lettre d'un ami à votre ennemi Bartenstein*. (XXXVI,
    329)
Stahl: *Chimie*. (XXXV, 443)
Stanislas: *Le Philosophe chrétien*. (XXXVI, 570)
Thomson: *Seasons*. (XXXIV, 460)
Tourreil: *Démosthène*. (XXXV, 235)
Tressan: *Dissertation sur Montaigne*. (XXXVI, 466)
Vadé: *Les Ecosseuses*. (XXXVI, 420)
Vanini: *Amphitheatrum*. 1615, in-8°. (XXXIII, 540)
Vauvenargues: *Introduction à la connaissance de l'esprit humain*.
    (XXXVI, 420)
Vauvenargues: *Réflexions critiques*. (XXXVI, 336)
Vauvenargues: *Eloge de Caumont*. (XXXVI, 332)
Villars: *Mémoires*. (XXXIII, 475)
Voisenon: *Le Sultan Misapouf*. 1746. (XXXVI, 420)
Wolff: *Cosmologia*. (XXXVI, 91)
Wolff: *Métaphysique*. (XXXIV, 241, 270, 295, 318)

Wotton: *Reflections on ancient and modern learning.* (XXXVI, 84)

(2)

Works cited anonymously:

L'Almanach du diable. (XXXIV, 208, 441)
Ample Disquisition. (XXXVII, 8)
Andronic. (XXXIV, 375)
Annals of Europe. (XXXVII, 8)
Castor et Pollux. (XXXIV, 339, 350)
Connaissance des temps. (XXXIV, 62)
De la Mécanique du feu des cheminées. (XXXIII, 511)
Etrennes de la St. Jean. 1742. (XXXVI, 420)
Histoire de Hongrie. (XXXVI, 182)
Histoire de l'inquisition. (XXXVI, 182)
Histoire de Naples (XXXVI, 182)
History of the Late Insurrection in Scotland. (XXXVII, 8)
La Présomption punie. (XXXVI, 231)
Le Philosophe guerrier. (XXXIV, 500)
Lettre sur la divisibilité de la matière à l'infini. (XXXIV, 253)
London magazine 1743-1745. (XXXVI, 403)
Mémoires de l'académie des sciences 1732. 1734. (XXXIV, 62)
Mercure de France (XXXV, 68)
Table of Histoire française de l'Académie des Sciences. 30 vols. (XXXIV, 308)
Traité du droit ecclésiastique. (XXXV, 194)
Transactions philosophiques. 9 vols. (XXXIV, 380)
Voyages du Nord. (XXXIV, 238)
Une suite du Langage des bêtes avec la réponse. (XXXV, 258)

(3)

Authors cited without titles of their works:

Bacon (XXXV, 206); Bernier (XXXVI, 182); Bion (XXXV, 215); Chardin (XXXVI, 182); Chubb (XXXIV, 141, 114-15); Cicero (XXXVII, 42); Clarke (XXXIV, 435); Darius (XXXV, 222); Desaguliers (XXXV, 23); Descartes (XXXIV, 114-15); Fra Paolo (XXXV, 194); Keill (XXXV, 215); Locke (XXXIII, 534, etc.); Machiavelli (XXXV, 342); Mézerai (XXXV, 194); Newton (XXXIV, 256, 157, 149, 141, 137, 116, 100); Plato

(XXXIV, 239) ; Plutarch (XXXVII, 42) ; Puffendorf (XXXIV, 238) ; Rollin (XXXVI, 111) ; St. Augustin (XXXVI, 111) ; Sallust (XXXVII, 42) ; S'Gravesande (XXXV, 215) ; Shaftesbury (XXXIV, 57) ; Tavernier (XXXVI, 182).

APPENDIX II

Comparison of Woolston's Discours sur les miracles *and the* Examen de la Genèse *of Mme du Châtelet*

Woolston.	*Examen.*

1. The driving out of the money-changers.

En effet il est bien difficile de comprendre comment un homme seul d'un extérieur qui ne devoit être que fort abject et peu imposant . . . un fouet à la main, ait pu exécuter une telle entreprise contre une troupe de gens qui n'étoient point ses disciples et qui n'avoient aucun respect pour lui. (I, 36)

Assurément il n'y a rien de si surprenant que cette action de Jésus et de voir un homme seul, sans autorité, et un homme méprisé chasser cette foule de marchands qui étoient dans les galeries extérieures du temple. (IV, 76)

Pourquoi s'étoit-il si fort enflammé de zèle à cause de la profanation d'un temple qu'il étoit venu renverser? (I, 37)

Mais on demande pourquoi Jésus étoit si dévoré de zèle pour une maison qu'il venoit détruire. (IV, 77)

2. The driving out of the demons into the swine.

Mais ce qui n'est pas moins incroyable, c'est qu'il pût y avoir dans ce pays-là un troupeau de cochons. (I, 48)

Il faut avouer qu'il est plaisant de trouver deux mille cochons dans un pays où ils étoient en horreur . . . (IV, 33)

Depuis qu'Antiochus eut souillé le temple en y faisant sacrifier un cochon, les Juifs avoient défendu sous peine d'anathême que qui que ce soit gardât des cochons dans le pays. (I, 48)

. . . et où il étoit deffendu sous peine de mort d'en avoir, depuis qu'Antiochus Epiphane avoit souillé le temple en y sacrifiant un pourceau. (IV, 33)

Les propriétaires des cochons dûrent souffrir une perte considérable . . . (I, 49)

. . . que je les (les cochons) plains bien véritablement ainsi que ceux à qui ils appartenaient, qui, moyennant ce miracle, durent être ruinés. (IV, 34)

Woolston.	*Examen.*
Ils le prièrent de se retirer de leur territoire vraisemblablement à cause de la perte qu'il leur avoit causée, et pour empêcher qu'il ne leur en causât quelqu'autre : ce qui fut en vérité une manière de se venger beaucoup plus généreuse qu'on n'eût dû l'attendre de ceux à qui on avoit causé un pareil domage. (I, 50)	Aussi imprima-t-il une telle frayeur dans le pays que les habitans vinrent prier Jésus de se retirer de chez eux ; et je trouve ces habitans bien doux. (IV, 34)
. . . mais si quelque exorciste de notre nation se fût avisé de nos jours de chasser des Démons du corps d'un possédé pour les faire entrer dans celui d'un troupeau de moutons, le peuple n'auroit pas manqué de crier au sorcier, et il est sûr que les loix et les juges l'en auroient puni très-sévèrement. (I, 50)	Si un enthousiaste en faisoit autant de nos jours, il seroit surement puni. (IV, 34)

3. The Transfiguration.

. . . ils me permettront de leur demander à mon tour quel étoit le motif et la fin de ce miracle ? (I, 60)	On demande quelle étoit la raison et l'usage de ce miracle ; car on n'en a jamais pu imaginer aucune . . . (IV, 63)
Mais que venoient faire Moyse et Elie avec Jésus sur la montagne ? Ont-ils paru en personne ou n'étoit-ce que leurs fantômes et leurs spectres ? Il est dit qu'ils s'entretenoient avec Jésus : de quoi pouvoient-ils s'entretenir ? Il est donc bien étrange que les Apôtres qui entendirent toute leur conversation ne l'ayent pas rapportée et transmise à la postérité pour notre instruction et pour notre édification. (I, 61)	On demande si Moïse ressuscita pour cette apparition, et s'il remourut ensuite. . . . d'autres disent que cette apparition ne fut pas réelle . . . (IV, 62)
	. . . mais on ne comprend pas pourquoi Jésus leur fit cette deffense (not to speak of the Transfiguration), et ils ont mieux gardé le secret sur la conversation qu'il eut avec Moïse et Elie, qu'ils durent entendre et qui n'étoit pas cependant ce qu'il y avoit de moins curieux dans cette avanture. (IV, 63)

4. The cure of the woman with the issue of blood.

S'ils étoient même assez mal intentionnés pour dire que la guérison de l'hémorragie de cette femme lui a été plutôt funeste qu'avantageuse, et qu'elle est morte peu de tems après . . . (I, 108)	Ainsi cette guérison paroit même lui avoir été funeste, comme une espèce de suppression, puisqu'elle a abrégé ses jours. (IV, 36)

Woolston.　　　　　　　　　　*Examen.*

5. Jesus and the Samaritan Woman.

Mais pourquoi M. l'Evêque et tous les autres Docteurs qui font tant d'efforts pour prouver que Jésus étoit le Messie, ne tirent-ils pas leurs preuves de ce qu'il a dit la bonne avanture à cette femme Samaritaine? (I, 149)

Pour les Samaritains ils l'attendoient apparemment comme un très-habile devin, et comme un fameux diseur de bonne avanture sans quoi il n'y auroit pas eu de bon sens dans ce que disoit la Samaritaine aux hommes de la ville. (I, 150)

Mais les hommes de Sichar eurent eux-mêmes le plaisir de se faire dire leur bonne avanture par Jésus, et d'en tirer la même conclusion qu'il étoit le Messie; sans quoi il n'y auroit pas eu de sens à ce qu'ils disent à la Samaritaine, verset 42 . . . (I, 153)

. . . et si Jésus, comme je ne doute pas, ayant l'art de deviner et de répondre juste à leurs questions, leur a dit tout ce qu'ils avoient fait, je suppose qu'il aura eu la précaution de ne pas dire tout haut à chacun d'eux ses débauches et ses adultères; cela auroit excité parmi eux des querelles domestiques et des haines entre les voisins . . . (I, 153)

Mais je sais bien qu'ils (priests) n'approuveront dans personne le métier de diseur de bonne avanture; ils n'ont pas trouvé mauvais qu'on ait puni et chassé comme des fripons des Bohémiens dont c'étoit l'unique talent . . . (I, 151)

Je suis bien surpris que les Bohémiens qui couroient autrefois le Pays ne se fondent pas sur cette histoire, pour insinuer qu'ils sont les vrais disciples de Jésus-Christ; puisqu'ils savent dire la bonne avanture, et que la profession qu'ils en faisoient n'étoit

On trouve dans ce chapitre l'histoire de la Samaritaine à laquelle Jésus dit sa bonne avanture. (IV, 178)

Mais il est plaisant que sur le récit de la Samaritaine, les habitans de Sichar aient, v. 29, pris Jésus pour le Messie; ils l'attendoient apparemment comme un diseur de bonne avanture. (IV, 178)

Les habitans de Sichar disent à la Samaritaine au v. 42, qu'ils croyoient qu'il étoit le Messie, moins sur ce qu'elle leur avoit dit, que sur ce qu'ils avoient entendu eux-mêmes. Apparemment que Jésus leur dit à tous leur bonne avanture. (IV, 178-9)

Je me flatte cependant qu'il n'aura pas été dire aux femmes devant leurs maris, combien elles avoient d'amans. (IV, 179)

Mais en supposant que les désordres de cette femme eussent été secrets, Jésus pouvoit très bien s'être informé d'elle; et il n'y a guères de Bohémiens qui ne disent des choses qui paroissent plus extraordinaires que cela; et cependant on a la sotise de les poursui-

Woolston.

que celle que Jésus-Christ exerça dans cette occasion. (I, 152)

6. The cursing of the fig-tree.

Les Pères comme Origène, S. Augustin, S. Jean de Jérusalem, ont écrit contre le sens littéral de cette histoire des choses aussi vives qu'auroient pu en dire les Incrédules les plus clairvoyants. (I, 184-5)

S. Augustin dit clairement que si on pouvoit soupçonner que Jésus ait été capable de faire une telle action, il en eût fait une très déraisonnable. *Hoc factum, nisi figuratum, stultum invenitur.* (I, 185)

Fort bien, en ce cas il devoit pourvoir à son dîner pour le tems à peu près qu'il prévoyoit qu'il auroit besoin de manger. (I, 186)

Quoi! parce qu'il se voyoit privé d'un repas de figues sur lequel il avoit compté, falloit-il qu'il se vengeât sur un arbre qui n'étoit pas la cause de son défaut de prévoyance? *Nulla esset ligni culpa, quia lignum sine sensu non habebat culpam.* August. in Serm. 89. (I, 186)

Ce qu'il y a de plus fâcheux dans cette circonstance, c'est que ce n'étoit pas la saison des figues. Jésus devoit le savoir avant que de s'approcher de l'arbre : s'il eût eu de la raison. *Quaerit poma; nesciebat tempus nondum esse? Quod cultor arboris sciebat, Creator arboris nesciebat?* August. in Serm. 89. (I, 187)

... un paysan de la province de Kent s'aviseroit-il dans le tems de Pâque d'aller chercher des pommes sur les arbres de son jardin? (I, 188)

Examen.

vre criminellement quoique certainement ils pussent prendre Jésus-Christ pour leur patron. (IV, 178)

Ce miracle est si ridicule et si revoltant que plusieurs Péres ont cru que cette histoire n'est qu'une allégorie et qu'elle n'est point arrivée. (IV, 77)

Origènes le dit nettement : *Si hoc factum, nisi figuratum, stultum invenitur.* Et St. Augustin avoue que si Jésus a fait cette action, il a fait une chose folle. (IV, 77-8)

... de plus, Jésus ne devoit-il pas prévoir sa faim, et y pourvoir avant de partir de Bethanie. (IV, 79)

Mais cette malédiction du figuier renferme encore une autre absurdité, car un arbre étant une chose insensible, n'est susceptible ni de malédiction ni de bénédiction. Aussi St. Augustin l'avoue-t-il dans son sermon 89, *nulla esset ligni culpa, quia lignum, sine sensu, non habebat culpam.* (IV, 78)

Mais il est plaisant de voir Jésus qui savoit tout ce qu'avoit fait la Samaritaine en sa vie, ne pas savoir qu'il n'y avoit pas de figues sur cet arbre, et que ce n'étoit pas le tems de figues, quoiqu'assurément il ne fut pas nécessaire d'être Dieu ni même prophête pour le savoir. (IV, 78)

St. Augustin, qui est inimitable sur ce miracle, s'exprime ainsi au Sermon 89 : *"Querit poma nesciebat tempus nondum esse, quod Cultor arboris sciebat."* (IV, 7)

Que diroit-on d'un païsan, qui ayant envie de manger des pêches à Pacques, s'en iroit en chercher dans son verger? (IV, 79)

Woolston.

Examen.

Si, faute d'en trouver il étoit assez sot pour se mettre en colère contre ses arbres, et pour les couper, qu'est-ce que ses voisins diroient de lui ? Le moins qu'ils pourroient lui faire, se-roit de lui rire au nez et de le re-garder comme un insensé. (I, 188)

Cette seule démarche suffiroit pour le faire croire fou : mais s'il prenoit sa cognée pour abattre tous ses pêchés parce qu'il n'y auroit pas trouvé de pêches, certainement on l'enfermeroit. (IV, 79)

... un de mes grands étonnements, c'est que le peuple n'éclate pas de rire devant nos prêtres, et ne démonte leur gravité lorsqu'ils lui racontent ce miracle en chaire, et quand ils le lui proposent comme un objet d'admi-ration. (I, 188)

Je ne sais comment on peut s'empêcher de rire quand on entend lire ce conte gravement à l'église, et les prédica-teurs le prendre pour le texte de leurs sermons, et en tirer les plus belles moralités. (IV, 79)

De plus je voudrois savoir à qui ap-partenoit ce figuier ; de quel droit Jésus y eût cueilli des figues, supposé que c'eût été la saison d'y en trouver ; enfin par quelle autorité il maudit ce pauvre arbre parce qu'il n'avoit pas alors de fruit ? (I, 188)

Quand à l'injustice de ce miracle, je voudrois bien savoir à qui étoit ce figuier dont Jésus prétendoit manger les figues, et si le maître avoit affaire que Jésus fit sécher son figuier parce qu'il n'y avoit pas trouvé de figues. (IV, 79)

St. Marc dit que les Apôtres en pas-sant le matin, virent le figuier sec jusque dans ses racines. Ce devoit être au moins le lendemain matin du jour que la malédiction avoit été pro-noncée ... (I, 196)

St. Marc dit au chap. 11, v. 20, que ce ne fut que le lendemain matin que les apôtres s'apperçurent que le fig-uier étoit séché. (IV, 80)

Les Juifs et les Incrédules pourront dire que Jésus dans la vue d'en im-poser à ses disciples, et à ceux qui le suivoient, avoit pris son tems pour venir furtivement faire périr les ra-cines de cet arbre ou y faire quelques incisions peu sensibles aux yeux ... (I, 196)

Or, cette circonstance de ne sécher que le lendemain, rendroit le miracle fort douteux, car un arbre ne meurt pas pour sécher ; et il se peut très bien que Jésus ayant prononcé cette malé-diction devant ses apôtres pour leur en imposer, ait dépouillé en cachette cet arbre de son écorce près de sa racine ; ce qui suffisoit pour faire sécher et tomber ses feuilles. (IV, 81)

7. The paralytic at the Pool of Bethesda.

Tout ce qu'on peut raisonnablement conjecturer de l'état de cet homme, c'est qu'il y avoit plus de lâcheté et de paresse dans son fait, que de vraie maladie ; que Jésus lui en avoit fait

Peut-être cet homme ne se tenoit-il près de cette piscine sous prétexte d'incommodité que pour demander l'aumône aux passants ; et peut-être Jésus ne fit-il que lui faire honte de

Woolston.

le reproche, et lui avoit dit d'emporter son lit . . . (I, 217)

. . . il n'étoit tout au plus que malade imaginaire, auquel cas Jésus lui auroit ranimé le courage par quelque discours consolant, de manière qu'-ayant guéri son imagination dérangée, il l'avoit vraiment guéri et lui avoit ordonné de s'en aller. (I, 217)

Nous ignorons quel étoit le genre de maladie de cet homme ; . . . (I, 232). Les Pères disent que la maladie de cet homme étoit une paralysie : sur quel fondement hazardent-ils cette décision ? (I, 233)

S'il y avoit quelque chose de vrai dans le fait en question, il ne seroit pas possible que quelque autre historien Juif n'eût fait mention d'un exemple aussi rare et aussi surprenant du soin et de l'affection particulière de cet Ange pour les malades de Jérusalem. Or c'est ce qui ne se trouve rapporté nulle part . . . (I, 221)

Pourquoi pour la guérison ne consultoit-on pas le besoin ou le mérite des malades ! Pourquoi cette faveur du ciel étoit-elle le prix de celui qui étoit assés heureux pour s'en emparer ? Comme c'est celui qui court le mieux qui gagne le prix de la course, de même aussi celui de tous les malades qui étoit le plus alerte, ou le plus attentif à épier le moment de la descente de l'ange et à se plonger dans la piscine, étoit celui qui gagnoit le prix de la santé ; moyen bien étrange et bien plaisant de conférer un don divin ! (I, 226-7)

. . . mais il me semble qu'on pourroit demander pourquoi il n'y avoit qu'une seule personne à la fois qui pût être

Examen.

sa paresse ; et lui ordonna-t-il d'emporter son lit pour qu'il n'y revint plus. (IV, 182)

Il n'avoit peut-être que des vapeurs, et son imagination étant échauffée par l'air d'enthousiasme avec lequel Jésus lui parla il aura cru être guéri de la maladie qu'il n'avoit pas. (IV, 182)

Ce qui est de sûr, c'est qu'on ne voit point par le texte que cet homme fût paralytique, ni quelle espèce de maladie il avoit ; et c'est gratuitement, et seulement pour fonder le miracle, que les péres ont supposé qu'il étoit paralytique. (IV, 182)

Il est à remarquer, premièrement, que Philon, ni aucun historien, sans en excepter Joseph, lui qui est cependant soigneux de rapporter tout ce qui peut faire croire que Dieu prenoit un soin particulier de sa nation, ni aucun des livres des Juifs ne parlent de cette merveilleuse piscine qui cependant en valoit bien la peine. (IV, 180)

Mais pourquoi cette grâce étoit-elle dispensée non à celui qui en avoit le plus de besoin, mais à celui qui étoit le plus alerte pour se jetter dans la piscine après que l'eau avoit été troublée ? (IV, 180-1)

Cette histoire, d'ailleurs contient beaucoup d'absurdités, car en supposant ce miracle, pourquoi à chaque

Woolston.	*Examen.*
guérie, et pourquoi ces pauvres malades n'y trouvoient pas tous leur guérison en même tems? (I, 224)	fois que l'eau étoit remuée n'y avoit-il qu'un malade de guéri? (IV, 180)
Comment est-il arrivé que, soit par un effet de la Providence divine, soit par les soins des Magistrats de Jérusalem, on n'ait pas mieux sçu faire profiter les malades de cette faveur de l'Ange? (I, 226)	Mais les magistrats de Jérusalem étoient bien négligens de ne pas établir l'ordre dans un lieu si important, et d'abandonner une si grande grâce à la dispute d'une vile populace. (IV, 181)
. . . pourquoi Jésus ne les guérit-il pas tous? (I, 235)	St. Augustin à l'occasion de ce miracle se fait cette objection: pourquoi
Quelle pourroit être la raison pour laquelle parmi cette multitude de malades il n'eût étendu ses bontés que sur un seul paralytique? C'est St. Augustin qui fait cette question par ma bouche . . . (I, 236)	Jésus ne guérit pas tous les malades de la piscine . . . Mais St. Augustin après s'être fait cette difficulté est obligé de la laisser sans réponse. (IV, 183)
St. Jean Chrisostôme qui s'est attaché à l'interprétation littérale des Ecritures plus qu'aucun autre, s'écarte de la lettre pour ce passage et s'écrie avec raison: ". . . il n'est pas possible que la chose se soit passée de la manière peu raisonnable dont elle est rapportée: il doit y avoir quelque chose de figuré pour l'avenir, ou bien cette histoire est si incroyable par elle-même qu'elle seroit un sujet de scandale pour plusieurs." (I, 243)	Voici comme St. Chrisostome sur St. Jean s'exprime au sujet de ce miracle. "Cette histoire est allégorique, et renferme quelque parabole; autrement elle est si peu vraisemblable, qu'elle offenseroit les oreilles de ceux qui l'entendroient raconter." (IV, 183)
St. Augustin sur le même sujet, dit: Y a-t-il un homme qui puisse croire que ces eaux de Bethsaïde ayent eu coutume d'être troublées de cette manière; à moins de supposer qu'il y ait un mystère et un sens spirituel caché sous ce récit? (I, 243-4)	St. Augustin ne paroit pas ajouter grande foi à ce miracle; car il dit à l'occasion de cet ange, "quelle apparence qu'un ange vint remuer ces eaux, comme on le rapporte?" (IV, 180)

8. The man born blind.

Il est vrai que voilà un remède bien étrange, dont on ne s'est guères servi devant ni depuis ce tems-là pour la guérison des maux d'yeux. (II, 9)	. . . mais il se servit pour cela d'une plaisante recette, il lui mit sous les yeux de la boue délayée avec son crachat . . . (IV, 193)
S'il vouloit nous expliquer en quoi consistoit la vertu de ce remède, quand même il devroit supposer que	Mais il me semble qu'en ne mettant rien sur les yeux de cet aveugle, il eût encore été mieux constaté; et

Woolston.

Jésus avoit adroitement glissé dans sa bouche quelque drogue balsamique et spécifique pour le mal d'yeux, qu'il auroit laissé dissoudre dans sa salive ; il rendroit un grand service à l'Église . . . (II, 10)

. . . pour moi je croirois volontiers avec Saint Jean Chrysostôme qu'un tel remède seroit plutôt capable de nuire à des yeux sains, que d'en guérir de malades. (II, 11)

Examen.

Jésus fit fort mal de rendre ce miracle ridicule par cette cérémonie ; car, on pouroit croire qu'il n'étoit pas né aveugle ; et que Jésus avoit une drogue dans sa bouche qui étoit bonne pour éclaircir la vuë. (IV, 193)

. . . car il lui mit sous les yeux de la boue délayée avec son crachat, v. 6, chose, dit St. Chrisostome, "qui auroit dû naturellement le rendre aveugle, s'il ne l'eût pas été." (IV, 193)

9. The wedding at Cana.

. . . pourquoi St. Jean s'est-il servi d'un terme qui signifie qu'ils étoient plus qu'à demi yvres ? (II, 32)

Mais on a de la peine à excuser le miracle que Jésus fit alors : car l'évangéliste fait entendre au v. 10, que les convives étoient à moitié ivres. (IV, 174)

"Femme, qu'y a-t-il entre vous et moi ? Mon heure n'est pas encore venue." Réponse peu décente dans la bouche d'un fils respectueux envers sa mère ; et surtout de Jésus qui, (excepté dans l'occasion où il s'enfuit de chez ses parens, ce qui leur causa tant de chagrin et leur donna tant de peine pour le trouver) a toujours été et est encore aujourd'hui . . . un enfant si docile aux volontés de sa mère. (II, 33)

Il commença par parler très durement à sa mére, qui lui disoit tout simplement que le vin manquoit, v. 3. . . . On voit par tout ce qui est raconté dans les évangiles que Jésus étoit un très mauvais fils ; car on a vu qu'il renia sa mére ; quand elle vint avec ses fréres pour l'emmener. (IV, 174)

Semblable à un habile faiseur de Punch il changea la saveur de l'eau et en composa une boisson que la compagnie prit pour du vin. (II, 35)

Car on peut dire que dans cette occasion Jésus ne fit autre chose que quelque mélange qu'il connoissoit, comme du punch, par exemple, et que les conviés à moitié ivres prirent pour du vin excellent. (IV, 175)

Il y a des hérétiques qui, de ces paroles femme qu'y a-t-il de commun entre nous, ont prétendu conclure que Marie n'étoit ni vierge ni la mère de Jésus, et que puisqu'il la traitoit si durement ils ne devoient pas être si proches parens qu'on le dit . . . (II, 35)

Mais plusieurs ont voulu inférer de ce titre de *femme* que Jésus donne toujours à sa mère, qu'elle n'étoit pas vierge, car Jésus devoit savoir qu'elle l'étoit, et il n'auroit pas dû induire les autres en erreur en l'appellant *femme.* (IV, 174)

Woolston.

Examen.

... Jésus avoit bien voulu épargner au marié la honte et le reproche de n'avoir pas fait une provision suffisante ; et qu'à l'aide du maître d'hôtel, il avoit fait semblant de faire un miracle, pour contenter tous ces yvrognes, ce qu'il fit par le moyen de quelque liqueur spiritueuse qu'il mêla dans une quantité d'eau ; que le maître d'hôtel donna cette composition pour de très-excellent vin qui venoit d'être fait miraculeusement par Jésus ; que ces bonnes gens qui étoient déjà ivres et par conséquent hors d'état de s'y connoître ou de découvrir la supercherie, s'étoient récriés sur la bonté du vin et sur la grandeur du miracle. (II, 39)

Il pouvoit s'entendre avec le maître d'hôtel, ou avec celui qu'on appelloit dans ce tems là, le roi du festin. (IV, 175)
[See also above]

S'il étoit vrai que Jésus eût miraculeusement et réellement fait du vin d'une façon que l'art humain n'eût pas été capable d'imiter, il eût dû le faire sans y employer le secours de l'eau pour prévenir tout soupçon de supercherie. (II, 42)

D'ailleurs, pourquoi faire mettre de l'eau dans ces cruches pour en faire du vin ? Jésus, puisqu'il vouloit en faire, auroit dû le faire sans eau. Cela auroit ôté tout prétexte de doute sur ce miracle, et on ne pourroit lui reprocher que son inutilité, et son indécence. Mais l'eau gâte tout ; ne pouvoit-il pas faire du vin sans eau ? Et s'il le pouvoit, pourquoi ne l'a-t-il pas fait ? (IV, 175)

Pourquoi ne remplit-il pas ces pots de vin sur le champ, et par un seul mot de sa bouche ? c'eût été là un miracle qu'il eût été impossible de révoquer en doute, et contre lequel les incrédules n'auroient eu rien à dire, si non qu'il étoit inutile et déplacé. (II, 42)

Mais cette eau affoiblit considérablement l'éclat de ce miracle. (II, 43)

Mais l'eau gâte tout. (IV, 175)

Tout ce qui me reste à dire là-dessus est que s'il est vrai que Jésus ait eu le secret de changer l'eau en vin, il seroit à souhaiter qu'il l'eût laissé à ses disciples, et à tous les Prêtres qui leur ont succédé ... Il est bien vrai que Jésus leur a promis qu'il leur don-

Mais Jésus auroit bien dû transmettre à ses disciples le don de répéter ce miracle ; cela vaudroit mieux que celui de transporter les montagnes, qu'il leur avoit promis. (IV, 175)

Woolston.   *Examen.*

neroit le pouvoir de faire des miracles,
de transporter des montagnes et d'ex-
communier des arbres . . . (II, 44)

10. The paralytic in Nazareth or Capernaum.

Qu'est-ce que le peuple avoit besoin
de se presser et de s'écraser à cette
porte? Etoit-ce donc pour lui voir
faire des miracles et guérir des ma-
ladies? . . . Mais cette raison-là même
auroit dû engager le peuple à laisser
un passage aux boiteux, aux aveugles
et aux paralytiques . . . (II, 56)

Mais qu'étoit-il besoin de prendre
tant de peines et de se hâter si fort
pour l'approcher de Jésus? Il n'y
avoit qu'à patienter un peu; la foule
ne pouvoit manquer de se dissiper au
bout de quelques heures et le passage
seroit devenu libre; mais il est bien
étrange et bien difficile à croire que
les porteurs de ce pauvre homme
ayent entrepris une chose qui de-
mandoit tant de travail et d'embarras,
et qui exigeoit pour le moins autant
de tems qu'il en eût fallu pour que la
foule se dissipât d'elle-même. (II, 57)

Il est sûr que Jésus, ses disciples et la
compagnie qui étoit dans la chambre,
ont été bienheureux si aucun d'eux
n'a eu la tête cassée par la chute de
quelque thuile ou de quelqu'autre dé-
combre . . . (II, 61)

Où se tenoit pendant tout ce tems-là
le bon homme à qui appartenoit la
maison? (II, 61)

Il est encore plus déraisonnable de
supposer que Jésus, pour prévenir
tant d'embarras, tant de travail et
pour garantir de dommage la maison
où on l'avoit reçu, n'eût pas prononcé
de loin les paroles qui devoient opérer

Il y a plusieurs difficultés sur la
façon dont ce paralytique entra dans
la maison où étoit Jésus: car, premièrement, on ne voit pas trop pourquoi le peuple qui l'écoutoit ne laissa
pas passer ceux qui portoient cet
homme. Car ils n'étoient là que dans
l'espérance de lui voir faire quelque
miracle; ainsi il n'y a nulle apparence
qu'ils ayent refusé de laisser passer ce
paralytique. (IV, 110)

De plus, la paralisie n'est pas une
maladie qui presse, témoin le malade
qui fut trente-neuf ans auprès de la
piscine de Jérusalem, et que l'on prétend qui étoit paralytique. Il n'y avoit
qu'à attendre quelques heures; la
foule se seroit dissipée, et ceux qui
portoient cet homme se seroient ap-
prochés de Jésus, sans être obligés de
découvrir le toict, et de couper la
charpente de la maison. Cette opéra-
tion devoit durer plus longtems que
le concours du peuple qui les empêch-
oit d'entrer. (IV, 110)

Mais, Jésus, et ceux qui étoient dans
la maison avec lui furent bien heureux de n'avoir pas la tête cassée par
quelques thuiles, ou par quelque morceau de charpente . . . (IV, 110)

Mais où étoit le propriétaire de la
maison? (IV, 111)

Mais Jésus, qui savoit tout, qui connoissoit la foi et les besoins de ce
paralytique, devoit bien le guérir de
loin, ou lui faire place par le peuple
et empêcher cette maison d'être dé-
gradée. (IV, 111)

Woolston.   *Examen.*

la guérison, ou n'eût pas dispersé
toute cette foule pour faire approcher
le paralytique. (II, 66)

11. The three resurrections (Jarius's daughter, the son of the
    widow of Naim, and Lazarus).

Le moindre des trois miracles en question est la résurrection de la fille de Jaïre. Toutes les apparences sont contre ce prétendu miracle. Le texte même dit que la fille n'étoit qu'endormie, ou tombée en défaillance à cause du bruit que faisoient ceux qui étoient autour d'elle. (II, 87)

Il paroit que Jésus ne donnoit pas ce miracle là pour grand-chose, puisqu'il dit lui-même que cette fille n'étoit qu'endormie . . . (IV, 37)

Le plus grand des trois comme je l'ai déjà remarqué est celui de la résurrection du Lazare; mais comme il n'y a que S. Jean qui en fasse mention, et comme il a écrit son Evangile long-tems après les autres Evangélistes, et plus de soixante ans après la résurrection de notre Seigneur, suivant le calcul qui est le plus universellement reçu, il n'y a que trop lieu de croire que c'est un conte dépourvu de fondement. Comment auroit-il été possible que S. Mathieu, S. Marc, et S. Luc qui avoient écrit leur évangile long-tems avant S. Jean, et dans un tems beaucoup moins éloigné de la source, eussent omis une circonstance de la vie de Jésus aussi considérable que celle de la résurrection du Lazare. (II, 89)

C'est dans ce chapitre que la résurrection du Lazare est rapportée . . . St. Jean est le seul évangéliste qui en parle; et il ne la raconte qu'après la dissolution des Juifs, lorsque les regîtres publics furent perdus, et brûlés et que les témoins et Lazare lui-même étoient morts. Car j'ai remarqué que supposé que l'évangile qui porte le nom de St. Jean soit de cet apôtre, il ne l'a écrit qu'à 95 ans passés. Or cette circonstance d'être rapportée par le seul St. Jean, suffit pour rendre cette résurrection fort suspecte; car, quelle apparence y a-t-il que les autres évangélistes eussent négligé de parler d'un miracle si éclatant, et dont le sujet étant encore vivant étoit lui-même un miracle subsistant qui atestoit ce qu'ils avançoient, et devoit suffire pour faire croire tout le reste. (IV, 196)

Une autre objection à faire contre la lettre de ces miracles, est de demander ce que sont devenues les trois personnes que Jésus a ressuscitées? Combien elles ont vécu depuis leur résurrection? De quel usage et de quel profit leur nouvelle vie a été à l'Eglise ou au genre-humain? (II, 99-100)

On est étonné de ne voir jouer aucun rôle, ni dans l'Evangile, ni dans les actes des apôtres, aux ressuscités, ni même aux malades que Jésus a guéris. Ce devoient être cependant les plus ardens de ses disciples . . . (IV, 202)

Woolston.

La reconnoissance du bienfait ne pouvoit moins exiger de lui; mais l'histoire ne nous apprend pas qu'il ait fait un tel usage de sa vie. (II, 100)

Suivant l'opinion de Grotius, que j'ai déjà cité, Lazare s'est tenu caché depuis sa résurrection et n'a fait qu'errer de côté et d'autre dans la crainte qu'il avoit des Juifs qui le cherchoient pour le faire mourir. Ce n'est là qu'une supposition qui non seulement nuit à la gloire de Jésus, vû que la même puissance qui avoit pu le rappeller à la vie, pouvoit et devoit le protéger contre les entreprises de ses ennemis; mais encore elle est honteuse pour Lazare lui-même, qui auroit dû s'exposer courageusement à une seconde mort, plutôt que d'éviter l'occasion de rendre un témoignage éclatant à Jésus qui l'avoit ressuscité. (II, 100)

La fille de Jaïre étoit un enfant d'environ douze ans qui n'étoit de nulle conséquence, et il n'y avoit d'autre raison pour la ressusciter que d'appaiser les pleurs et la douleur de ses parens . . . (II, 106)

Mais puisque je me suis mis à examiner si les personnes sur lesquelles Jésus a opéré un si grand miracle, méritoient de sa part une telle grâce, je demande pourquoi il n'a pas ressuscité Jean Baptiste? (III) Mais Jean Baptiste, cet homme d'un mérite si rare et qui avoit rendu des services si essentiels à Jésus-Christ, ayant été négligé, et une faveur aussi grande que celle de rappeller de la mort à la vie, n'ayant été accordée qu'à des personnes de nulle considération, on peut raisonnablement douter de la vérité de telles histoires, et à moins d'avoir recours au mystère on les prendra pour des contes faits à plaisir. (II, 114)

Examen.

. . . et surtout Lazare, qui d'ailleurs son ami; et il y avoit bien de l'ingratitude à lui de ne pas employer la vie qu'il lui avoit rendue à confirmer sa doctrine. (IV, 202)

Lazare, dit on, craignoit les Juifs; mais cela étoit bien lâche à lui; et de plus cela n'est guère vraisemblable; car il devoit croire que celui qui avoit été puissant pour le ressusciter, le seroit assés pour le defendre. (IV, 202)

. . . mais Jésus ne devant ressusciter que trois morts, choisit bien mal, car cette petite fille n'avoit que douze ans; sa vie ne paroissoit ni importante ni nécessaire . . . (IV, 37)

. . . il auroit bien mieux fait de ressusciter Jean Baptiste ou le putatif Joseph, . . . La résurrection de Jean Baptiste n'eût pas été équivoque, et eût fait beaucoup de conversions; mais on lui avoit coupé la tête, cela étoit plus difficile. (IV, 37)

Woolston.

Examen.

Quant au fils de la veuve de Naim, il y avoit plus d'apparence qu'il étoit réellement mort, vû qu'on le portoit à la sépulture; d'où l'on peut raisonnablement présumer qu'il étoit réellement mort; mais ne pouvoit-il pas y avoir de la fraude ou de l'erreur? (II, 114)

L'histoire n'est-elle pas remplie d'exemples de personnes qui ont été crues mortes, et qui ont été malheureusement enterrées toutes vives, et d'autres qui ont été tirées de cet état par quelque heureux hazard? (II, 114)

Ne pouvoit-il pas y avoir en cela une fourberie concertée? (II, 114)

Mais les Incrédules . . . ne s'aviseront-ils pas de demander si Lazare qui étoit un des amis de Jésus, n'avoit pas pris des mesures avec son maître pour faire éclater sa gloire et pour étendre sa renommée? (II, 116)

Quant à ce qui est dit que le cadavre de Lazare sentoit mauvais, les Incrédules diront que c'étoit un propos avancé par sa sœur pour faire valoir la chose et pour servir d'introduction ou de prologue à la farce qui se jouoit. (II, 117)

Et afin qu'il ne manque rien à la malignité de ces Incrédules, ils diront encore que Jésus appella Lazare à haute voix comme s'il eût été aussi sourd que le devoit être un homme mort; néanmoins comme ce prétendu mort étoit resté enveloppé d'un linceuil de façon à ôter aux spectateurs la liberté d'observer le changement merveilleux qui pouvoit se faire dans la couleur du visage d'un cadavre presque corrompu, qui reprend la vie (en quoi pourtant consistoit toute l'essence de ce miracle) ils conclueront de cette seule circonstance

Des trois morts ressuscités par Jésus, c'est celui là qui paroit avoir été le mieux mort; car on le portoit en terre, et Jésus semble le rencontrer par hazard; cependant l'Évangéliste en dit si peu au sujet de cette résurrection, qu'on ne peut prononcer que dans son récit ce miracle paroisse sans fraude . . . (IV, 150)

Il y a plus d'un exemple de gens qu'on alloit enterrer, et que des hazards ont fait découvrir n'être point morts. (IV, 150)

Jésus pouvoit s'entendre avec la mère de cet enfant . . . (IV, 150)

. . . et il étoit tout simple que Lazare qui étoit ami de Jésus aussi bien que ses sœurs, se soit entendu avec lui pour donner cette scène. (IV, 198)

On voit que Marthe qui paroît, par tout le récit, se mêler beaucoup plus de tout cela que sa sœur . . . Marthe lui dit Seigneur il sent mauvais . . . Discours dans lequel on sent aisément l'affectation . . . (IV, 198)

Et puis il crie de toute sa force à Lazare de sortir dehors, v. 43 . . . Chose très ridicule! si Lazare étoit réellement mort, puisqu'il l'est extrêmement de parler à un mort; mais qui étoit très utile à Jésus pour avertir Lazare de commencer son rôle. . . . Les interprêtes ont fait des efforts incroyables pour expliquer comment Lazare put sortir de sa caverne quoiqu'il eût les pieds attachés. D'autant qu'il est marqué dans ce v. 44, que Lazare avoit le visage couvert . . . circonstance remarquable et fort suspecte, car si Lazare avoit eu le visage

Woolston.

Examen.

que le tout n'a été qu'une fourberie et une imposture préméditée. (II, 117)

découvert, avant de ressusciter, on auroit pû voir s'il avoit la mine d'un mort, et d'un mort de quatre jours. (IV, 199)

Au reste il est clair par tout ce qui vient d'être dit, que Lazare n'a pas été assés longtems dans le tombeau pour qu'il ne reste aucun doute sur le miracle de sa résurrection. (II, 118)

Enfin Lazare ne fut point assés longtems dans son caveau pour ôter tout soupçon ... (IV, 199)

... aucune des trois personnes ressuscitées n'a rendu compte de l'état où elle s'est trouvée durant la séparation de son âme d'avec son corps ... (II, 119)

... aucun ne nous a appris ce qui se faisoit dans l'autre vie. (IV, 202)

... une opinion qui suppose qu'un des amis de Jésus-Christ ait pû aller en Enfer ne doit pas être bien reçu des prédicateurs de nos jours qui se vantent fort d'être de ce nombre; si l'âme de Lazare étoit dans le Paradis, ce n'étoit pas lui rendre un grand service que de l'en tirer. (II, 122)

On demande où fut l'âme de Lazare pendant les quatre jours qu'il fut mort? S'il étoit en enfer dit on, cela n'est guères honnorable à Jésus d'avoir pour ami intime un réprouvé; et s'il étoit en paradis, il n'y a pas de charité à Jésus de l'en avoir tiré, et de l'avoir résuscité. (IV, 202)

Si donc nous ne trouvons dans les Saints Pères une explication mystique des pleurs de Jésus, on ne peut les regarder que comme le prélude ridicule de la farce qu'il alloit jouer dans la prétendue résurrection de Lazare. (II, 127)

Quoiqu'assurément, il ne soit pas trop naturel de pleurer quelqu'un qu'on và résusciter; mais c'étoit apparemment un prélude qu'il croyoit nécessaire à cette comédie. (IV, 197)

... ils auront des idées trop justes de la nature humaine dans toutes les nations et dans tous les siècles, pour se laisser persuader qu'on puisse avoir haï et persécuté un homme dans le cas de Lazare, par la seule raison qu'il avoit été l'objet d'une grâce aussi éclatante que celle d'être rappellé de la mort à la vie. Quelle auroit donc été la cause de la haine qu'on lui portoit, et de la persécution qu'on lui faisoit éprouver? C'étoit parce qu'il fut regardé comme un des complices de Jésus dans l'horrible imposture qu'il avoit voulu jouer. (II, 133)

Mais ce que St. Jean marque au chap. 12, v. 10, que les princes des prêtres cherchoient à faire mourir Lazare est tout à fait absurde. Je voudrois bien savoir si on fait mourir un homme pour s'être laissé résusciter? Mais il étoit tout simple qu'on voulut le punir de s'être prêté à la fraude. (IV, 201)

Woolston.   *Examen.*

. . . c'est une opinion reçue parmi nous autres Juifs et qui est même une espèce de tradition, que les Chefs des prêtres et les magistrats civils de Béthanie pour décider la dispute avec connoissance de cause, et pour appaiser l'esprit de tout le peuple, avoient ordonné que Jésus fit un autre miracle pareil sur une autre personne qui étoit morte et enterrée depuis peu; mais que Jésus n'ayant pas voulu se soumettre à une pareille épreuve . . . (II, 142)

. . . la tradition des Juifs porte qu'on proposa à Jésus de recommencer mais qu'il refusa . . . (IV, 201)

12.   The Ressurrection of the Christ.

Je m'en rapporte aux chefs des prêtres de votre Eglise, je les somme de me dire si l'enlèvement de ce cadavre avant le tems désigné n'est pas une preuve évidente de fourberie et d'imposture, et s'il ne démontre pas d'une manière convaincante que les disciples de Jésus ne furent pas assés hardis, pour laisser le cadavre de leur maître dans le tombeau jusqu'au jour fixé pour sa résurrection, à cause de l'impossibilité qu'ils prévoyoient de l'en tirer alors et d'oser parler de ce miracle. (II, 183)

Il y a apparence que les disciples de Jésus, qui méditoient leur coup ne voulurent pas manquer leur belle, quand ils la trouvèrent, et qu'ils aimèrent mieux qu'il passât pour avoir ressuscité plustôt qu'il n'avoit dit, que pour n'être point ressuscité du tout. (IV, 102)

Quoique les soldats qui étoient Romains pussent avoir autant de fidélité et d'intégrité qu'aucun de ceux de leur profession, personne n'ignore qu'il n'est pas trop ordinaire que des gens de cet état soient difficiles à corrompre; mais quand même ils auroient été incorruptibles, il n'étoit pas impossible que Pilate, qui trouvoit son compte à entretenir le trouble et la division parmi nous, eût donné ordre à leurs officiers de ne pas s'opposer avec trop de rigueur à la fourberie qui pouvoit se commettre au tombeau. (II, 188-9)

Effectivement, ils purent fort bien gagner, ou enivrer ses gardes; peut être même Pilate, dont la politique trouvoit son compte dans les divisions des Juifs, favorisât-il cette fraude. (IV, 104)

Où seroit l'absurdité de supposer que les apôtres eux-mêmes avoient contribué à enyvrer les soldats? (II, 190)

D'ailleurs, cette garde, qui n'étoit là que contre la fraude, et non pas contre la violence, étoit, sans doute,

Woolston.   *Examen.*

peu nombreuse, et par conséquent, plus aisée à gagner, ou à enivrer. (IV, 105)

Vos évangélistes voudroient insinuer que les chefs des prêtres donnèrent de l'argent à ces soldats pour leur faire avouer qu'ils s'étoient endormis, et que pendant leur sommeil les disciples avoient enlevé le cadavre. Il faut supposer qu'ils étoient capables de rendre un faux témoignage, ce qui n'a pu arriver; en effet s'il eût été vrai qu'ils eussent été frappés d'étonnement et de terreur, à la vue d'une véritable résurrection, il n'y auroit pas eu de somme d'argent capable de les engager à rendre un faux témoignage dans la juste crainte qu'ils auroient eu de Dieu et de Jésus. (II, 191)

Mais j'aime ce que les apôtres imputent aux Juifs sur cette résurrection de Jésus. St. Mathieu rapporte v. 12 et 13, que les princes des prêtres et les sénateurs donnèrent une grande somme d'argent aux soldats qui gardoient le sépulchre de Jésus pour dire que ses disciples avoient dérobé son corps pendant qu'ils dormoient . . . Ce qui est assurément le comble de l'absurdité, et digne d'avoir été inventé par les apôtres. Mais cela marque que les soldats n'avoient pas vû ressusciter Jésus: car il n'y a point d'argent qui pût engager à rendre témoignage contre une résurrection qu'on auroit vûe. (IV, 106)

APPENDIX III

Mme du Châtelet's Preface to her Translation of the *Fable of the Bees*

PRÉFACE DU TRADUCTEUR

1735

Depuis que i'ay commencé a vivre avec moy, et a faire attention au prix du tems, a la brieveté de la vie, a l'inutilité des choses auxquelles on la passe dans le monde, ie me suis étonnée d'avoir eu un soin extreme de mes dents, de mes cheveux, et d'avoir negligé mon esprit et mon entendement. J'ay senti que l'esprit se roüille plus aisément que le fer, mais qu'il est bien plus difficille de luy rendre son premier poli.

Des reflexions si sensées, ne rendent pas a l'ame, cette flexibilité que le manque d'exercice lui otte quand on a passé la premiere jeunesse. Les fackirs des Indes perdent l'usage des muscles de leurs bras, a force de les laisser dans la mesme posture, et de ne s'en point servir. Aussi perd-t-on ses idées quand on neglige de les cultiver. C'est un feu qui meurt, si on n'y iette pas continuellement le bois qui sert a l'entretenir. Voulant donc reparer, s'il est possible une si grande faute, et tacher de replier cet arbre desia trop avancé, et de luy faire porter les fruits qu'on peut encor s'en promettre, i'ay cherché quelque genre d'occupation qui pust en fixant mon esprit, luy donner cette consistance (si ie puis m'exprimer ainsi) qu'on n'acquiert iamais en ne se proposant pas un but dans ses etudes. Il faut s'y conduire comme dans la vie civile bien savoir ce qu'on veut estre. L'irresolution produisant dans l'une les fausses demarches, et dans l'autre les idées confuses.

Ceux qui ont reçû de la nature un talent bien decidé, n'ont qu'a se laisser aller a l'impulsion de leur genie, mais il est peu de ces ames qu'elle conduit par la main, dans le champ qu'elles doivent defricher, ou embellir. Il est encor moins de ces genies sublimes, qui ont en eux, le germe de tous les talents, et dont la superiorité embrasse et exécute tout. Ceux qui pouroient pretendre le plus a cette monarchie universelle des baux arts atteignent cependant la perfection d'un seul avec plus de facilité, et en font leur favori. Mr. de Voltaire par exemple quoyque grand metaphysicien, grand historien, grand philosophe, etc. a donné la preference a la poesie, et l'epithete du plus grand poete français sera aussi bien son caractere distinctif que celui d'homme universel.

Il arive quelquesfois que le travail et l'etude forcent le genie a se déclarer comme ces fruits que l'art fait eclore dans un terrain pour lequel la nature ne les avoit pas faits, mais ces efforts de l'art sont presque aussi rares, que le genie naturel. Le plus grand nombre des gens pensans car les autres sont une espece a part sont ceux qui ont besoin de chercher en eux leur talent. Ils connaissent les difficultés de chaque art, et les fautes de ceux qui en courent la cariere, mais le courage qui n'en est pas rebuté, et cette superiorité qui les fait franchir leur a esté refusée. La mediocrité est mesme parmi les elus le partage du plus grand nombre. Les uns s'occupent a arracher les épines qui retarderoient les vrais genies dans leur course, et c'est ce qui procure tant de dictionaires, et d'ouvrages de cette espece qui sont d'un si grand secours dans la litterature. Il faut bien broyer les couleurs des grands peintres. Les autres rendent compte periodiquement au public de tout ce qui se passe dans la republique des lettres. Enfin d'autres transmettent d'un pays a un autre les decouvertes et les pensées des grands hommes, et remedient autant qu'il est en eux a ce malheur de la multiplicité des langues tant de fois deploré par les vrais amateurs.

Je sçais que c'est rendre un plus grand service a son pays de lui procurer des richesses tirées de son propre fonds que de luy faire part des decouvertes etrangeres et que Van Robés a esté plus utile a la France, que celuy qui a fait venir le premier des draps d'Angleterre. Mais il faut tacher de faire valoir le peu qu'on a receu en partage et ne pas entrer en desespoir parce qu'on n'a que deux arpents a cultiver et qu'il y a des gens qui ont dix lieües de pays.

On peut appliquer aux arts ce passage de l'Evangile *sunt plures mansiones in domo patris mei.* Il est certain qu'il vaut mieux donner une bonne traduction d'un livre anglais ou italien estimé que de faire un mauvais livre français.

Les traducteurs sont les negocians de la republique des lettres et ils meritent du moins cette louange qu'ils sentent et connoissent leurs forces, et qu'ils n'entreprennent point de produire d'eux-mesmes et de porter un fardeau sous lequel ils succomberoient. D'ailleurs si leur ouvrage ne demande pas ce genie createur, qui tient sans doute le premier rang dans l'empire des baux arts, il exige une application dont on doit leur savoir d'autant plus de gré, qu'ils en attendent moins de gloire.

De tous les ouvrages ceux de raisonnement me semblent les plus susceptibles d'une bonne traduction. La raison et la morale sont de tout pays. Le genie de la langue, ce fléau des traducteurs, se fait bien moins sentir dans des ouvrages ou les idées sont les seules choses qu'on ait a rendre, et ou les graces du style, ne sont pas le premier merite, au lieu que les ouvrages d'imagination peuvent estre rarement transmis de peuple a peuple, car pour bien traduire un bon poete, il faudroit estre presque aussi bon poete que luy.

Mais s'il est impossible d'avoir des memoires bien fidels de l'imagination des hommes, il ne l'est pas d'en avoir de leur raison, et c'est une des obligations qu'on a aux traducteurs. Ainsi si la nature humaine en general est redevable au sage Mr. Lock de luy avoir appris a connoitre la plus belle partie d'elle-mesme, son entendement, les Français le sont sans doute a Mr. Coste de leur avoir fait connoitre ce grand philosophe. Car combien de gens mesme parmi les lecteurs de Lock ignorent la langue angloise, et combien peu parmi ceux qui ont appris cette langue de la philosophie moderne, seroient en etat d'entendre Mr. Lock en anglois, et de surmonter en mesme tems les difficultés de la langue, et celles de la matiere.

Il faut, sans doute, pour se resoudre a traduire, se bien persuader que c'est aux commentateurs et non aux traducteurs qu'on a fait dire dans le temple du goût :

Le goût n'est rien, nous avons l'habitude
De rediger au long de point en point
Ce qu'on pense, mais nous ne pensons point.

Le iudicieux autheur de ce charmant ouvrage a bien senti la difference qu'il y a de composer de gros volumes sur un passage de Dictis de Crete qu'on n'entend point et dont on n'a que faire, ou de rendre propres a son pays les travaux et les decouvertes de tous les autres.

Mais comme on abuse de tout, l'envie de gagner de l'argent et d'estre imprimé a produit presques autant de mauvaises traductions que de mauvais livres.

Si une bonne traduction n'est pas sans quelque difficulté, il sembleroit du moins qu'il devroit estre aisé de choisir un bon livre pour l'obiet de son travail. Cependant on voit souvent paroitre des traductions dont l'original est desia oublié. Les Anglais tombent encor plus souvent que nous dans cet inconvenient. Il n'y a gueres de mauvais livres français qu'ils ne traduisent, temoin Sethos et tant d'autres. Cependant le genie profond des anglais devroit les rendre moins avides de nos livres qui sont frivoles pour la plus part, en comparaison des leurs. Il me semble qu'on pouvoit appliquer aux livres français ce que le comte de Roscomon a dit de nos vers : que tout l'or d'une ligne angloise tirée a la filiere françoise rempliroit plusieurs pages.

The weighti bullion of one sterling line
Drawn to a french wire would through all pages shine.

(Le mot *line* en anglais signifie *ligne* et *vers* egallement)

Je crois que ce qui rend les traductions si communes ches les anglais c'est que l'etude du français faisant partie de leur education, il y a plus de gens parmi eux a portée de traduire.

Il y a bien des traducteurs infidelles, les uns traduisant mot a mot le deviennent crainte de l'estre. Les autres par la difficulté de saisir le sens de leur autheur donnent a costé, et rendent obscurément une pensée lumineuse que leur esprit n'a fait qu'entrevoir. Pour ceux qui mettent leurs sotises a la place de celles de l'autheur qu'ils traduisent je les regarde comme les voyageurs qui abusent du proverbe : *a beau mentir qui vient de loin.* Il n'y a gueres, ie crois, que les traducteurs des ouvrages en langue orientalle, qui soient tombés dans cet exces.

Les difficultés de chaque art sont pour les artistes ce que les circonstances des plus petits evenements sont pour les contemporains. L'interest qu'ils y prennent et le point de veüe dans lequel ils les envisagent, grossissent aux uns et aux autres les obiets. La posterité et le public en iugent bien différément. Ainsi quoyqu'il soit vrai de dire qu'une bonne traduction demande de l'application et du travail, il est certain cependant que la meilleure est un ouvrage tres mediocre.

Cependant tout mediocre que soit ce genre de litterature, on trouvera peut-estre encor qu'il est bien hardi a une femme d'y pretendre. Je sens tout le poids du preiugé qui nous exclud si universellement des sciences, et c'est une des contradictions de ce monde, qui m'a touiours le plus etonnée, car il y a de grands pays, dont la loy nous permet de regler la destinée, mais, il n'y en a point ou nous soyions elevées a penser.

Une reflection sur ce preiugé qui est assés singuliere c'est que la comedie est la seulle profession qui exige quelque etude et quelque culture d'esprit, dans laquelle les femmes soient admises, et c'est en mesme tems la seulle qui soit declarée infame.

Qu'on fasse un peu reflection pourquoy depuis tant de siecles iamais une bonne tragedie, un bon poëme, une histoire estimée, un beau tableau, un bon livre de physique n'est sorti de la main des femmes? Pourquoy ces creatures dont l'entendement paroit en tout si semblable a celuy des hommes semblent pourtant arrestées par une force invincible en deça de la barriere, et qu'on m'en donne la raison si l'on peut. Je laisse aux naturalistes a en chercher une phisique, mais iusques a ce qu'ils l'ayent trouvée, les femmes seront en droit de reclamer contre leur education. Por moy j'avoüe que si i'etois roy, je voudrois faire cette experience de physique. Je reformerois un abus qui retranche pour ainsi dire la moitié du genre humain. Je ferois participer les femmes a tous les droits de l'humanité, et surtout a ceux de l'esprit. Il semble qu'elles soient nées pour tromper, et on ne laisse gueres que cet exercice a leur ame. Cette education nouvelle feroit en tout un grand bien a l'espece humaine. Les femmes en vaudroient mieux et les hommes y gagneroient un nouveau suiet d'emulation et nostre commerce qui en polissant leur esprit l'affoiblit et le retrecit trop souvent ne serviroit alors qu'a étendre leurs connoissances. On me dira sans doute que ie devrois prier Mr. l'abbé de St. Pierre de ioindre ce proiet aux siens. Il poura paroitre d'une execution aussi difficille, quoyqu'il soit peut-estre plus raisonable.

Je suis persuadée que bien des femmes ou ignorent leurs talents, par le vice de leur education, ou les enfoüissent par preiugé, et faute de courage dans l'esprit. Ce que i'ay eprouvé en moy, me confirme dans cette opinion. Le hazard me fit connoitre de gens de lettres qui prirent de l'amitié pour moy, et je vis avec un etonnement extreme qu'ils en faisoient quelque cas. Je commençai a croire alors que i'etois une creature pensante. Mais ie ne fis que l'entrevoir, et le monde, la dissipation, pour lesquels seuls ie me croyois née, emportant tout mon tems et toute mon ame ie ne l'ay crû bien serieusement que dans un age ou il est encor tems de devenir raisonable, mais ou il ne l'est plus d'acquerir des talents.

Cette reflection ne m'a point decouragée. Je me suis encor trouvée bien heureuse d'avoir renoncé au milieu de ma course aux choses frivoles qui occupent la plus part des femmes toute leur vie, voulant donc employer ce qui m'en reste a cultiver mon ame, et sentant que la nature m'avoit refusé le genie createur qui fait trouver des verités nouvelles, ie me suis rendüe iustice, et ie me suis bornée a rendre avec clarté, celles que les autres ont decouvertes et que la diversité des langues rendent inutilles pour la pluspart des lecteurs.

M'etant determinée a ce genre de travail, mon estime pour les Anglais et le goût que i'ay touiours eu pour la façon libre et masle de penser et de s'exprimer de ce peuple philosophe m'ont fait preferer leurs livres a ceux des autres nations, et i'ay choisi ce livre qui a pour titre *La Fable des Abeilles* parmi tous ceux que i'aurois pû traduire parce qu'il me semble que c'est un des ouvrages du monde qui est le plus fait pour l'humanité en general. C'est ie crois le meilleur livre de morale qui ait iamais esté fait c'est a dire celuy qui ramene le plus les hommes a la veritable source des sentimens auxquels ils s'abandonnent presque tous sans les examiner. Mandeville* qui en est l'autheur peut estre appellé le Montagne des Anglois a cela pres qu'il a plus de methode et des idées plus saines des choses que Montagne.

* C'etoit le petit fils d'un refugié français. Il prouve par son example que les esprits français ont besoin d'estre transplantés en Angleterre pour acquerir de la force.

Je n'ay point pour mon autheur le respect idolatre de tous les traducteurs. J'avoüe qu'il est assés mal ecrit en anglais, et qu'il est quelques fois plein de longueurs, et qu'il passe quelques fois le but come quand il dit par exemple qu'un voleur est aussi utile a la societé qu'un eveque qui done l'aumone, et qu'il n'y a point de merite a sauver des flammes un enfant pret a en estre devoré, et dans bien d'autres endroits, il avance plusieurs choses qui ne sont pas vraies et qui pouroient estre dangereuses. J'ay eu soin de mettre un correctif a ces endroits afin d'empecher qu'ils n'ayent des suites dangereuses. J'ay pris la liberté d'élaguer son stile en plusieurs endroits, et de retrancher tout ce qui n'etoit fait que pour les anglais, et qui avoit un raport trop unique a leurs coutumes.

J'ay pris aussi la liberté d'y ajouter mes propres reflexions, quand la matiere sur laquelle ie travaillois m'en suggeroit que ie croyois meriter la peine d'estre ecrites. Mais affin que le lecteur puisse les discerner, i'ay eu soin de les marquer par des guillemets.

On trouvera dans ce livre des pensées qui pouront paroitre un peu hardies, mais il ne s'agit, ie crois, que d'examiner si elles sont iustes, car si elles sont vraies, et si elles apprennent aux hommes a se connoitre, elles ne peuvent manquer d'estre utiles aux gens qui pensent, et c'est pour ceux-la seullement que ce livre est destiné. Odi prophanum vulgus et arceo.

J'avoüe qu'ayant eu la temerité d'entreprendre cet ouvrage, i'ay celle de desirer d'y reussir. Je me crois d'autant plus obligée d'y donner tous mes soins que le succes seul peut me iustifier. Il faut du moins que l'iniustice que les hommes ont eu de nous exclure des sciences, nous serve a nous empecher de faire de mauvais livres. Tachons d'avoir cet avantage sur eux, et que cette tyranie soit une heureuse necessité pour nous, de ne leur laisser que nostre nom a condamner dans nos ouvrages.

INDEX

INDEX